The Music Industries

The Music Industries

From Conception to Consumption

By

Michael L. Jones
University of Liverpool, UK

First published 2012 by
PALGRAVE MACMILLAN

Palgrave Macmillan in the UK is an imprint of Macmillan Publishers Limited, registered in England, company number 785998, of Houndmills, Basingstoke, Hampshire RG21 6XS.

Palgrave Macmillan in the US is a division of St Martin's Press LLC, 175 Fifth Avenue, New York, NY 10010.

Palgrave Macmillan is the global academic imprint of the above companies and has companies and representatives throughout the world.

Palgrave® and Macmillan® are registered trademarks in the United States, the United Kingdom, Europe and other countries.

ISBN 978–0–230–29148–5

This book is printed on paper suitable for recycling and made from fully managed and sustained forest sources. Logging, pulping and manufacturing processes are expected to conform to the environmental regulations of the country of origin.

A catalogue record for this book is available from the British Library.

A catalog record for this book is available from the Library of Congress.

10 9 8 7 6 5 4 3 2 1
21 20 19 18 17 16 15 14 13 12

Printed and bound in Great Britain by
CPI Antony Rowe, Chippenham and Eastbourne

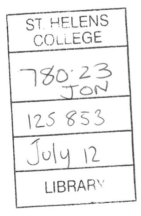

To Gertrude Emma West, who taught me how to read, and to Stephen Howard Marks, who insisted I should write

Contents

Acknowledgements

For consistent support and encouragement, I have to single out Holly Tessler, who has read and commented on chapters both ancient and modern.

For outstanding help: Mat Flynn and Keith Mullin.

I would like to thank all my students at the University of Liverpool, UK, in the MBA in music industries degree and then the MA in music industry studies. I have made great friends, and learned much that I formerly did not understand or appreciate as a result of years of lively debate with a stream of intelligent and dedicated people.

I would like to thank all the musicians, artist managers and music industry personnel who have shared their experiences with me. I made a pledge of anonymity to everyone, so I cannot thank you all by name, but I have tried faithfully to make sense of all that was said to me and all the reflection that our encounters encouraged.

I would like to thank colleagues past and present at the Institute of Popular Music, University of Liverpool, UK, and in the School of Music at the University of Liverpool, UK, notably Sara Cohen, Philip Tagg, David Horn, Marion Leonard, Rob Strachan, Anahid Kassabian, Hae-Kyung Um, Mike Brocken, Michael Spitzer, Nedim Hassan, Phil Kirby, Ellen Loudon and Emilia Barna. I would also like to thank other university colleagues who commented on drafts: Andrew Davies, Phil Davis, Paul Jones and Peter Goddard.

For good company and insights: Kate Smith, Jo Wright and Dave McTague.

Sheffield contingent: Josie Robson, Rinella Cere, Frank Wilkes, Adam Morris, John Ball and Frances Ball.

Nationally and internationally: for more music than you can shake a stick at – Andrew Beck; for close reading and insightful comments – James Wyllie, Simon Frith, Peter Bailey, Mark Pulman, Roger Smith, Karen Collins, Richard Ekins, Christoph Jacke and Byron Dueck.

For help and assistance: Paul Thompson, Lynne Segal and Marcus Russell.

Honourable mentions: David Loscos, Kelly Wood, Hwan-ho Choi, David Southworth and Ann Harrison.

Finally, thanks to Rosanna Brown, whose love, care, support and incredible patience have helped me to finish what I began a long time ago. Words are not enough.

Introduction: Music Industry and the Music Industries

While working on this book during a train journey, I became conscious of the iPod or some such MP3 player of someone sitting behind me. He was listening to heavy metal. I could tell it was heavy metal by the relentless shuddering kick drum, the pounding two-note bass line and the screaming guitars. Every aspect of listening to someone else's music choices intrigued me. It intrigued me because I was the last link in a very long chain whose individual links would all be difficult to specify, but which all existed or had existed in the moments leading to my fellow passenger's sounds arresting my attention. Why that kick drum sound? Why that bass line? Why those players together in that band? Why choose to immerse himself in listening to them? How had he encountered them? Who created the conditions for that encounter? Who paid who to have the record made and promoted? Why did they choose this band to invest in and not some other when there are so many others? How had the investment been organised? Were the investors happy with the end product? Were the musicians happy?

This list is not endless but these are only a few of the questions that are raised when an individual chooses to play a commercial recording for pleasure. I cannot know what specific meanings the listener was deriving from his choice of soundtrack but it is certain that he chose it for its impact on his mood. Either the track was a background to reflection on immediate or past issues or it was chosen because it evoked pleasurable associations. For whatever set of reasons, as it thundered relentlessly on, that soundtrack was doing complex work: it was helping him reach aspects of his memory, his personality and his values that staring out of the window or reading a book could not, or else could not do as effectively. I write this with certainty because, had I reverted to my MP3 player, then my own soundtrack would have done this work for me; except that the only real certainty on that train would have been that my soundtrack would have been a different one, as would all of the soundtracks available in all of the players carried that day.

We 'use' music because music has its own, potent capacity to allow a play of meanings that we 'control' only to the extent that we choose the encounter. Not all – perhaps very few – of our encounters with music are as consciously chosen as inserting a pair of speaker buds into our ears. It is blasted at us in bars and blared at us in TV adverts (when broadcast volume noticeably rises). Music forms part of 'occasions' we either choose or have thrust upon us – weddings, funerals, parties of all kinds. It is an essential ingredient of sporting events and state occasions. It is an essential component of every film and TV programme we watch; even 'talk' radio is punctuated by theme tunes and trailers with jingles. The object of this book is to discuss what connects the originators of all of this music with its users.

Making music is an activity that occupies musicians; selling music goods is an activity that occupies music businesses. At the very least, these actions need to be brokered in some way so that both parties get what they want from their interactions. Further, this brokering must be organised in some way so that the supply of music goes on meeting the demand for it, which is obviously an extensive and multi-faceted activity. My argument will be that, because the demand for music is indeed extensive and multi-faceted, its supply cannot be left to chance, and has not been left to chance for a considerable period of time. Clearly, some of the originators of the music we listen to – either willingly or not – lived and worked long before recording, broadcast and MP3, so their experience of connecting with audiences for their music was pre-industrial. What is interesting in their case is how such pre-industrial works have become irresistibly bound up with industrial processes. But this is a study for another work; the originators of music I am concerned with are those whose efforts reach users through the intervention of investors in music as a saleable outcome.

Companies which supply music to music users as a commercial activity became fully industrialised during the 19th century. Industry, here, will be taken to be a routinised relationship between investors in the production of music goods and forms of labour that realise profit from the sale of those goods. This is not a particularly attractive formulation but nothing else explains the heavy metal leaking on the train journey; nothing else explains the film and TV soundtracks, iTunes or Spotify. The reasons for the cultural aversion to music's implication with industry will be discussed in Chapter 1, but it is safe to say that it is the notion of 'routine' together with the implied impersonality of the term 'industry' that is at the root of the offence. Music tends to be represented as the outcome of imagination, while 'industry' seems suffused with regimentation. Equally, music is an intimate, sense-making practice and the idea that it reaches us through processes that are calculated to induce this intimacy can also be offensive. Taken together, this resistance presents a formidable amount of cultural baggage that needs to be both clambered over and tunnelled through in order to reveal the object of study. What complicates the matter is that this 'object' itself needs to be unpacked like a 'Russian nesting doll'. To confuse metaphors, it is as if the links in the chain are coiled one on top of the other – to tug at one is not just to reveal the others but to have them insist on their ability to affect each other.

The industrialisation of music is a complex whole and the first step in beginning to identify its complexities is to accept that it takes place. Where it does not take place, though, is somewhere called 'the Music Industry'. To think of the Music Industry as a 'place' is to miss the all-important point that music industry is a process – a continuously active process that allows demand for music to be met by supply. This process involves every stage of the chain that takes a heavy metal drumbeat from the imagination of a drummer to the speaker buds of a train passenger. It involves people becoming and behaving as musicians and it involves those musicians making music. (For a detailed explanation of the usage of the terms 'music industries', 'the Music Industry' and 'music industry' in this book, see Chapter 1.)

The total of performance and presentation is a musical text. For the drummer to become recognised as a drummer – to be acclaimed for this and to be validated by such recognition – they need to work, with others, on fashioning texts for entry into music markets. Only through market-entry activities can the drummer and the others reach a potentially appreciative audience for their texts. Drummers and all other musicians find it hard, if not impossible, to mount and sustain market entry projects; their expertise lies in hitting skins, not creating market awareness and servicing points of market entry. To complete the work of market entry, musicians need to work with companies whose expertise lies in these activities. This expertise has developed over a lengthy period of time into specific specialisms. Broadly, these are recording, music publishing and live performance, but each of these industries is supported by, and so sustains, a range of ancillary industries. It is this interdependence, together with its remoteness from musicians who are just beginning to aim at market success, that gives rise to notions of the Music Industry as a separate and special place.

Certainly, when the drummer began drumming they were not, yet, being invested in by music companies seeking to make a profit from their actions and from the abilities they were seeking to develop. Even so, we should recognise that in choosing to become a drummer, the individual was already investing in themselves. They were likely to be listening to records of other drummers: ones they wanted to emulate; ones whose technique they believed they could learn from and adapt to their own style; ones they felt they were good enough to surpass. In this concentrated activity the drummer was setting aside time and investing not just money but hope and effort to become someone who would be recognised and acclaimed for the performances they and their fellow musicians offered. In this way, being a musician is, in part, a competitive role aimed at to defeating the competition, or at least trying to do so. Therefore musicians need the value that music companies of different kinds can add to what they already do for themselves. As mentioned above, these companies have different types of expertise. How those companies go about their separate businesses has taken on the routine as well as the scale of industry.

That musicians need music companies does mean that they are necessarily separate from each other. This is because they both have a joint interest in the market success of the texts that musicians originate. They are distinct entities that bring different specialisms to the business of market entry of texts. For the purpose of this argument, these texts will be specified as 'symbolic goods in music'. This is a slightly cumbersome designation, but it is important to recognise that musicians seek music companies to add value to what they already do and if what they do is to make music texts then there needs to be a way of distinguishing texts which have value added to them from those that do not. Musicians seeking market entry covet the value-adding abilities of music companies in the three main music industries and this tends to give those companies tremendous power in their 'collaboration' with musicians. Further, because being a musician seeking market success, and attempting to sustain it once created, is a demanding business, musicians tend to appoint managers to act as their representative in negotiations with companies from the different music industries. In all of these ways, musicians become bound up in a process that is industrial for three main reasons:

1. It is aimed at successful market entry. This involves recognising that there is market competition and taking courses of action that will

create competitive advantage for their work. These courses of action are undertaken on the advice of music companies whose first loyalty is to themselves and to an industrial system characterised by interdependencies.
2. The courses of action taken are similar in all cases. There are routines in perspective and action that market entry companies follow as a matter of course regardless of the originality of the musicians they work with.
3. It is based on a mode of production of symbolic goods which involves investors of capital seeking to manage their investments even as, in the case of musicians, those whose efforts they seek to manage are not their direct employees. The strategies for dealing with this particular contingency marks out the music industries as particular instances of cultural industry.

The term 'the Music Industry' is an attractive one because it exists as a shorthand descriptive term for mass or repeated actions taken by record companies, music publishers and live agents. It also appeals because as a mass they are difficult to isolate or even to apprehend, which makes their confinement to a mysterious 'place' all the more attractive. These actions, together with the rationalisations that justify them, are difficult to apprehend because the expertise embodied by the music companies that make up the music industries is not one that has ever been codified as a set of professional standards. In essence, music industry, from the perspectives of music companies, is an unstable mixture of entrepreneurial 'instinct' together with the industrial and business latitude this requires, held together by a legal framework of contract and intellectual property law. Further, almost all music-industrial actions proceed informally, often as one-to-one discussions and decisions. Further still, as these discussions are about intangible outcomes (symbolic goods) whose organisation is conducted out of a substantially intangible expertise practised by a cast of constantly changing characters, the likelihood of professional standards and explicit forms of knowledge being generated in music industry is highly unlikely. The organisation and motive force of this book is guided by this observation.

Structure of the book

Chapter 1 explores the tensions that surround the notion of the Music Industry and examines the discursive mechanisms that keep it in place – often for want of an alternative approach to understanding the industrialisation of music. This allows a platform to be created from which to discuss recent attempts to analyse cultural industries more generally. In critiquing the predominant school in this field ('the Cultural Industries Approach') the conclusion is that in exploring music industry, rather than enter at the level of the text (as did the Frankfurt School) or the level of company practice (as do so much media, music industry and cultural industries theory), the most productive starting point is to see the music industry as a process that connects music makers to music users. The emergence and embedding of this process is then discussed in Chapters 2 and 3–6, inclusively, concentrating on the key factors in this process: the complexities of the role of musician; the practice of artist management; the practice of music companies; and the role and nature of contracts in actively connecting all of these distinctive 'players' in the pursuit of market success. Within the context established by this identification of who contributes to the industrialisation of music and under what conditions and circumstances, actual examples of such alliances are discussed in Chapter 7. Chapter 8 then explores the impact of digitisation on music industry where the argument is that to understand what is changing in music industry as a result of the rise of the internet and the impact of MP3 technology we need to understand the continuities that persist in giving music industry its shape and purchase, even as it experiences a place at the sharp end of an industrial revolution.

The thrust of this book is that music industry is a human experience. It involves one set of human beings – musicians – believing that they create texts that other human beings will find delightful or diverting or inspiring if only they could achieve access to the mechanism that might bring this about. This 'mechanism' exists in the form of the actions of a further set of human beings who believe they have evolved a set of principles and procedures for realising exactly these aims. The problem is that there are so many musicians who believe they have the ability to fashion texts as good as, or even better than, those that already exist. A further problem is that the mechanisms that exist as the Music Industry are substantially indiscriminate and inefficient despite the huge stars that they create. This 'mix' has existed since Music Hall became an industry in the 19th century, and the evidence seems to indicate that, for all its power, digitisation has not liberated musicians from their dependencies. These dependencies derive, ultimately, from our need to alleviate train journeys with susurrating iPods and to travel to inner landscapes as we do.

To celebrate the musicians who accompany us on journeys by taking us on other ones is what inspires the study of music industry, but this study reveals, or should reveal, how challenging the journeys of musicians are. It is the musicians' journey that informs this account, but that journey is pieced together from the accounts, and with the cooperation, of other often equally idealistic and ambitious people who attempt to realise what they see as the promise of such musicians. That so much promise is unrealised is the condemnation of the process. That some promise is realised is not entirely the result of the abilities of musicians working alone. Creating a productive balance between the two as a method for explaining music industry is the challenge of this study.

1
Music and Industry

We are entering a territory in which terminological uncertainty is a strong feature but this confusion is not accidental, it derives from the conflicting conceptions of 'music' and 'industry' embedded, generally, in cultural and social usage. Consider these comments which appeared on a BBC website for its children's service:

> Most manufactured bands are highly successful, but I think truly talented people should come forward and make their mark without people interfering!! They should find their talent within their heart, not within the 'manufacturing' studio.
>
> Ella, 14, London

> I think most of the top 40 is rubbish but some songs are brilliant because the artists wrote them themselves and really thought about the lyrics!
>
> Eva, 11, Derry

> The top 40 nowadays is full of groups which are owned. This annoys me as we never get to see people who have formed a band themselves, and produce their own music. The companies which own the groups make the band go on different TV programmes and magazines, and the single turns out to be awful. The question is when are non-owned bands going to enter the charts?
>
> Paul, 15, Cheadle.
> (news.bbc.co.uk/cbbcnews/hi/chat/your_comments/.../
> 2248416.stm 10Sep 2002 – accessed 3 October 2011)

These comments form a point of departure for studying the relationship between industrial processes and the making and enjoying of music.

They do so because what swirls around in them is a set of popular prejudices, structured as binary opposites, which can obscure that study: 'manufactured' versus 'talented'; 'heart' versus 'people interfering'; 'owned' versus 'own music'; 'companies' versus 'groups' (of musicians). These binaries derive from and exemplify a deeply and pervasively entrenched social and cultural aversion to the idea that music we might like is an outcome of industry. So deeply is it entrenched that an 11-year-old has already absorbed the prejudice, but what makes the study even more difficult is the passion with which those prejudices are held.

All popular music is industrial: in all its multiplicity of genres, popular music emerges through the joint effort of musicians working with music companies whose expertise lies in taking music, in a range of saleable forms, to market. This 'effort' is not solely musical; it is industrial in ways that follow from the (continuing) fact that musicians lack the means to enter markets unsupported. The support offered to them comes at a price and is offered on the basis that it will lead to profit for those making the offer. Consequently, different types of effort are made towards market entry and market success, and these must be coordinated. This need for coordination then raises the issues of who controls the coordination of effort, on what basis, with what justification and towards what goal(s).

Once we understand that popular music reaches us out of the joint effort of musicians and music companies, we should be better placed to understand how the types of popular music we like give us what we want regardless of the industrial circumstances of its reaching us implied in this joint effort. This then allows us to go on enjoying it without making that enjoyment dependent on a strategy of exceptionalising what we like from what we don't like, where the basis of this strategy rests in an unsustainable separation of music from industry. Under contemporary conditions this aim is unrealistic. That is because, as they impact on musicians and commerce in symbolic goods, recent and ongoing changes in technology, and in society more generally, have been and continue to be profound, suggesting that old forms and models of conducting joint effort are irrelevant. More than this, so much of the new music business pivots, through database-mining, on rewarding music users for allowing and facilitating access to the ways (e.g. via Amazon and Facebook) that individually and as groups they make exactly these exceptions. In this way the entrepreneurial exploitation of digital applications is driving new forms of business, but whether this is making for a new music industry is what needs to be assessed.

Before exploring, or as a way to begin exploring, the ways in which music and industry are connected, it is important to indicate that three variants on the connections between these terms will be used in the course of this study. The need for this separate usage should become apparent as the exploration progresses.

1. **Music industries**

   There are three main music industries: recording, music publishing and live performance. If popular music is a product (the clarification of this claim will be the work of the following chapter), then the commodity form taken by the product can and does vary. For example, the commodities dealt in by music publishers are licences to use songs. Publishers are in the business of attracting other business to the wares of their writers. Their clients include record companies, advertising agencies, film-makers, game designers, and telecommunications and TV companies. Their role is to make 'deals' with such companies; to set prices for the use of songs and to collect payments for this use. These activities are substantially different from making records and from organising live performances, which suggests that the three industries should not be merged together as if they face identical conditions of existence. Further, there are considerable differences of scale and power between companies active in each industry – from the major ones (e.g. the publishing arm of Universal Music, Sony Music, which is a major record company, and Live Nation, which is the dominant force in live music), to the myriad and miniscule 'bedroom' independent record companies (Strachan, 2007), to small-scale publishers and self-publishing efforts, and to the equally myriad promoters of individual gigs and club nights throughout the western world. The use of music industries should also reflect the range of experiences subsumed by the use of 'industry' to describe the activities involved in making music commodities available, whether to companies in other sectors or to paying audiences, directly or indirectly.

2. **The Music Industry**

   This term indicates that different skill-sets and markets aside, industries in publishing, recording and live performance have practices and perspectives in common. For example, companies in each industry choose from the work of all the musicians available to them and they make their choices based on almost identical data and on almost identical prejudices. This choice needs to be actualised in the form of legally binding agreements with musicians to provide music for sale (whether in the form of songs, recordings of songs or the live performance of songs). Further, the approach of those companies to creating such agreements is comparable across the music industries – it is a product of calculated risk where calculation involves estimating whether particular musicians and their music are likely to make money. Finally, and decisively, a success in one industry is likely to be a success in the others, so interactions and inter-dependencies between the three industries are both necessary and commonplace. The degree of unity of purpose and practice, and all this calls for on the part of music companies – of different types and sizes – then justifies the use of the singular term 'the Music Industry'. Even so, there is a danger in using it as a discursive, shorthand construct. The Music Industry is not a tangible 'place' and neither is it a single, conscious entity; rather, as the next point insists, it is a process more than it is a place. To ensure that this distinction is maintained, the term will be capitalised throughout this study.

3. **Music industry**

This term should be used when indicating the 'doing' of the practices referred to in points 1 and 2. By this I mean the actions taken by the people who comprise the record companies, the publishers, the live agencies and all of the networks of companies they engage with in entering music markets and attempting to succeed there. This means considering that rather than these actions being somehow 'neutral' where music and musicians are concerned there is a constant *realpolitik* to the choices made by the personnel of music companies and to the prosecution of those choices. For example, it is not enough to report that agents for live performances 'take on' musicians and organise tours for them. Instead we need to ask, how, for what reasons, through what methods, on the basis of what arguments and with what arguable results and consequences do live music agents persuade promoters and venue managers to accept a particular act, for a particular price, on a particular date in the face of the clamouring of agents and managers representing other acts? We need to ask these questions because, unless we do, we do not see music industry, or the Music Industry, at all: the entire thrust of what follows is that music industry is how the people who make up music companies work with and through the efforts of musicians to make a profit on the investment of time, money and effort they expend on taking musicians and their music to market.

This study is concerned with exploring the music industries by specifying the practice of music industry. It will focus on unpacking the one-on-one relationships that drive the production of music as a symbolic good. These can be argued to define the industrialisation of music even as this industrialisation experiences the enormous impacts of digitisation – notably in sound recording and in the distribution and marketing capabilities offered by the internet. 'Relationships' do not necessarily form naturally: they are constructed from existing cultural materials, such as discourses, forms of knowledge and the kinds of popular prejudices we have already met. In later chapters these relationships will be discussed as working 'alliances' or as 'joint endeavours' between key parties who invest time, energy, money and differing types of expertise in the creation of symbolic goods in music. Before exploring the dynamics of such alliances, their key constituencies can be identified in the following ways:

(i) **Music companies** I use the term 'music companies' in place of the perhaps more likely 'music businesses' for three main reasons. Firstly, the term 'the music business' is an over-familiar one – one that is used too frequently to stand for the Music Industry. In this way, referring to music businesses would simply add to this confusion. Rather, what needs to be uncovered and examined is how, in a fast-moving world, the hectic intensity of business decisions involving music and musicians is shaped by the consistencies of industry. Secondly, by electing to use 'music companies' I hope to keep at the forefront of discussion the actions of people (rather than faceless entities) who are working, with musicians, towards goals that, while they are expressed in the same terms, are not necessarily identical. Thirdly, there is a need to find an expression that does not ignore or sublimate the actions of very small companies for a preoccupation with the actions of very large ones. It is seductive to think of the Music Industry as if it were equivalent, for example, to the activities and perspectives of the major record companies, but it is not – much music-industrial activity takes place away from the corporations. Further, the experience of personnel recruited to those corporations is very often formed in the milieu of tiny companies and is taken into those corporations in a more or less unreconstructed manner. In all of this the term 'companies' helps to focus concentration on what I will argue is the heart of music industry – the actions and activities, together with the justifications made for them, taken towards the production of music commodities.

(ii) **Musicians** There are many different types of musicians and many different types of experiences of making music. In this study I am concerned with musicians who are bent on achieving a particular kind of 'success'. Success, of course, can be defined widely as economic success; as celebrity and fame; or as acclaim by their peers and by what musicians would see as discerning audiences, but mostly it will entail all three in varying proportions. I am concerned with the life experiences of musicians who set out to become 'visible', to become acclaimed and to sustain that acclaim so that their role and identity is that of a 'popular' musician. Clearly, these criteria could apply to 'classical' musicians but I am not concerned with their routes into what I will discuss in the following chapter as an overtly institutionalised form of music. They could also apply to 'session' musicians but these are not my concern – their careers tend to consist of a self-contained servicing of demand for specific types of performances on a client basis. I am interested in the bands that are the obsession of the music press; the proto-pop stars who queue for hours for 'reality' show auditions; the 'bedroom' DJs who covet the headliner spot in the club scene they take an enthusiastic part in; the hip-hop and R&B acts who think often simultaneously of their music and their brands. Each of these is, very broadly, a 'genre world' of its own and will have its own rules and peculiarities. However, to a greater or lesser extent, and always decisively, 'progress' involves partnership with one or more music companies. Somehow such partnerships – such joint endeavours and the alliances they entail – will always come to obey industrial logics; and these logics will work against the likelihood of success for the vast majority who chase it.

(iii) **Music users** The reasons for choosing the term 'music users' over 'music consumers' has already been broached: not only do music consumers derive meaning from a text but they are able to put this meaning to work in social contexts – for example, in the creation and dissemination of an intended identity. Further, 'identity' is a moveable feast – we can feel a particular sense of self in isolation from others; or we can choose to be with others; or else the occasion for being with others might be chosen for us (a wedding, a birthday, a funeral) when, in each context, music can facilitate the experience of self, and self in relation to others. This capacity of music will be returned to in Chapter 2. Here the continued attraction of music can be argued to derive from its versatility and, for want of a better term, its intimacy. As with any text, meaning is made on reception through sense-making practices based on the codal competences of the receiver. The wider and deeper versatility of music is that receivers decode in ways that satisfy them. There is no ultimate 'message' in this form of communication, so individual allegiances to individual music texts can be passionate (as 'Eva's' comment exemplifies) or they can be pleasingly disengaged (as in ambient music and 'chill out' music, for example, where music choices will still reflect identity). In these combined and complex ways, music consumers are willing to elect for symbolic goods in music because they offer uses or have 'use values' that other goods do not enjoy.

(iv) **Music** If music is the centre but not the entirety of a symbolic good with music at its core, then other, key textual dimensions concern the performances of musicians in making that music. Further, such performances are not made in isolation – whether from the input of technical personnel (producers and sound engineers) or business associates (artist managers and music company personnel), as well as from a range of 'significant others' (family, friends, partners and fans). When a symbolic good is bought, what is bought can be argued to be a complex combination of the sound that the musicians made originally that attracted music companies to them; the sound they become responsible for following inputs received willingly or not; the image they adopt, any changes they make to it and how they use this image in representational material; the stories they tell or that can be told about why they sound and look the way they do; and how all of this is configured in marketing campaigns. The implications and consequences of this for the idea of music industry are considerable, not least because while the industry is far from being confined to matters of music, the habits of all concerned – music company personnel, artist managers, musicians, music users, musicians and those involved in the media and marketing apparatus – are to focus on music above and beyond its contexts and to attribute all musical decisions to musicians as if they exist in inviolable isolation from those contexts. Both of these positions will be argued to be unsustainable, but this representation of the centrality of music rather than texts (and the actions of text-makers) to industry can be argued to distort the experience of musicians within that industry by reducing a complex reality to a disempowering, one-dimensional focus on the manipulation of sound. Rather than always being authors of their own fate, musicians find themselves as simultaneously commodifiers and the commoditised. More complicated still, to be in both conditions at once means inhabiting three concurrent realities: as business partners with music companies; as the workforce of the music industry; and as objects of consumption. It is the triple-reality of the condition of being a musician chasing success, and of how this success-chasing is managed, that compounds the challenges faced by students of music industry because the fate of music and musicians is an outcome of actions taken in their name but ones that express or impact upon dimensions of their whole as a text.

(v) **Music markets** Markets for music can only be markets for music commodities – buyers have to be able to take something away with them in exchange for the money they are prepared to spend on the item of choice. What is taken away is the experience of the symbolic good on offer; clearly, though, as an intangible, textual and symbolic, commodity music's pleasurable decoding cannot be ensured in advance. In fundamental ways the work of music companies is work associated with the preparation of the experience of the text and of the text for experience. For example, a record company engages in promotion and marketing of its releases. These activities involve encouraging favourable associations within potential buyers in advance of the 'release' of the symbolic good ('release' here in quotes to draw attention to the text as an active, pent-up force). Where concert promoters are concerned, they too engage in preparing potential audiences – building their anticipation for a proposed event – and then, on the night, seek to ensure that the intended experience is created by dressing the space and providing sound and lighting systems towards this end. Considered in these ways, music markets are 'experience' markets – no buyer knows, on purchase, whether the good will bring pleasure; they can only trust that the anticipation they have built from the materials made available to them in advance will be satisfied. So it is that much of the work of music companies consists of 'value-adding': adding further textual dimensions to existing texts and encouraging texts-in-production to anticipate their likely reception. Further, music companies tend not to sell direct to the public but indirectly through 'filters', notably through a critical apparatus which itself needs to be courted and brought 'on side' if promotional and marketing materials are to be validated. Markets for intangible goods, then, present investors with complex problems, so it should be no wonder that they seek solutions to those problems that favour their stake in the production of those goods rather than, and often at the expense of, the originators of the texts from which those goods are fashioned.

The 'stake' that investors in symbolic goods in music have in individual commodities is not just considerable, it is, in its own defining ways, vulnerable. The commodity that enters a music market is the commodity as finished by music companies and, consequently, it is the total of their investment (in the utilisation of promotional networks; in financing marketing campaigns; in paying in advance for musicians to work on their texts) that is at risk in taking the commodity to market. This many-sided risk is the source of the vulnerability of music companies. If they produce too many market failures, the reputation of the company is harmed. Consequently there can be considerable staff turnover in such companies. Mounting music projects (e.g. album releases, major tours) can be an extremely costly business. Thus risk-reduction strategies can impact all and any moment of the production process. Assessing when to take risks and when to avoid them is an intricate and demanding affair, and high staff turnover militates against the development of this expertise. In many ways, music companies, notably the larger ones, are little more than shells populated by different regimes of staff who enjoy differential rates of market success. It is into these inherently unstable, simultaneously risk-taking and risk-reducing environments that always ambitious and often headstrong musicians march.

Musicians and music companies – forms of representation

Approaching music industry as the comparatively regularised ways in which disparate alliances of musicians and music companies go about the work of producing productive outcomes in the form of symbolic goods in music is to fly in the face of commonsense accounts of the Music Industry. For example, the business press, government and the education system habitually rehearse exactly the same sets of binaries evident in the contributions to the CBBC website. Even in the academic literature most alert to cultural industries there is a palpable reluctance to situate musicians inside an industrial production system. In each instance the blindness to musicians' willing implication in industry can be argued to derive from the same source as that exhibited by the young people already quoted. This is the distinction between 'art' and 'commerce' associated with 19th-century Romanticism.

Within the boundaries of this compelling, if hazy, construct, each of these formations then inflects the separation of musicians from the

Music Industry in different ways. The business press is concerned with the performance of companies and concentrates its attention on company reports and press statements. By implication, musicians exist in some other realm. Government, at least when 'creative industries' policies were in vogue under the Labour administration led by Tony Blair, made an identity of the practices of musicians with a superficial account of the Music Industry in order to promote the former as creative spirits who could be facilitated in their efforts by the expertise of the latter. In the education system, where this is concerned with vocational outcomes, the Music Industry is taught as a mysterious and powerful place of expertise for which musicians need to be prepared. Where academic studies of cultural industries are concerned, it can be argued that there is a tension between a desire to specify cultural-industrial production as industrial (as a set of relations between forms of capital and types of labour), which is inhibited by an equivalent desire to extract and relocate musicians from such relations lest their efforts be tainted by earlier, far more deterministic accounts of cultural labour. Taken together, in order to discuss music industry as a process, it is first necessary to consider the discursive construction of the Music Industry associated with these various interested parties, encouraged as they tend to be by the trade bodies of the main music industries.

The business press and the Music Industry

The wider formal discussion of the music industry is a phenomenon of the comparatively recent past. For example, a search of the archives of the *Financial Times* after 1950 for the terms 'music business', 'music industries' and 'the music industry' yields interesting and consistent results – few before 1992, the bulk afterwards. This, of course, could reflect a change in editorial policy, but this then begs the question as to why coverage of the music industry should suddenly become acceptable to the *Financial Times* only during the 1990s. The answer, perhaps, is to do with the global insistence of popular music and, with it, the music industry, which had arguably become a social and cultural fact by the early 1990s. With the cultural impact of MTV at a gathering pace throughout the 1980s and *Live Aid* as an MTV-inspired, 'global' triumph for satellite TV, by 1990 popular music had become as much a visual as an aural medium. Although its negative aspects would quickly register themselves with the major record companies, satellite broadcasting transformed the marketing of records. In turn the centrality of the music video to marketing campaigns emphasised the performance dimension of pop, after a period marked by the comparative non-performance of introspective singer-songwriters as 'album artists' in the early 1970s, and the apparent anti-performance of punk bands as predominantly singles acts during the late 1970s and early 1980s. In turn, the major record companies were able to rise to the economic challenge of video marketing by the windfall super-profits they enjoyed from the boom in catalogue sales brought about by the introduction of the CD.

Michael Jackson's album *Thriller* is emblematic of all the key changes of the 1980s: the recording of the album was a very expensive process; it involved other songwriters as well as Jackson; its musical themes reflected the rise of club culture as well as the predominance of mainstream rock music; and all of this was spearheaded and mobilised by a music video that lasted for 14 minutes, was shot by an established film director and cost a reputed $0.5 million to make[1] (half the cost of the very expensive album itself). *Thriller* is the biggest-selling record of all time. It made Jackson a 'global' star in a way that, thanks to the reach of satellite TV and the music video, outstripped even the success of Elvis Presley and the Beatles. In turn, Jackson's achievements offered a template for other acts to emulate, and the snowballing success of acts such as Madonna and George Michael – who were able to make records that translated into strong videos – ushered in a period of enormous expansion in the recording industry during the 1980s and 1990s. This expansion then came to the attention of the business press when it began to involve processes of takeover and merger (e.g. Sony's takeover of CBS in 1988, Bertellsman's takeover and merger of RCA and Arista in 1987) – processes that, by their very nature, involved very large sums of money which necessarily tended to come from outside the wider music industry and from sources that the business press was more familiar with and receptive to.

In the case of the business press, the over-arching problem with this reporting is that it is the reporting of company performance, as if what companies do is somehow distanced from what musicians do and from what they do together. The music industry becomes an abstract field of balance sheets combined with a glamorised playground of 'stars' to the exclusion of an account of the effortful interactions between companies and musicians that make market success (and failure) happen.

Government and the Music Industry

Where the UK Government is concerned, three drivers towards an overt public policy embrace of popular music can be identified, all of which emerged in exactly the period when the recording industry enjoyed the surges of the 1980s and then the 1990s (in the USA as a consequence of the rise of hip-hop and R&B; in the UK as an outcome of 'Britpop'). These were the cultural policy template established by the Labour Party administration of the Greater London Council (GLC) which contributed to a wider (though not identical) embrace of creative industries policies; the need to respond to, and anticipate, the onset of the internet as a medium for commerce, as flagged by the World Intellectual Property Organization 1996 conference; and the formulation of music creativity as a well-spring of entrepreneurship in a period of manufacturing decline. All of these topics are far too much to discuss in this context but they coalesced and crystallised around the notion of 'Cool Britannia' and were given a governmental 'seal of approval' through the re-designation of the (backward-looking) Department of Heritage as the (forward-looking) Department of Culture, Media and Sport in 1997. In short, the coincidence of a resurgent UK recording industry with the election of a newly media-savvy Labour Party appeared, or was contrived, to presage a future in which UK creativity could seize the initiative offered by ecommerce and its implication with trade in forms of intellectual property.

The lessons the Labour Party had learned from four successive general election defeats were many. The largest of them was that their lengthy association with social welfare capitalism needed to be jettisoned. What replaced it was a philosophy of the 'Third Way' – namely steering a path between social welfarism and neoliberalism. Neoliberalism had rapidly become a global ideology in the twin senses that the key global financial organisations (the International Monetary Fund and the World Bank) endorsed it; and its cornerstone policies of privatisation and the deregulation of capital movements out of and into the UK had produced pronounced effects on the domestic economy. These can be summarised as the accelerated decline of primary industries (subsequently extending a dependence on foreign trade) and the dispersal of key stages of manufacturing to other countries (notably to those in South-East Asia). Taken together, Labour set itself the objectives of re-inventing its voting base by securing a place in the sympathies of non-unionised young people. One strategy for accomplishing this goal was to ally themselves with successful pop musicians of the day (a dilution of the precedent set by the GLC which emphasised socialist politics in its own connection with musicians). This in turn allowed them to endorse pop music as a business product as well as a cultural one, by emphasising its ability to bring in foreign earnings; to act as an employer; and to encourage entrepreneurship and with it the self-reliance of self-employment.

As described in *Creative Britain* (1998) by Chris Smith, the first secretary of state for the Department of Culture, Media and Sport, the single most notable cultural policy enacted by the Labour administration was the 'New Deal for Musicians', a measure which sought to allow unemployed musicians time and assistance to develop their careers. Although deeply compromised from the outset and, over time, substantially an abject failure, the willingness of government to take musicians (and, through them, the music industry) 'seriously' stimulated both the creation of reports into the (apparent) condition of the industry and lobbying by the industry's representative bodies, both of which have persisted to the present day. In a parallel and associated development, various cities and regions advanced their own creative industries policies, with, notably, Sheffield – a city that enjoyed a council much in the same vein as the GLC – pursuing interventionist music industry strategies, especially Red Tape Studios and the National Centre for Popular Music. Significant about these initiatives was the way in which they all endorsed the same set of claims about the vibrancy of the music industry, where these claims tended to originate from within the industry itself – especially from within the British Phonographic Industry (BPI), the trade association of the (major) record companies (see Frith et al., 1993; Jones, 1999; Cloonan, 2007). This representation of 'vibrancy' then obscured the working methods of music companies, which tend to produce the market failure of the vast bulk of aspiring musicians as a condition of the success of the very few.

The over-arching problem with this embrace was that it was based largely on a conflation of New Labour ambitions for a new voting base with the determination of the major record companies to win government support for its own version of the nature and strength of the recording industry – one in which the actual activity of music industry (the preparation of market entry and its role in the high market mortality rate of musicians) is never broached. In this way the experience of music companies in relation to musicians as the basis of music industry is separated from music making as an apparently autonomous activity which happily follows its own paths.

Education and the Music Industry

More by its own route than necessarily one impelled by actual developments in the recording industry or the wider tides of social, political and economic change, higher education began to admit popular music to the curriculum in the late 1980s. Such is the independence of universities as institutions that popular music teaching had disparate roots and was uncoordinated. For example, the interests of sociologists or English literature teachers were an individual spur to such teaching in some institutions while, in others, music departments eventually conceded that there was music of value and interest beyond the classical canon. Especially in tertiary education, the rhetoric of economic and cultural renewal quickened this expansion but with a slant towards studio production and music performance. The various levels of tertiary qualification expanded their subject areas to meet the decline in primary and manufacturing industries, where their address was not only to the severe reduction in the technical apprenticeships that these industries had always fostered but to what was arguably the dissolution of the very notion of apprenticeship in an age of increasing digitisation.

Even in this severely abbreviated account, tensions should be apparent within the education system's approach to teaching music industry, but these should not be automatically read as a product of the differences between tertiary and higher education. Instead, the key tensions are threefold. Firstly, there are those which are created by teaching popular music substantially in the absence of teaching music industry. Secondly, there is a lack of interdisciplinarity evident, such as when a business studies approach is not informed by concepts and perspectives of popular music studies. Thirdly, there are tensions between academic and vocational approaches to teaching popular music and notably the music industry. In the first case the music industry became an adjunct to popular music teaching as one of the 'contexts' of popular music. This approach tends to represent the music industry almost as an incidental dimension of popular music rather than its *seat*. Conversely, in the absence of popular music (and cultural studies) concerns, the defining specificities of music as an industry can be lost if music is treated solely as a business. This, then, becomes a particular problem where vocationally inflected courses are concerned: here all that counts is what companies do and therefore what musicians might do in relation to them to improve their market chances. Further, it is an approach that relies on the same sources of information on music industry as government and the business press – on the representation of what happens and why offered by the industry's trade bodies (the BPI and the Performing Right Society among them), supplemented by testimony from music industry professionals. This mixture is repeated in the para-music industry education sector, in the privately run recording courses; in the 'New Deal for Musicians'; and in the music industry conferences sector that continues to grow in the UK.

The over-arching problem here is that there is a lack of criticality about music industry because there is a fixation with the Music Industry, as if this is confined to the actions taken by companies; while 'popular music' describes the actions taken by musicians as if, in their joint ventures with music companies, their self-expression and self-organisation as musicians is somehow insulated from impact by the former (except for lurid, cautionary tales of musicians 'ripped off' by 'unscrupulous' music business people).

The 'cultural industries approach' to the Music Industry

Taken as a whole, and to use a cliché, the Music Industry is frequently discussed but barely analysed. When it is, the discussion tends to follow the patterns identified above: the actions of music companies are separated from those of musicians, with music hovering above them as a third and independent element which, because it is deemed to be judged by criteria inaccessible to business practices, allows music companies to be absolved of any responsibility for 'its' market fate. But this is exactly the territory of the young people's remarks quoted previously – it is as if the Music Industry boils down to companies allowing music to be heard which, when it is, is judged on its merits, where the merits or otherwise of any piece of music are entirely the responsibility of its composers and performers. This appeals to the over-arching 'commonsense' so deeply absorbed by those quoted, but it begs some very big questions: if music is 'untouched' by music companies, what do they do; why do they exist; and why do we use the term 'the Music Industry' if music is not industrial? Further, if there is a 'Music Industry', what is industrial about music?

The most compelling account we have of music as an industry is that offered by David Hesmondhalgh. His principal work is *The Cultural Industries*, first published in 2002 and revised and updated in 2007, where the later work, *Creative Labour* (2011), amplifies and deepens the earlier one through an attention to specific working conditions in music industry, TV and publishing. For the purposes of these remarks I will concentrate on the first edition of *The Cultural Industries* as the core statement of a position that the later works modify in limited ways but certainly do not repudiate. Thus in that work Hesmondhalgh demonstrates his awareness of the need for theorists of culture and of cultural production to restore a sense of industry to culture after its abandonment in the rise of cultural studies in the 1980s. In mounting this task he distinguishes 'the cultural industries approach' from two closer traditions. The first of these is a political economy of (substantially) media industries which tends to be preoccupied with the scale of their political power and, consequently, tends to ignore or downplay day-to-day processes that make them industrial. Secondly, he retrieves the term 'the cultural industries' from the disabling pessimism of its origins in the work of the (Marxist) Frankfurt School theorists, most notably Adorno and Horkheimer. In seeking to generate 'a *historical* (sic) sociology of cultural production' (2002: 1), Hesmondhalgh draws on, and cites, a comparatively limited range of theorists, such is the relative novelty of his position. The most prominent of these are Bernard Miège and Nicholas Garnham. These two, though, are not overly concerned about studying the music industry; rather it is the work of Jason Toynbee (2000; together with the later contribution of Mark Banks (2007)) – along with his own – which comprises a new, cultural industries approach to the study.

This approach is novel and persuasive because it originated as a synthesis of attempts to come to terms with what Hesmondhalgh describes as the 'remarkable transformation' experienced in and by the cultural industries since the early 1980s (2002: 1). It is also particularly germane to this study because he is alive to the 'many important continuities which might be obscured by an over-emphasis on change' (2002: 2). His synthesis is a persuasive one because it situates its analysis in the heartlands of cultural studies but in a way that fully confronts their neglect of industry studies. Hesmondhalgh then seeks to specify how, through a series of coping strategies and in the face of a set of specific constraints, industries control their production processes. At the same time, however, he remains aware of the major theoretical gains of cultural studies – that media producers do not determine the meanings made of media texts, of symbolic goods. The significance – and with it the great gain made by the cultural industries approach – is that, through it, sociologists of culture are able to discuss cultural-industrial production without being hobbled by the deeply negative conclusions drawn about them by Adorno and Horkheimer. This is extremely valuable because with the production of symbolic goods being such a vital dimension of contemporary economies, there is a desperate need for a theory, or for a way of theorising, which allows that these goods are made under industrial conditions but ones that do not determine the uses made of them. All of this noted, the account offered by a cultural industries approach can still be shown to be 'part of the problem' when discussing, in this instance, music industry. That's because in order to come out from under the gloomy weight of, especially, Adorno's work (where the music industry is concerned), the means created to accomplish this distance and the renewal it brings bear too close a resemblance to existing, and flawed, representations of how music, musicians and music companies (fail to) connect.

Early in the work, Hesmondhalgh identifies (Miège, 1979, 1987; Garnham, 1990) what he determines are the 'distinctive features' of 'industries that make texts' (2002: 17). He divides these into a set of three 'problems' and five 'responses' to them. The problems are that:

1. cultural industries are in a 'risky business';
2. cultural industries face high costs of production but low costs of reproduction;
3. because cultural goods are not used up in consumption (a film is still a film after it has been watched), cultural-industrial firms are forced to create an artificial scarcity of the goods they are attempting to sell.

The five responses to dealing with the operating problems they face are as follows:

1. They 'offset (misses) against hits' (they over-produce goods in the knowledge that a market success of one will meet the costs of the others).
2. They adopt familiar strategies from other industrial sectors – companies merge with each other and they seek to control the product value chain. Further, they seek to control the paths of entry to the market place.
3. They use their forms of business organisation to limit access to their goods.
4. They reduce risk by producing goods that can be easily categorised – whether by genre, or because they involve an already successful 'star', or because they represent the next release in a series of some kind.
5. As companies, they focus their energies on controlling the marketing and distribution of the products they make rather than on how those products are originated – they exercise 'loose control of symbol creators'.

Hesmondhalgh cites a range of studies of different aspects of cultural production in assembling his table of problems and responses, and it is his assembly which yields 'the cultural industries approach' – the originality of the work is its demonstration that, in ways that connect with each other, there are theorists willing to confront the fact that culture is produced by industry, but they are also able to argue that this should not be a cause for pessimism. It should not be a cause for pessimism because, as he argues,

> Abandoning extreme pessimism is not the same thing as complacently celebrating the cultural industries as they are. The key words...are **complex, ambivalent and contested** (emphasis in original)
>
> (2002: 17)

So determined is Hesmondhalgh that we understand his position as one in favour of a representation of cultural-industrial production as 'contested' that the above quote is a re-emphasis of exactly this sentiment made on page 3. In arguing this point, and as evidence of it, he makes his entire argument pivot on a specific claim:

> More than other types of production, the cultural industries are involved in the making of products – that is, texts – that have an influence on our understanding of the world....I prefer the phrase **symbol creators** for those who make up...songs....symbol creators are the primary workers in the making of texts (-) symbol creators are granted considerable autonomy within the process of production – far more, in fact, than most workers in other forms of industry. (emphasis in original)
>
> (Hesmondhalgh, 2002, pp. 3, 4/5, 22)

Again, because the idea of 'creative autonomy' of musicians inside the industrial production of music commodities is central to his representation of those industries as contested (and, by implication, its production processes as 'contestable') Hesmondhalgh also repeats this assertion:

> **This point about creative autonomy is absolutely crucial for an understanding of the cultural industries in the late twentieth century** (emphasis in the original). It shows that the metaphor of the traditional factory production line, often used in critiques of industrial cultural production, entirely misses the point (emphasis in original; a point also made by Negus, 1992, p. 46).
>
> (2001, p. 55)

We will need to return to the 'factory production line' metaphor and its usefulness, or otherwise, as a conceptual tool for understanding the music industries. Here what needs to be considered is that even though he is careful to qualify this statement,

> This is by no means complete autonomy: it is carried out under the supervision of creative managers
>
> (2002, p. 55)

An exploration of what the 'supervision' of 'managers' means for autonomy is never engaged. This means that we are left to imagine or, in our case, envisage the musician in a state that is very much the one that Ella describes at the start of this chapter – somewhere away from the 'manufacturing studio' – and only impacted by these managers somehow after the event. But if aspects of production take place away from companies (under conditions of creative autonomy), how, then, are they 'industrial'; or else, what happens to them when they arrive at companies that make them become industrial? Taken as a whole, Hesmondhalgh's determination to create the cultural industries approach out of the pioneering work of Miège and Garnham, but added to by his own work and his synthesis of other satellite works in media production, leads to a fusing of what are almost tectonic plates of theory that then obscure the working alliances of musicians and music companies and tend to leave them separated rather than united in much the way that less rigorous accounts do.

This is a severe judgement but it is not intended to be a confrontational one. There needs to be a refreshed political economy of cultural production, especially when this approach has been so long crippled by the influence of Adorno, but this needs to be a political economy that is capable of movement between the various levels identified previously – of music industries (as a distinct cultural-industrial sector); the Music Industry as a necessary amalgamation of them but, as a descriptive term, one whose use needs careful handling; and, most importantly of all, music industry as the practice of working alliances that lead to the commodities that demand an analysis of their production as an outcome of industry. For all its deftness, one could argue that Hesmondhalgh's study 'bends the stick' too far away from the Frankfurt School. His desire to refuse a portrayal of the cultural industries as 'top down' monoliths – to render them as sites of struggle and negotiation rather than mechanisms of regimentation – urges him too far towards industry as 'contested' and so an equivalent distance away from accepting them for what he recognises them to be – the province of 'corporations, [that] like all businesses, have an interest in making profits' (2002: 3). This can be seen in the ways discussed below.

Where the responses to the problems that Hesmondhalgh argues are distinctive features of the cultural industries are concerned, three can be argued to misrepresent the industrial experience of musicians. The first of these concerns the observation that 'misses are offset against hits'. The problem here is that he does not show that 'misses' are the outcome of exactly the same managed process as 'hits', which tends to 'naturalise' 'misses' (market failures) as the product of musical weaknesses and so weakens a framework for understanding the management of music commodities within the working alliance between music companies and musicians. In turn, that management takes place at all is not explored – in either its practice (as a servant to the music companies' desire for profit) or its implication – that musicians enter business partnerships inside which they become managed subjects. If this latter logic is then teased out, what musicians enter into when they sign their contracts may well be a working alliance but this partnership is nonetheless re-composed as a set of production relations. Inside these relations, musicians assume the place of sellers of labour power in relation to the capital invested in commodity production, a position far removed from one of 'creative autonomy' and far closer to 'the factory production line' than is comfortable either for Hesmondhalgh's argument or for the sensibilities of all of us who prefer to think of the music we like as not industrial.

The second response that can be questioned is the practice of 'formatting'. As an industrial practice it brings into question the entirety of Ella's point:

> Most manufactured bands are highly successful, but I think truly talented people should come forward and make their mark without people interfering!! They should find their talent within their heart, not within the 'manufacturing' studio.
>
> (news.bbc.co.uk *op cit*)

It does so because if formatting is an industrial strategy then this is a pre-determined approach to engaging with 'creative' people – no matter what is in their 'hearts', it is the 'manufacturing studio' which decides what will enter the market for the reason that, as Hesmondhalgh argues, it is the imperative of a company engaged in cultural production to maximise its audience share. At the very least, this suggests that such companies are likely to overlook or reject, in our case, musicians who do not obey the formatting imperative, but this is a convenient myth (the one that underpins exceptionalising some musicians from an imputed common, industrial, experience for all the rest) and it is one that actually runs counter to the point Hesmondhalgh is attempting to make with his insistence that cultural industries are 'complex, ambivalent and contested'. It does so because what picture of them he wants to create is that cultural industries are so dependent on the creativity of creative people that it needs to allow them scope to work on their creations – which then become industrialised we don't know how. But by insisting on formatting as a response, he suggests that the culture companies are in the driving seat with regard to creativity (because they know what they want and recognise it when they see it), which then problematises his conception of 'creative managers' and the 'supervision' they exercise – if this is so 'light touch', and if so much of commodity production goes on outside their control, how is it management at all? And if it is the case that it is management of market entry of finished commodities, then doesn't this sudden switch in the power to decide the fitness of a commodity for market entry become the all-powerful, all-embracing one in cultural production?

Clearly there are more questions here than the cultural industries approach would seem to have answers for; and the lack of answers can be argued to derive directly from the claim that 'creative autonomy' is 'absolutely crucial' to understanding how cultural industries function. As we have just seen, if musicians are creatively autonomous then it is not clear how, if at all, what they do is engaged with industrial processes of commodity production. This is especially the case when Hesmondhalgh insists on the characterisation of cultural industries as exhibiting 'loose control of symbol creators; tight control of distribution and marketing' (2002, p. 17). In an unstated way, it is in this claim that he repudiates 'the metaphor of the traditional factory production line' (2002, p. 55). It is not my intention to fight for the re-instatement of this metaphor, but it is to suggest that the metaphor of 'traditional factory production line' only 'misses the point' if we think of musicians as workers working under physically direct managerial control in the performance of physically prescribed tasks. If we substitute 'physical' for 'metaphysical' control and prescription we can begin to see musicians as forms of labour whose actions are controlled through discursive regimes in which the construction of knowledge and the disposition of power favour their compliance with industrial processes that do not necessarily favour their needs or aspirations.

We will return to this notion of music industry as substantially discursive and informal throughout this study. We can begin to appreciate its general contours and main dynamics if we re-commence Hesmondhalgh's analysis from two further 'distinctive features of the cultural industries' that he references but gives no prominence to. These are the twin facts that there is a huge over-supply of musicians, and that 'nobody knows' (Caves, 2000, p. 3)[2] what cultural commodities are likely to offer a substantial return on investment following market entry. That Hesmondhalgh is aware of the significance of these conditions is clear: under his outlining of the problem posed by 'high production costs', he refers to the 'volatile and unpredictable nature of demand'. Similarly, he quotes Miège's observation that 'cultural firms' rely on the existence of 'vast reservoirs underemployed artists' (2002, p. 70; Miège, 1989, p. 72). In failing to feature them in his summary of the problems faced by the cultural industries, Hesmondhalgh misses an opportunity to engage with the day-to-day realities of musicians seeking success through market entry. He does this by failing to consider what it means to be an investor in making music commodities; what it means to face in two directions at once (in one towards a mass of hungry hopefuls, many of whom probably write and perform reasonably well, and in another towards markets that are hugely difficult to predict). Certainly, as he suggests, one strategy for coping with the latter is to over-produce – at least in the sense that, for example, record companies might initiate the making of more commodities than they can hope to sell at any one time. But this is not as indiscriminate as he represents it nor is this commodity-making left substantially to the actions of musicians working autonomously. Further, if 'over-production' can be likened to throwing 'mud against the wall' (2002, pp. 20–21) – when this 'mud' consists of creative, ambitious and optimistic human beings and their efforts – how is this brutality managed, face to face, on a day-to-day basis?

While the 'distinctive features' that Hesmondhalgh identifies certainly apply, it is over-supply and the fact that 'nobody knows' that are the truly 'distinctive features of the cultural industries'. What these conditions instil in investors in music commodities is a double need: to choose and to create an apparatus that actualises those choices as commodities generated by routine measures. Further, these choices are made throughout the commodification process: by musicians about themselves and their address to music markets in the earliest days of their self-organisation; by the artist managers they engage to manage their pursuit of competitive advantage over other musicians; and then by music companies that first choose from the vast army of aspiring musicians and, following this, during the stages of the commodification process, organise and choose again – selecting those they suspect might become market successes and rejecting those they fear might not.

All of this choosing is about the market potential of symbolic goods and therefore itself involves symbolisation – discussing meanings that appear to be being made in the present by musicians and that might be made in some version of the future by possible audiences. In this way, to study music industry is to study two key phases or dimensions of music-industrial praxis. Firstly, we need to understand the generation of knowledge about symbolic goods and their likely market performance as the commonsense of music industry. Secondly, we then need to consider how the application or mobilisation of this knowledge comes to have material effects – about what to play, how to look as one plays, where to play, how to record sounds, and how to represent musicians and their efforts in marketing and promotional activities. This puts terminology or, more accurately, discourse at the centre of music industry. This is the reason for beginning this study by highlighting how common formulations of 'music' and 'industry' influence the understanding of their points of connection and disconnection – for the reason that if music is considered to be compromised by its implication with industry, then this problematises how people who practise music industry behave. Further, it also shapes how music industry is represented by interested parties where, together, this representation accumulates as an entity referred to widely and more or less colloquially as the Music Industry when no such place exists; rather, music industry is a practice more than it is a place, and it is a practice not just characterised but defined by the modes and methods through which people who believe they can make market-successful music commodities come to work with musicians who believe that they can be market successes.

This approach gives rise to many questions. Who are these 'people'? Why do they believe they can make successful commodities? How do they actualise this belief? Who are musicians? Why do they believe they can be successful? How do they come to work with music companies? What does this 'work' consist of – how is it organised, practised and rationalised? And what is its object – how can we understand the music text as a symbolic good, as the outcome of a industrial production process? Chapter 2 will discuss the origins of the music-industrial process. Chapter 3 will consider musicians seeking market entry. Chapter 4 will discuss the role of artist managers in the organisation of musicians for securing working alliances with music companies towards market entry.

Chapter 5 will discuss music companies. Chapter 6 will consider the role and arguable effects of the contracts that musicians and music companies agree in their working relations. Chapter 7 will discuss how all of these constituent components interact as a distinctive form of industrialised music. Finally, Chapter 8 will consider whether, and if so to what extent, digitisation has changed music industry along with the music industries.

2
Industry and Music

The previous chapter can be summarised as series of propositions:

1. Even though the term 'the Music Industry' is used as if industrialised music is a social and cultural fact, there is a parallel and contradictory cultural resistance to music's implication with industry.
2. The co-existence of resistance to, and yet comparatively casual acceptance of, the idea that there is a 'music industry' is a barrier to analysis because in neither accounts are the working relations between musicians and music companies specified.
3. The term 'the Music Industry' is a problematic one and its use needs to be supplemented by application of 'the music industries' and 'music industry' when and where appropriate. Further the music industry is not to be confused with or reduced to 'the recording industry'.
4. There is major digitally driven change across the music industries but there are underlying continuities that continue to give music an industrial character.
5. These continuities involve the relations that exist between music companies, musicians, music users, music and music markets but the 'industrial character' of music must be sought in the inter-relations between music companies and musicians.
6. The inter-relations between musicians and music companies are a form of production relations. Rather than consider their actions separately, it is of greater analytical benefit to consider how the actions of one party bears on another in a joint effort that results in the production of symbolic goods in music.

The object of this chapter is to explore the origins of industrialised music. Once the historically and culturally deep-rooted nature of music industry has been explored it will be easier to consider the roles of the constituent elements in the music-industrial process. This will be the work of the next four chapters. It is by isolating these 'constituent elements' – musicians, artist managers, music companies, and the contracts they create between each other – that music industry can be specified and the weaknesses in existing cultural industries theory can be addressed.

Industries are not identical but it is fair to assert that they are driven by identifiable and defining characteristics and practices. Among these, the most salient could be argued to be the following: the decision to invest capital as an anticipation that profit can be derived from investment, the creation of companies as the vehicle for the investment of capital, the organisation of production by consistent and comparatively transparent methods that are accessible to managerial intervention and an imperative to seek competitive advantage over rival companies selling products that are close substitutes. Musicians become embroiled in these practices because, in order to survive, they too are driven to seek competitive advantage over rivals. It is how they then become embroiled that counts, and it counts not just for them but for what music users receive as music or, more accurately, as symbolic goods with music at their core. In this way, whatever the biographies of individual musicians and whatever the often apparently deep segregation between music genres, consistencies in the inter-relations between musicians and music companies can be identified across apparently unique and dissimilar experiences and over time.

Once we appreciate how the actions of music companies bear on those of musicians we should be better placed to confront the huge changes in and across the music industries that are being driven by digitisation, especially in the form of the internet and the economic, social and cultural transformations it is stimulating. These transformations continue to be represented in either extremely optimistic or pessimistic ways depending on the position of the commentator.[1] Although it is the recording industry which has been most affected by digitisation, its turmoil has had significant consequences for the other music industries. These developments will be discussed in Chapter 8, but it is worth noting here that not all of the turmoil in the recording industry has been produced by the internet. Furthermore, change is not a new phenomenon where music industry is concerned; music is sensitive to social and cultural change because it is an expressive, symbolic medium and the defining point is that, throughout its history, music industry has continued to be practised in the face of massive social and cultural change as well as through periods of intense technological innovation. Given this, it is the versatility and resilience of music industry as a practice that begs to be explored.

Popular music has never reached us by musicians working alone. As with all suppliers and sellers of goods, musicians need to enter markets. What musicians face when allying with companies whose focus is the market entry of symbolic goods is that music companies must follow the logic of profit-making and are therefore driven to manage their business relationships so that profit is made. At the very least this means that, in their collaboration, the limits of the managerial actions of music companies are never clear and never fixed: when both parties want market success, where do the interests of a company end and those of the musician begin? As the 'cultural industries approach' indicates, conflict does indeed lie at the heart of the Music Industry but it is not necessarily a conflict between what companies want and what musicians would prefer; rather it is a conflict between what musicians want and what they must experience in order for these wants to be realised. This is an opaque claim but what we are dealing with is not a clear-cut industrial process of the conversion of raw materials into finished products. It is not clear-cut because the raw materials are human beings and their actions and the outcomes of their joint effort with artist managers and music companies are symbolic intangibles. Even so, industrial processes producing marketable goods is a comparatively constant process across all industries; establishing what is comparable and what is specific to music industry is the challenge posed by its study.

Music industry – change and continuity

As the previous chapter argued, there is change in the music industries, but there are continuities in the practice of music industry that gives them their coherence. Music industry and popular music gave birth to each other in the 19th century. Since then the foundational consistencies that give character to music industry are that there is always music and there are always musicians, music companies, music users and markets in which all four are connected for profit. Certainly, none of these constituencies is static and none of this 'connecting' is straightforward. All of the constituencies are continuously dynamic and changes in the total dynamic of their inter-connectedness can be stimulated by changes in one or more of them at any one time. Just to pluck examples from within each constituency from comparatively recent pop history, consider the emergence of hip-hop and dance music partly as a consequence of digital instruments, or the abrupt emergence of 'grunge' in the USA as an aesthetic among musicians or the rise of independent record companies and distribution networks characteristic of punk rock in Britain and their impact on the majors record companies, or the enthusiastic take-up of downloading by music users with its consequences for the concept of the 'album' as an object of consumption.

Each innovation has triggered a need for adjustment and innovation in each other constituent of the music-industrial process; but music industry went on, and goes on, being recognisably music industry whatever the nature and scale of disruption and change. This is substantially because however much musicians want to make music and music users want to enjoy it, it is only music companies that are both equipped and invested in connecting them. Further, this 'connecting' has to obey business logics. Considered in this way, music companies all want to realise the 'promise' of new acts and the quality of existing ones, but they need to make these unique configurations of symbolic producers fit their own prescribed routines and match their own business imperatives and goals. This does not necessarily mean that all acts are powerless in their dealings with music companies – acts that have already created some kind of enthusiastic popular profile may well be able to dictate favourable terms of engagement with companies – but these 'terms' are not unlimited, they will always be based on industry standards and expectations.

Where these standards are concerned, they should, but rarely do, act as a grim warning to aspirant acts; for example, a staple statistic of the recording industry was always that nine out of ten records failed to recoup their costs of production while only 1 in 20 made significant profits – and market failures were always summarily dropped from their contracts. No other industry could exist with a 90 per cent failure rate; the record industry existed this way because musicians rather than companies always took 'the fall'. To configure an industry this way then suggests that music industry as a practice is one stacked against the market success of musicians. 'Stacking against' does not happen by its own volition; the reality behind these statistics is that each and every act anticipates and expects market success. Market failure is always a managed outcome of an industrial process which involves human beings making decisions about the form and content of symbolic goods in production. The challenge is to specify this as music industry.

While musicians may have gained the ability, through digital audio workstations (DAW) and the internet, to make recordings and to distribute them cheaply, what they cannot contrive is the investment necessary for them to 'grow' themselves as businesses. Equally, beyond working on their sound, their look, and their 'story', they are unlikely to be able to develop, manage and sustain strategies of competitive advantage over rivals. At the same time the digital applications that empower musicians simultaneously intensify competition among them so, again, whether they combine with record companies or other providers of marketing, they are forced into working alliances with companies. It is the dynamic of individual alliance, especially in terms of how they are led that counts for the coherence of the symbolic good that emerges from them; where, as Chapter 7 will examine, it this coherence that is pivotal in the good's chance of market success.

Even as the Music Industry is experiencing a period of defining and historic change, demand for music persists and the most efficient way of meeting demand is to establish systematic means of supply. Whether any music commodity will sell remains unknown during the earliest phases of the forming of working alliances, in virtual as in real space. Furthermore, success in virtual space is seen as a platform to real-world music industry activities – recording on bigger budgets in dedicated studios, touring on as large and as extensive a scale as possible, making significant and sustained media appearances, gaining sponsorship for live performances, selling clothing and other goods that often are only fully meaningful, and therefore pleasurable, when used in the company of like-minded people. Consequently, even as the internet short-circuits industrial production in important ways, the maximisation of return on investment continues to be guided by a persistent logic along familiar paths by familiar beliefs and prejudices about how a desired market outcome might be achieved. The questions then are how and where do such beliefs come from, who holds them, and with what arguable effects?

New business practices are becoming evident as offline and online practices combine, but whether these are new industrial practices is what is at issue. It is at issue because what is not truly changing is the need for musicians to work with companies, when this 'working' can be demonstrated to be characterised by what it has always been characterised by – the creation of a working context for joint endeavours established by the needs of profit-making. This does not mean that there cannot be change and innovation in music industry. Even so, music-industrial work continues to proceed on the basis that companies know best how to enter markets. Musicians ally with them because they seek an edge over their rivals and so they covet what they believe is the skill, expertise and knowledge of those music companies. By exploring music's industrialisation in the 19th century, the formulation and the persistence of these relations can be better appreciated. This persistence will be argued to drive from a social construction of music driven by the re-formulation of society around the needs of capital and its expansion. This was to be a period in which industry 'came to' music but one in which music was also enshrined as a practice that was antithetical to industry. Perversely, from the perspective of music companies, the practice of music industry was facilitated rather than hindered by the notion of an antithesis between music and industry. Forms of knowledge about music were created in this period that the new music entrepreneurs could exploit to their advantage; an advantage they can be demonstrated to have enjoyed ever since.

Music, demand and industry

There could be no industry in music unless such an industry had become socially and culturally possible and desirable. This may seem an obscure statement, but there was a time before popular music and that time, from an historical perspective, was not so long ago. In order for there to be popular music, and with it, as both its guarantee and outcome, an industrial mode of producing popular music, a range of substantial, and substantially new, social, political, legal, economic and cultural conditions needed to have become operable.

As Attali (1985) has speculated, music is likely to have become consolidated and codified through its place in rituals in pre-history. The fact that it came to enjoy such an important place in the social order tells us something about the special characteristics of music. Music is a form of communication that has its own codes: ones that, because they rely on patterned relations between instruments (including the voice), differentiate it from both speech (Tagg 2002, p. 8 and *passim*) and noise. Ritual gives music a particular power for several reasons. For example, even to the uninitiated it will be powerful because powerful people use it to say something about their position in political and social hierarchies and about the ideas and values they represent. More than this, music draws a separate attention to itself so that, in its way, it is the equivalent of the priest or the monarch. We attend to 'the music' at a ceremony because it is essential to that ceremony; it 'speaks' of the powerful matters at hand even when we do not know why; it comes after and before the voice of the priest or the monarch, pre-figuring, reiterating and consolidating their pronouncements and authority by other means. Because we often do not know why music has the effect it does then its place in ritual can seem magical to us; almost as if the music produces the expected behaviour in and of itself.

Perhaps because of its power, music could not be contained to, or limited by, its place in official ritual. Music was either always present in, or else leaked into and permeated, the orders of those without power, but always in a way that saw it retain its usefulness as a peculiarly expressive and yet substantially ineffable practice. In this way and from the perspective of this study, the issue of the origin of music is a red herring. Making music may well have existed before and beyond its use in rites and ceremonies, but the very fact that its power was 'revealed', sealed and maintained through such usage meant that, in its permeation of the social order beyond the ruling levels, it came to be used by the powerless to perform their own rites (cf. Frith, 1996).

In its role in the performance of social rites in the very widest sense, music can be said to be 'useful'. It is useful because it helps us to be alone and to be with others, to dance, to cry, to apologise, to celebrate birthdays and to bury the dead. It has facility and authority, and it continues to feel and seem magical far beyond the church or the royal court. Consider the rapture evident in crowds at festivals or in arenas, the happy chaos of a karaoke session, or the intimacy of an 'acoustic' event in a gallery or art space of some kind. In these senses, music is valuable because not only does it help to bind social groups and to reproduce core values that are often difficult to express but it also helps to articulate differences, conflicts and tensions. Music only takes on industrial significance when companies offer it, in exchange for money, to people who find music useful.

The value of music is a function of its continuing social recognition as useful; its 'use value', in the narrower economic sense, is brought into being when an apparatus of manufacture and exchange is established to sell music goods. This apparatus was one of the many industrial ones that came into full effect during the 19th century. The broad emergence of industrial, capitalist society created new relations between music, musicians, and music users by systematising and vastly expanding the role of music companies in connecting them. It did this as one of the many effects of the breaks from, and adaptations to, the previous power system accomplished by the new capitalist class. The rise of new social groups to political power resulted in music becoming celebrated for its supposed capacity to connect users to a transcendent, supernatural sphere. More, this was newly composed music that no longer needed to be tied to praise or worship of God to demonstrate this capacity.

To clarify this point, in the 19th century the basis for the creation of wealth shifted away from the ownership of land and towards the generation of capital. The immediate object of the investment of capital is profit, but its driving aim overall is, more accurately and profoundly, to generate new capital. In turn this means that a capitalist system is focused on growth as the condition of the creation of wealth. What made pursuit of capital expansion such an unstoppable social and economic force was that its growth is not limited by physical factors in the way that income from land is. Consequently, the scale of the wealth of the new capitalist class quickly outstripped that of the previously dominant class. In the ascendancy of new, non-aristocratic groups to power, what did not change was the fact that this new ruling class needed to secure its position.

As previous incoming rulers had learned, social disruption is to no one's benefit and the quickest way to settle the social order after major change is to adapt whatever is serviceable in the old order and, where this cannot be accomplished, to make change seem an improvement on what came before. Where music was concerned, its intrinsic usefulness in the facilitation of rites remained active. This meant that the incoming ruling class re-defined music by adapting existing rituals to its own needs and creating new ones that declared not just their accession to power but the rewarding, new and better way of life this accession heralded. In this way, the creation of new official rituals, together with the insertion of new faces and new values into old ones, involved more than writing new music, it meant re-configuring music in ways that gave new legitimacy to a newly reconstructed social order.

How this was accomplished was by imbuing certain music and certain composers with a supernatural status, as artistic geniuses inspired by God. This, then, reflected glory onto those who enjoyed the ability to recognise which composers and which music embodied this state of grace. In turn, by elevating and celebrating some music and specific compositions and composers in a very public way (through the creation of orchestras and concert halls) this legitimacy was restricted to those who could patronise the new music where their patronage could be re-positioned as accomplishing the work of God, or reason, or both. This newly endorsed music could itself be re-positioned as a universal good because it was taken to exemplify the 'best' of civilisation in its classical symmetries.

'Classical music' as it became known could enjoy the capacity to act as a socially unifying force once an apparatus to spread and consolidate its widest appreciation could be established. So it was that, alongside the orchestras and concert halls, what arose was an apparatus of institution: a canon of composers, conservatoires for the training of the players and conductors of their works, grade exams to ensure standardised recruitment to orchestras, music criticism to maintain the canon and to judge admission to it, and musicology to theorise challenges to this music's fitness to be considered ever-valuable. In this way, institutionalisation 'froze' not just a body of music and a set of music practices but, more importantly, a way of thinking about, and a way of forming knowledge about, music.

In a parallel process, a further aspect of the rise of a new class to social power involved the impact of the philosophy in and through which its aims were formulated. Couched in France as a pursuit to establish the 'rights of man', what had galvanised the masses of the poor, along with the low- and middle-income strata, to overthrow feudal relations and monarchical rule was that the prize for sacrifice would be their individual right to self-expression and self-determination. As it transpired what was truly achieved was the individual right to own and dispose of property and to restrict its taxation. Even so, if this was a far narrower realisation of the revolutionary goals and dreams than had seemed desirable to some (consider also the Diggers and the Levellers in the English Civil War), the triumph of the rule of law over the arbitrary, hereditary rule of monarchs, had a significant impact on expression.

Within the constraints of censorship laws, the recognition of Intellectual Property (IP) was an advance over the restrictions associated with absolutist monarchy. Recognition and consolidation of this form of property helped to distinguish capitalist from pre-capitalist societies. Under IP, authors of original works earned from the use of those works for a prescribed period. In the UK, for example, it was initially the privilege of the monarch to grant the right to authors to make copies of their work. Earnings from this 'copyright' were called 'royalties' to reflect the initial royal assent. What key impact this had on the industrialisation of music was that once the work of the intellect could be treated as property it could be bought and sold. The buying and selling of music then became an attractive business proposition once a demand for music began to register as an economic force.

The demand for what became industrialised music was a new demand created by a new social class. Capitalism brought not only a new set of rulers into being; the industrialisation stimulated by capitalism brought an industrial workforce into being. This 'working class' was composed, initially, of land labourers drawn into industrial centres. Such urban immigrants brought with them the culture of rural life and they would go on to generate new music associated with industrial work. Even so, the history of this new workforce was defined by the search for power rather than its exercise. The new working class lacked political resources and, consequently, rather than configuring an equivalent but different institution of music on its own terms, the new working class had their use of music substantially transfigured for them by commercial forces. This transfiguration though, paralleled the rise of classical music. It did so by re-situating the practice of 'hierarchising' music.

The classical institution had not just taken on itself the work of rank-ordering composers and compositions: it had made its mission the realisation of itself as the designated arbitration mechanism for the worth of music. One consequence of this was that if the 'best' music was ineffable, then those inside the institution became bathed in the ineffable belief that only they had the power to declare and decide. As individual music businesses came to merge and meld into music industries of live performance and music publishing, they came to practise a similarly institutionalised ordering of music. The difference, of course, was that while the classical institution judged the fitness of music to be admitted to the canon, the popular institution decided on the fitness of music to be admitted to the market. The process of accession to the market is every bit as searching as admission to the canon and the actions of both selecting groups takes place on essentially the same premise – that music decides its own outcome, all that counts is that it conform to the expectations of the selectors and to their criteria. The point of divergence is, then, that the classical institution makes its knowledge of music transparent, while the popular institution continues to rely on knowledge that is inaccessible; that is arcane and mysterious and all the more powerful for being arcane and mysterious.

Popular music as a commercial form of culture developed once private companies took up the business of meeting demand for forms of entertainment, including the performance of new compositions, expressed by a new market. The commercial process was defined by a combination of two powerful general forces: the institutionalisation of music and the formation of a legal framework for protecting copyright holders which facilitated the buying and selling of compositions. The demand for music which drove its commercialisation expanded exponentially partly because, in changing times, there was a great need to express new ties and lament the loss of old ones, in part because, as populations expanded so many more came to need it, and to a degree because demand, as a result of the IP framework, could be responded to in the form of new music businesses. These businesses were the 'music halls', and the writing and publishing of songs to be sung in them.

Music hall, music and music Industry

Before the rise of industrial society, payment for music existed, primarily, as payment for 'broadside' ballads – payment for sheets of words rather than for songs or for music, as such. Vague in their origin and, given the regularity and simplicity of their metrical structures, easily adaptable to existing melodies and to recent events, the ballads could be bought at fairs and markets and also in the streets of the largest cities. The ballads covered a fairly limited range of topics. To an extent this reflected the limited lives of their users. More, they tended to reflect the restricted, but still potent concerns of a population rooted in the regularities of land-centred society. The ballads discussed and rehearsed the supernatural as well as religious forces that were believed to give an order to existence and, through their tales of love, morality and mortality they contributed to the self-regulation of social life. Through them, the places of the land-owning rich and powerful as well as of the poor and powerless were read as unchanging explanations for, and reconciliations to earthly, rather than social and political, experiences. When, at last, the rural poor had mostly been re-located to industrial centres – where their numbers grew despite the appalling conditions – music continued to do this work, but with markets and fairs of less relevance to industrial workers, where they came to engage with music as a commercially structured negotiation of a life made of new, changed, social relations was in music halls.

Kift argues that the first music hall in Britain was The Star which opened in Bolton in 1832 (1996, p. 19).[2] Kift's work is heterodox because it challenges the conventional wisdom that Music Hall was almost entirely a phenomenon associated with London and one with a later starting date than she identifies. The significance of citing a dispute in Music Hall scholarship is not to contest it in order to offer a separate perspective, only to draw attention to how deep can Music Hall's roots in industrial history be argued to be and how its coming was a phenomenon of industrial urbanisation. Bolton, as a town, is almost a microcosm of the industrial revolution – a place with roots traceable to the Stone Age, a continuous history from Roman times and a tradition of weaving that became re-cast as a teeming mill town, in a matter of decades, from the turn of the 19th century. It was in such towns, such urban industrial centres, that Music Hall took root and formed the industry in music which is the subject of this study. Rather than deal with this formation in a continuous way it is more useful to identify its key dimensions as a series of points:

1. Demand

The existence of IP laws does not mean that all music suddenly became 'industrial'; rather what it meant was that all original music composed under its rule became notionally saleable. Music publishing was the first music business to adapt to the rise in demand for light music and songs to be played and sung in a range of new social settings associated with the rise of industrial towns and in the face of the reduced importance of markets and fairs. Alongside these public and private settings – park bandstands and the homes of the more prosperous citizens – Music Hall became the new commercial focus for the consumption of music, of songs that needed to be specially written for a novel type of performance. Even so, these songs needed to satisfy not just the quantity of demand but also its specific qualities. In effect, the songs that became the staple of Music Hall as an experience needed to carry on the work of the ballads by helping what were now industrial workers to make sense of their new lives.

2. Music and brevity

It took several decades for the emergent form to consolidate itself as a genre. Towards the end of the 19th century, the typical bill of a Music Hall show was one of eclectic variety. For example, various authors[3] quote various bills that include a wide range of often exotic speciality acts, but the staples remained the teller of funny stories and the singer of mostly comic but also sentimental songs. In the larger towns and especially in the cities, there would be many music halls. The practice of acts would be to appear at as many halls as they could on a single night. Eventually this practice coalesced into a system of 'circuits'. Singers relied on material they did not always write themselves. Further, as bills featured many acts then singers would sing very few songs; the songs they sang tended to vary little over time and became associated with them as signatures, even 'trademarks'. These songs tended to be rousing and to emphasise choruses because, as selling drink as well as food to patrons was a further income stream for hall owners, a drunken audience enjoyed 'joining in' with the singer, a fact that also compensated for the lack of amplification. In turn, the song form and song content were dictated by these requirements. Where song form was concerned, time constraints meant that the singer, as all 'turns', had only a limited time to perform and so they favoured brief 'numbers'. Secondly, they favoured songs with choruses that were simple, memorable and which captured or re-stated the sentiment of the song's title. Such songs encouraged 'joining in' but there was more to them than this, as the following point should clarify.

3. Performance and knowingness

In Music Hall, along with sentimental songs it was the 'comic' songs which succeeded the most. Even so, comic songs are only effective if they are funny, and what characterised Music Hall humour, generally, was what Bailey (1994) has referred to as 'knowingness'. The detailed analysis of Music Hall performance Bailey offers is beyond the limits of reference here, but, for these immediate purposes, what we need to consider is that in their earliest forms, music halls were rowdy places. Faced with this clamour and generalised inattention, the Music Hall performer needed to constitute an audience from the crowd facing them. The nature of the songs together with the nature of their performance were a response to the need to control this rowdiness and, once established, fixed the 'genre rules' for the medium.[4] Bailey explains the centrality of comic song through Althusser's concept of interpellation:

> 'interpellation' is suggestive here as the form of ideological address or hailing that recruits individuals into a particular subject-role or identity. In some such way, the performer's knowingness activates the corporate subjectivity of the crowd, and calls an audience into place.
>
> (1994, p. 146)

What reinforces the form and content of the comic song is the work of social reproduction the audience can be argued to accomplish through enjoying, participating in and so completing the performer's act:

> It is knowingness that ignites this effect by pulling the crowd inside a closed yet allusive frame of reference, and implicating them in a select conspiracy of meaning that animates them as a specific audience.
>
> (1994, p. 151)

The 'conspiracy of meaning' is a crucial phrase because it reflects the audience's own power and understanding – its activity rather than its passivity. The importance of this distinction cannot be underestimated when discussing popular music and the Music Industry and will be returned to in this and subsequent chapters. Here we need to recognise that, as Bailey argues, the music hall was more than a place of consolation for the new working class, it was a place to make sense of new conditions and so forge a new way of life; a place of resistance and negotiation as much as one of diversion and distraction. In this, humour played a vital role in giving vent to, and allowing pleasure to be taken in, the subversive power of being disrespectful.

In turn this reveals one of the central contradictions of popular music: it is 'popular' because 'the people' use it for important, even essential, purposes, but they neither make nor own what is so vital to them. Music Hall as a means of social reproduction was in private hands; commercial forces created the dedicated spaces, the bills, the acts and the material to resist with and negotiate through. This recognition then leads to one of the key sets of questions in popular culture, generally: does the public get what it wants, or want what it gets? This binary will also need to be returned to but Bailey's observation will set the tone for that return:

> Interpellation is not just the calling into position of a particular subjectivity, but is more in the nature of a transaction or co-production. Where a performance takes [place], the crowd/audience registers recognition and identification, certainly, but it also asserts its own collective authorship/authority in the performance.
>
> (1994, p. 146)

4. Product, commodities and symbolic goods

A previous observation made with regard to the impact of IP laws on music is not entirely accurate: it is not so much that 'a demand for music began to register as an economic force', it was more a demand for this music expressed in these ways that led to the industrialisation of music. 'This' music was the sentimental and the comic song and 'these' ways of expressing demand were to pay for entry to music halls and to enjoy a drink there as part of, in Music Hall's earliest decades at least, a raucous assembly in a new and teeming urban environment. This is not to entirely suggest that demand calls a specific form of industry into being, but it is to indicate that, if a cultural experience is desired, and if it can be contrived to be provided on a regular, satisfying and comparable way across an entire country, then what is called into being is a product and, consequently, an industry geared to a form of its production that can be organised and controlled to the satisfaction of investors.

The reasoning here is that if the product is a cultural one – one that reflects and reproduces ways of making sense of social relations – then it only works as a product when it is able to go on effecting or pretending to effect this reflection and reproduction. As later remarks will discuss, the over-arching product needs constant feeding to retain its relevance and appeal. The social place of powerless people is by its very nature an insecure one. The powerless are easily and strongly buffeted by social, political and economic contingencies and events and symbolic goods go on being called on to help survive and make sense of vicissitudes. Not all texts survive change and there is a constant demand for new material, driven as much by the needs of users as by the imperatives of production for profit. The industry of popular music thus became not just the building and maintenance of halls and a mechanism for organising events, it became the process of converting men and women who sang and played into 'acts' that could be advertised for their specific attributes and special abilities. In this way, popular music is the product; musical acts are popular cultural commodities – ones intended to exemplify the general usefulness of the product that was Music Hall. In making and performing popular music, acts then furnished the texts that music companies offered for sale as symbolic goods. In all of this, determining the potential effectiveness of any act, of any symbolic good, became central to the industrial production of music.

5. Entrepreneurship

Music industry developed from demand – a demand that was capitalised by entrepreneurs. Early forerunners of Music Hall came in the form of increasingly formalised versions of what will have begun as informal 'sing songs' or 'free and easies'. These would take place in a pub or hostelry of some kind and would involve members of a comparatively regular circle of people standing up and giving a turn – more accurately taking a turn to sing or to recite or to tell a funny story. Formalisation, in the role of a chairman, was required to ensure that turn-taking was respected and to bring some order to proceedings. Astute pub landlords quickly came to see the benefit of providing dedicated spaces and food and drink to these gatherings. From there, the encouragement of particularly good 'turns' to repeat performances for payment for the benefit of other customers was a brief but decisive step. In fact, this was more than a 'step'; truly it was a flashing over from the pole of amateurism to that of professionalism. In the move from pub landlord to host of a regularised form of entertainment, such individuals instigated a new branch of commercial music and their formalisation of their practices quickly yielded the industry of live performance.

Entrepreneurs are individuals either with funds or who enjoy the persuasive ability to access funds. They see chances for profit and use great energy in taking them. Entrepreneurs are risk takers and they are exemplary of the 'heroic' capitalism described and analysed by Schumpeter.[5] In this account, entrepreneurialism involves a clutch of abilities; among them to innovate, to read emerging and changing markets rapidly and astutely, and to be attuned almost instinctively to seek competitive advantage over rivals. Popular culture can move very quickly; 'the position' in Bailey's words, of 'particular subjectivit(ies)' can be extremely volatile, so many and so dynamic and unstable are the social and cultural variables that constitute those positions. Consequently, many entrepreneurial gambits and gambles fail, but the mercurial nature of popular culture goes on throwing up new money-making opportunities; creating new 'angles'; encouraging new risks to be taken.

The challenges faced in pursuing such opportunities are threefold: firstly, entrepreneurial forays need to be formalised legally through the constitution of companies and the agreeing of contracts; entrepreneurialism needs flexibility but the legal frameworks for doing business come with a rigidity than can be restrictive. Secondly, industry is about routine more than it is about any mercurial element; investors of capital want its realisation as profit to be secure and repeatable rather then insecure and left to chance. Thirdly, these 'chances', 'angles' and 'risks' involve living human beings: managing the conversion of texts into symbolic goods means managing relationships with people who may well see the world differently from the entrepreneur. The neglect of this human dimension to cultural production is one of the aspects of Hesmondhalgh's account of the contemporary incarnations of these processes that was identified as of concern in the previous chapter. It is the active, working reconciliation of the challenges emblematic of the entrepreneurial nature of cultural production that is the centre of music industry in all its tension and complexity.

6. Standardisation and institutionalisation

Before it could take on the attributes of an industry, Music Hall needed first to become standardised. Once standardised, the music companies that made up this music industry could then begin to behave as an institution – as a repository of knowledge about music. In turn, in behaving as 'experts' in the popular taste, a way of positioning music companies and musicians was initiated which, arguably, has persisted to the present day. If we take the earliest developments in Music Hall as regionally driven, the sheer scale of London as a metropolis was always likely to give it the momentum to standardise the composition of bills, the time slots afforded to acts, levels and types of payment, contracts, marketing, the internal organisation of venues and the emergence of settled companies over *ad hoc* entrepreneurial efforts. Bolton may well be the site of the first true music hall, but, rather like railway gauges in the same period, the most successful examples eventually became generalised across the country. Aided by the standardised spread of railways, the generalisation of London's commercial-infrastructural norms led, eventually, to the emergence of circuits with the building of bespoke theatres under single ownership in numerous cities – the Stoll 'Coliseum' chain and the Moss 'Empires' as the two most notable examples. These latter developments occurred towards the end of the 19th century and it gave Music Hall 'respectability' as a now nationally dominant form of commercial entertainment. The climactic and also pivotal moment of the relentlessness of standardisation was reached with the hosting, by Oswald Stoll, of the first Royal Variety Performance held at the Palace Theatre on 1 July 1912. The bill featured the cream of the Music Hall acts of the day – including Vesta Tilley, Little Titch and Harry Lauder, but notably excluding Marie Lloyd who was considered too risqué. Royal approval acted as an unimpeachable seal of the embedding of Music Hall as a national, cultural institution with all the significance and import the status of institution has for the nature and conduct of music industry.

Music industry's templates

The reason for breaking Music Hall down into a set of dimensions rather than attempting to write a summarised account of its history is to draw attention to what might be regarded as the templates it established for the previously discussed conduct of music industry. Commercial music making for mass markets was a phenomenon of industrial society. In responding to demand, the emergent music businesses of the 19th century not only stimulated further demand, they regularised the supply of a particular product, the Music Hall. It is important to maintain the distinction between product and commodity and also to see that commodity as one of a specific type, the symbolic good. Further, it is the intangibility of the symbolic good that makes music industry, and its study, such contentious undertakings. As a way of elucidating this comment it will be productive to map the defining dimensions of Music Hall onto the constituent aspects of music industry identified in the previous chapter – onto music, music users, music companies and musicians

Before beginning that process it is worth reiterating that music industry is a practice undertaken between music companies and musicians. To this extent, the study of music use and of music itself will play only 'walk-on' parts from here forwards while the study of markets as a phenomenon will be entirely absent. This is not to diminish their importance; all of the efforts of musicians and music industry personnel take place around music and in the name of and in anticipation of the actions of music users in the marketplace. There is insufficient space to discuss all of the constituents of music industry, but it is essential to begin with considering the connections between Music Hall and music users for the impulse the use of music gave, and still gives, to music industry.

Template 1: Music Hall, Music Users and Music

To return to Bailey's argument that music hall performers (and here I want to imagine these solely as singers) constituted a crowd as an audience by recruiting 'individuals into a particular subject role or identity' (1994, p. 146). Here the pivotal point is that these roles and identities were ones that were rapidly becoming familiar as a new 'people' negotiated a profoundly changed set of social relations experienced in the new settings of industrial towns. What sealed successful recruitment 'into … identity' was a particular quality of the total performance. This quality was the performer's ability to encourage the formation of a 'conspiracy of meaning' with individuals in the crowd so that the crowd became an audience. Arguably, it is exactly this process which continues to characterise popular music. Not all people like all music but when music connects with 'hearers' and transforms them into listeners this transformation is an outcome of the performer's activating some form of 'knowingness' they share with the hearer.

Specifying 'knowingness' on a case-by-case basis would require an enormous empirical research project but the contours of knowingness are captured in Bailey's identification of the condition that allows this conspiracy to form itself: the 'closed yet allusive frame of reference' that the performer and crowd members create between them. Another way of understanding an 'allusive frame of reference' is as a 'structure of feeling'. This is a concept developed by Raymond Williams in and through his work on culture and the development and importance of popular culture as a political resource for the emergent industrial working class of the period under discussion. Williams describes a structure of feeling as 'meanings and values as they are actively lived and felt' (Williams, 1983, p. 132) and Bailey's point is that these 'meanings and values' were exactly what music hall singers drew from and spoke to in their songs and performances of songs. By extrapolation we can then argue that alluding to 'lived values' lies at the heart of the successful symbolic good with music at its core. It does so because alluding to lived values in the form of a text of short duration allows those values to be focused and reaffirmed for the period that meaning is made from the text – but only if the text connects to and activates the relevant structure of feeling. If a text does this, then a proportion of the total number of hearers is transformed into an audience for as long as the performance lasts.

What it is vital to recognise at this juncture is that, while structures of feeling are what help integrate individual hearers into listening groups (and with group membership into a 'subject role or identity'), the plethora of roles we choose or are forced to play in life suggest that there are many such structures of feeling in constant, dynamic operation. Consequently there is a need for most music on a wide scale to be accessed fleetingly or at greater duration throughout the course of a day and the course of a life. Even so, not just any music will do or will connect with the palette of feelings socially and culturally available to potential audience members. Consequently, in order for any performance of any song to demonstrate the requisite type and degree of allusiveness it must be appropriate to a hearer in the instance of hearing, otherwise it will not be 'used' to take up the identities Bailey indicates. Considered in this way, in order to have their effect, music performances (whether 'live' or on record) must be expressed in an idiom that listeners respond to and would expect to be addressed in given the context of listening. Further, that idiom must demonstrate currency.

Currency has a dual meaning and both must be activated if the text is to 'work'. Firstly, the signifying materials must be coded in such a way that pleasurable meanings can be made through attending to them. Secondly, they must signify productively in ways that allow 'meanings and values' to circulate. These meanings and values will then activate and become active in specific structures of feeling. For example, while I might attend a Liverpool F.C. home match and roar along to a recording of 'You'll Never Walk Alone', I would never choose to attend a performance by that song's popularisers, Gerry and the Pacemakers. In the first instance the song's sentiments together with the significance for home fans of the act as one from the historic 'Merseybeat' era make the perfect and enduring text for galvanising home supporters as a unified crowd. In the second, the act and its texts have lost almost all currency, save the connection of one of their hit records to the culture of football in Liverpool specifically and in the UK generally. In both cases, idiom is the saviour of the text in the sense that the popular cultural dynamics of football exhibit different modalities and different temporalities from those of popular music; 'old fashioned' music can still evoke and re-affirm meanings and values partly because it is 'old-fashioned'; redolent of an era which is now a nostalgic treasure trove for the self-construction of football fans as believers in what could be considered an almost Victorian value-set.

So it is that all music performances strive to generate and demonstrate idiomatic currency in order that audiences for music are created. Not all idioms are appropriate to all listeners on all occasions, so there are different audiences with differing degrees of loyalty over time for different types of music and for differing qualities of music performance within those types. Moreover, not all musicians can strike the right degrees and balance of idiom and currency in a particular genre and for a particular audience and so fail to create audiences they desire for their performances. What complicates all of this, of course, is that where music industry is concerned, 'musicians' are not musicians, they are 'acts' and music is not music it is the centre of a symbolic good created from a text originated by musicians whose every aspect of the performance of music and of themselves as musicians makes up that text. Acts need music companies in order to enter music markets and so constitute audiences through commercial operations. In this they must accede to, or certainly negotiate with, the apparatus established for deciding degrees of idiomatic currency formed by those companies in pursuit of their own profit.

Template 2: Music Hall, Music Companies and Musicians

The significance for music industry of the institutionalisation of music in the 19th century was that, in the very era of the industrialisation of society, certain forms of music were collected together as a pinnacle of human endeavour. The fact that a defining characteristic of this music was identified as its not being tainted with industry was a problem for popular cultural production; music from outside the canon was lesser music for the simple fact of being outside the canon. Yet the creators of the Music Hall, as successful entrepreneurs, were rich and influential enough to be considered as men of substance and this was reflected in the migration of the term 'impresario' from opera to Music Hall to describe their role and activities. The principal difference between the classical and the popular institutions as they both crystallised out across the late 18th to early 20th centuries was that the former was backward-looking, it specified defining aspects of the form and content of the art works of antiquity and looked for them in existing and new works as the basis for forming judgements about their worth; but the pop institution looked forward and, by definition, must do so always.

The impresarios of the Music Hall, as too the A&R (Artists and Repertoire) personnel emblematic of the recording industry at its height, attempted to estimate the degree to which a performer, a performance or the performed exhibited, or would exhibit when encountered by the market, a sufficient degree of idiomatic currency to engage with a particular structure of feeling in a way that would bring a profitable return on investment. Not all the choices of Music Hall impresarios bore fruit. This is because, as noted in Chapter 1, cultural production is characterised by 'demand uncertainty'; 'nobody knows' what symbolic goods are likely to sell. The role of impresarios was to 'add value' to the acts they engaged and, in some instances, managed. Again, there was more to this than building theatres and organising regular and reliable circuits, important and vital though they were. Rather, and from the perspective of acts, the value-adding undertaken by impresarios was in choosing them to perform.

By plucking an act from the ranks of aspirants, impresarios added value to that act by signalling to potential users that they offered a symbolic good that would be 'useful' to consume. The challenge faced by the act was then not so much that it needed to 'deliver' on this promise (although, of course, it did) but that it did not necessarily control the configuration of this promise or the means of access to its realisation. Acts, especially in their earliest contact with music companies when moving towards joint endeavour, lack power and control over the means of production of symbolic goods. On first contact with an aspirant act, a music company always enjoys a starting advantage because of the twin effects of institutionalisation and standardisation. Where institutionalisation is concerned, rather than its polar opposite, the popular music industry became, effectively, a sub-set of the dominant form of the institutionalisation of music. What institutionalism not only allowed and encouraged, but depended on, was the granting of the right to a designated group of people to speak with authority about music. In turn, this authority could only be effective if it was subscribed to by society more generally. In the classical institution it was scholars who judged; in industry it was impresarios but, crucially, both deferred to 'the music' as if music itself decided who should be acclaimed or who should be top of the bill. In this way, music retained its ineffability and the institutional figures became the judges of the worth of music. It is this capacity which then allowed impresarios to represent themselves as 'all-knowing' (when nobody can know) but also to absolve themselves of responsibility for any negative effects of their own actions because, if acts failed in the marketplace, it was their music making that governed this fate.

Considered in these terms, there is no essential difference or distance between Oswald Stoll and Simon Cowell. *X Factor* judges habitually defer to 'great songs' but what music users use is a symbolic good and the symbolic good exceeds music – it is the total of the text created by the originators of music and, in offering such texts for sale, music impresarios signalled the likely worth of the text through production and marketing practices. So it was, and remains, that the form of goods and the basis on which they enter markets has a bearing on their market performance. Whether those taking the actions are Stoll in the Edwardian era or Cowell in the current one, the fact that actions are taken to prefigure potential meanings is what counts. This is not to argue that the actions of companies determine meanings – this is the weakness of Adorno's argument – but nonetheless when texts are set in contexts to be accessed by potential customers, then contexts play their part in how texts may come to be read. If the impresarios of the past or the 'brand managers' of today mishandle the creation of contexts for access to texts they have already impacted upon then market failure is the likely outcome. Even so, it is the act that pays the ultimate cost of this mishandling regardless of the music it makes.

Template 3: Music Hall and Markets

Marketing is a key practice in the operation of markets. If markets are the names we give to processes of exchange, then alerting those with the power to demand goods to the virtues of specific goods and making them available for purchase are powerful factors in facilitating exchanges. These are the attributes music companies argue they have in regard to symbolic goods in music and this is why musicians are eager to seek them out. Even so, the centrality of markets to social existence and the nature of market competition between goods of a similar type can be argued to have distinctive repercussions for all parties involved in the music-industrial process. To take musicians, first, the problems they face in regard to markets and their associated practices is that there is an over-supply of musicians and, therefore, of music. Music companies are forms of capital and are necessarily driven to seek profits and to grow. They enjoy the luxury of choice where aspirant acts are concerned but, equally, they all face the pressure of competition from each other which makes the over-supply of musicians a problem more than a boon. It is a problem because when nobody knows which symbolic goods will sell, any act might supply the texts from which market-successful goods might be furnished. The coping strategies evolved by music companies in the face of market competition then negatively impact on musicians but they also limit the scope of the entrepreneurialism which gives some music companies their market advantage.

The 'coping strategies' of music companies negatively impact on musicians in two main ways. Firstly, the form of knowledge associated with the institutionalisation of popular music lacks transparency. The standards of the classical institution are transparent because they need to be; the entire enterprise of the classical institution comes down to the maintenance of verifiable standards of composition and performance. In popular music, what counts are sales. Those 'at the top' of the pop institution are there because their efforts have, at some point and perhaps over time, resulted in high sales figures – of concert tickets, sheet music, or records. How these sales were accomplished is regularly attributed to 'the music' and, by inference, to the particular entrepreneur's ability to 'spot' and 'nurture' 'talent'. In this way, knowledge in the Music Industry is tacit rather than explicit, and it pays to have it remain tacit lest awkward questions are asked about all the 'talent' that does not enjoy market success. Because it remains 'arcane and mysterious', acts have little chance to evaluate the claims made by companies and they have little opportunity (and often little time) to decide between companies. Worse, the pressures of over-supply mean that acts are likely to ally with the first company which shows an interest in working with them and they enter alliances often in states of severe under-preparation.

The second negative impact on musicians derives from the ways in which the opportunism of the original music entrepreneurs addressed, but did not solve a market conundrum. As has already been noted, what the original music entrepreneurs did was to re-cast an existing cultural practice involving amateur music making – the 'free and easy' – as a product. Because they did, they also created the market and the market conditions for that product. In creating regularised spaces and a regularised 'bill of fare', they established the expectations of music users and acts. What this meant for acts was that because they knew in advance about what to expect of contexts of performance, they were encouraged to invent performances for payment not on their own terms but to serve a profit-driven business – they created texts with industry in mind and so practised within the ideological boundaries of the Music Industry. Because they want to enter markets, acts implicitly accept the protocols of market entry: even when, as Hesmondhalgh demonstrates, the protocols of market entry are predicated on the market failure of the majority of acts. The risk management strategy of music companies means that companies can be profligate with acts; acts, though, cannot afford to be profligate with themselves.

It is market competition and the risk this poses to capital investment in the production of symbolic goods that takes us to the heart of the defining contradictions of music industry. The formalisation of informal entertainment became generalised across the UK. This generalisation involved the previously identified forms of standardisation. The problem was and remains, though, that the 'meanings and values' potential audiences create and exhibit are not static. In (commercial) cultural contexts in which currency needs to remain current and idiom is dynamic and mobile, then gesture and nuance are all important. Entrepreneurs seek out often fine differences in nuance and emphasis; but the running of companies demands standard practices and processes for the purposes of predictability and reliability in all aspects of production. Similarly, acts demonstrating difference demand bespoke regimes to deliver their nuanced texts as symbolic goods; but standardisation offers formula instead. A formulaic approach to marketing acts reduces risk by allowing control over difference to be maximised, but if formula is too rigidly applied then the energy that difference offers can be stifled. Ultimately, music entrepreneurs want, and need, the 'new' but they want it to behave like the 'old'; they are risk takers who can only operate by being risk averse.

Conclusion

The goals of this study are to specify music industry and to argue that it demonstrates resilience in the face of change. If music industry as a practice involving the joint efforts of musicians and music companies can be specified, the weaknesses in existing theories of cultural-industrial production will be easier to address. Furthermore, the various and substantial impacts of digitisation on the Music Industry will be more readily assessable. The purpose of tracing music industry to the rise of Music Hall in the 19th century was to identify defining consistencies that were established in and through Music Hall as a form of music industry. These defining consistencies have been described as 'templates'. These templates were established in the inter-relations between music companies and musicians in their joint attempt to satisfy demand for entertainment in the 19th century. Music enjoys specific characteristics that make it adept at forming and expressing bonds between people.

It does this through a capacity to articulate and animate structures of feeling as the lived expression of the meanings and values associated with roles and identities that we choose to enter or have thrust upon us. Music does not make itself. It has to be made and its making involves performances that create a text with music as the core, but not sole, signifying practice within that text. Musicians make music with audiences in mind but audiences are not naturally occurring; they too have to be made. The role of music companies is to alert hearers to available texts, but in making texts available as symbolic goods, music companies expect to play a role in their formation and in preparing the groundwork for the contexts of their reception. Companies have these expectations because their contribution to the production of symbolic good comes in the capital they invest in their production. All forms of production devolve onto managed relationships between capital and labour. The symbolic labour of musicians is demanding to understand and demanding to organise for profit; but the fact of its profitable organisation goes back deep into the 19th century.

Ultimately, the templates of organisation established in the earliest years of popular music as a commercial, industrial form of culture solved an enormously demanding conundrum; namely, how to produce symbolic goods in alliances with musicians who are simultaneously business partners, forms of labour and essential components of the commodity produced. The solution to this conundrum involves a balancing act of managerial strategies. These will be explored in the following four chapters, but the strategies can be traced to the form of knowledge represented by the Music Industry as an institution and to the leeway that the over-supply of musicians allows music companies in their constant search for idiomatic currency. This 'solution' though is only ever provisional.

The volatility of subjectivities Bailey cites derives from the permanent but always mutating challenges faced by people whose stake in life is never fully secure. Demand for texts is constant but what specific texts are demanded goes on changing. No formula works forever because few symbolic goods retain their currency intact over time; but formula still works better than any other industrial strategy. There are always audiences for music but there is a constant churn in their membership, in their tastes and in their responses to specific symbolic goods over time. Music companies rely on musicians anticipating these changes in the texts they fashion; musicians rely on music companies retaining their astuteness in terms of the value they add to texts in the fashioning of symbolic goods. Music industry is, to an extent, a symbiotic relationship between music companies and musicians, but it is a contested and unequal symbiosis in that not all parties benefit equally from its conduct. In order to explore the contemporary condition of this particular symbiosis it is necessary to look at each component of music industry separately and then jointly. This will be the work of the following five chapters. The eighth and final chapter will then use the lens they provided to estimate the impact of the recent waves of change that have crashed against the resilient pragmatics of the Music Industry. In this, whether music industry as a practice has been similarly impacted remains to be seen.

3
Musicians in Four Dimensions

The object of the previous chapter was to establish the roots of the three terms used at the outset of Chapter 1: music industry as the activity of industrialising music, the music industries and the Music Industry. The concentration on the rise and consolidation of Music Hall over an 80-year period was intended to demonstrate that a new industry of live performance became established from the 1840s onwards. In creating popular music by generalising and systematising amateur music making practices associated with the emergence of an urban populace, the live performance industry also helped to transform the existing music publishing business by encouraging writers and publishers to produce for the vast new market created by entrepreneurial innovation. It would take a far more detailed historical study to explore the full impact of Music Hall on music publishing and, similarly, the discussion of the rise of an industry in live performance was necessarily schematic. The point remains that new industries in music were called into being in the 19th century. These became substantially inter-dependent, standardised in their practices. They then took on the trappings and, more importantly, institutional power through their growing centrality to commercial entertainment. The purpose of this chapter is to explore the ongoing effects of this embedded, industrial framework on musicians, organised as popular music acts, seeking market success.

As Chapters 1 and 2 argued, to separate popular music from music industry is unsustainable for the reason that there would not and could not be one without the other. Popular music and music industry are inseparable because, for all its contemporary genre distinctions, the music that resonates with large numbers of people within and across all of those categories is an outcome of unified, commercial effort around constructing a symbolic good. Ultimately, management can be understood as control over effort and the conflict that characterises music industry is that different actors (musicians and music companies) have different investments in the effort involved in creating symbolic goods in music for public consumption. Ultimately, musicians must manage their own efforts, but they must somehow make their own efforts complement rather than conflict with the managerial actions taken by the companies they work with. Introducing their own personal manager to co-ordinate this joint effort then introduces a third force into an already complex matrix of managerial practice. Further, there is an enormously wide range of points of possible managerial intervention in the production of symbolic goods – from the portrayal of an act in a video to the place of an act on a festival bill. When all parties to the process have opinions about an array of matters, and when all actions bear on all other actions, establishing a management strategy and sticking to it are huge challenges; challenges made greater still by the fact that the role of musician can be shown to be an inherently conflicted one.

The focus of this chapter will be on the self-managerial challenges musicians face when they decide to go in search of acclaim for their actions. How they meet those challenges is in part inflected by how they understand the role of the music companies they need to ally with. Equally, however much those companies need acts to work with, they are impelled to operate in their own interests and so seek to control their investment through a suite of management practices evolved over a lengthy passage of time. On this basis, acts and companies need each other but need each other in ways that are constitutionally incompatible: acts need companies to help them in realising the recognition and acclaim they seek; companies need acts to produce profit for them. Acclaim and profit can both be found in markets, but these outcomes are not identical. Further, both hinge on market address but, again, different modes of market address can produce different outcomes. To a substantial extent music industry consists of creating, on a case-by-case basis, forms of market address that satisfy two incompatible partners in ways that produce results with which both parties are happy. It should be no surprise that this rarely occurs.

Given the complexities of their joint endeavours, acts and companies can experience conflict in ways and from sources that neither party is necessarily equipped to locate and to extinguish. In all of this, musicians must accept the place in the production relations of music goods offered to them by the industrial system of music. This is not to argue that there is only one way of experiencing that place or that it is a necessarily always an entirely restrictive one, but what is obvious is that musicians come and go while the industrial system, for all its current upheaval, persists. The argument of this chapter will be, firstly, that this persistence must have its consequences for musicians and, secondly, that in seeking out investment, musicians lend themselves to subservient places in the production relations of symbolic goods in music. Given these general, analytically structural aims, this particular chapter should be seen as a relatively freestanding account of a general process that involves musicians, artist managers, music companies and music contracts. The discussion of individual cases and examples will need to be held over to Chapter 7 in order that all the elements that bear on music-industrial practice can be seen in play.

Musicians and symbolic goods

The indivisibility of music and industry remains a contentious notion because our commonsense tells us that, if we can play an instrument, sing, programme a track or all three, we can do this at home and away from any involvement with music companies and their personnel and, if we so choose, in deliberate disregard of the market. As Jason Toynbee has argued very persuasively,[1] innovation is always an idiosyncratic, personal field. The problem with Toynbee's argument is that what influences new musicians is not simply music, it is music they access in a textual form and mostly, overwhelmingly until the coming of the internet, in the form of industrially produced symbolic goods. It is in constructing themselves through what are industrial commodities as much as they are music performances that, as the previous chapter argued, acts create texts with industry in mind and so practise within the ideological boundaries of the Music Industry.

These 'ideological boundaries' are blurred in the ways discussed at the beginning of Chapter 1; through hostile constructions of industry and through misleading conceptions of musicians as autonomous 'artists'. All acts can then be argued to be a strange brew of prejudice and determination; ambition and submission. By this I mean that acts can convince themselves of what they imagine is a huge potential, but they can be equally convinced that they need the assistance of companies to realise this potential. In seeking the attention of companies they are simultaneously drawn to them but may also be equally suspicious of, and hostile towards, them. At the very least, this conflicted condition is not an effective preparation through which to enter a business partnership; worse it is an almost destructive prelude to a place in the production relations of an industry. The problem for musicians, and by inference music companies, is that these are not the only conflicts that musicians experience when deciding to become popular music acts.

Towards an examination of these further conflicts it is useful to re-state the ways in which Music Hall's consolidation of music-industrial templates problematised the industrial position of 'acts' from then on:

1. Because music companies controlled access to the music market, musicians had to first convince companies of their market potential before being allowed access to that market. In this way music companies were, and remain, both intermediaries between music users and musicians and also a decisive, first-stage, 'surrogate market' to which musicians must demonstrate potential market value as the condition of being allowed to work with those companies on market entry. Music companies are, therefore, trebly powerful – they control access to the market, it was established by them and favours their conceptions of what makes music popular, and musicians must accept these two positions in order to undertake the joint endeavours that might win them the acclaim they seek. As one of the inescapable conditions of popular music as a cultural-industrial form, this means that when musicians create texts to take to market they must always factor in, or allow for, the reactions to their music of potential investors: symbolic goods in music neither sell themselves nor organise themselves as saleable.

2. Once in the market, musicians must organise themselves not just to remain there but to face the challenge of working to intensify their market value. I say 'intensify' rather than simply 'maintain' because what is deemed valuable about specific music, and therefore about specific musicians, can alter very rapidly. Except for what are now referred to as 'heritage acts' such as the Rolling Stones, no new acts can afford, or can afford to appear, to be standing still creatively. In turn, this need for maintenance and intensification of value requires musicians to behave in a more self-consciously 'business-like' way; where this can negatively affect the textual dimensions of their 'anti-industrial' credibility in some cases. It is to deal with these contingencies that musicians seek their own managers. In its turn artist management is never a clear-cut process, as the next chapter discusses. Further, and decisively, this need for management and for the industrial awareness it concedes makes the need to interact with music companies on their terms all the more stark.

3. As the previous chapters have argued, where popular music is concerned, musicians are 'music acts'. Acts can be seen as tradable

embodiments or expressions of a capitalised professional practice that was once the province of amateur music makers. As such commodities, musicians can often be hostage to fortune and experience negative career development for reasons that are not traceable to their degree of musical ability alone. In any industry, no commodity can control its own fate in a market, but when the market is one for symbolic goods, the musician becomes 'responsible' for all dimensions of the signification of the commodity they have become, whether or not they author the entirety of those materials. In this way, the conception of musicians as always and entirely self-determining – except when somehow 'manipulated' by music companies – is denied. The reality is that working within an industrial system means working through a system you do not control. In attempting to assert control, the musician need not always lose the struggle, but the need for such a struggle is inescapable.

The in-built tension between acts and companies is fertile ground for musicians' tales of 'rip offs', and of the generalised bad faith in music industry personnel. Rather than be distracted by these familiar tropes, what needs to be recognised is that this tension is one rooted in the contradictions of generating texts by industrial means. The reality of a company is that it must make profit and that it must always grow; the reality for a musician, while it involves generating an income, is constructed from different materials. Cultural production presents capital investment with specific and quite intractable challenges but capital remains capital and so retains its core imperatives. If one of these imperatives is to create a product as efficiently as possible, then the often-inefficient behaviours of musicians become a 'control' issue almost of a technical order. What makes this control issue particularly intractable is that, from an industrial perspective, the role of popular musician encourages inefficiency, whatever other distractions might preoccupy them.

When discussing music industry, what so complicates the issue is not just that musicians themselves become commodities (although this is complicated enough), it is that, strictly speaking, the Music Industry is not an industry of music, it is an industry that produces symbolic goods with music as an important element of a complex array of signifying systems. This is what the analysis of Music Hall was intended to demonstrate. In order for Music Hall bills to be profitable, a system involving musicians creating performances and writing songs, or having those songs written for them, needed to be created. Impresarios and agents became the arbiters of whether or not performances by acts exhibited sufficient degrees of idiomatic currency to animate structures of feeling associated with likely audiences. Currency was then exhibited not solely through the music performed, but through the sum of the performing materials woven into the text represented by the total of the actions of the musicians in question. The evidence for this can be seen in the surviving footage of Music Hall performances when singers often dressed in costume, taking on perhaps a caricatured version of the stereotypical garb and mannerisms of a particular song's subject. Variations on this practice then continued to characterise popular music performance – from the tears of Johnnie Ray, to Janis Joplin's bottle of Southern Comfort, to the mouse head of Deadmau5.

As the previous chapter argued, what makes an audience for popular music (and this can be as much a TV, radio or internet audience as a physical body of people in a physical space) is when a performer and the performance they give, connects with structures of feeling, with the 'lived and felt' meanings and values held by individual crowd members. This is not to suggest that all audience members react in identical ways to a performance or that, for the period of the performance, an individual takes on a collective 'crowd' identity that supersedes his or her own, but that when a crowd has gathered to attend a performance, they bring to it expectations which are comparable and similar. What is industrial about popular music is that musicians create far more than music, they conjure a total text out of all the signifying materials they can generate – from the way they look and behave to the stories they tell about why they look, behave and make the music they do – but all of these signifying elements need to be carefully integrated with each other and with the further materials produced to market symbolic goods. The work of music companies is to sequence and contextualise those materials in ways that encourage a preferred reading of them. Musicians who have only just begun to play can often be seen working hard at their own attempts at self-promotion, with the aim to present themselves as integrated and excitingly new texts. They do this by associating with what they hope and imagine are influential figures in an endless effort that becomes more sophisticated, high-powered and costly, as musicians are taken up by the companies with the resources to accelerate and manage these efforts.

In wanting to be 'taken up' in these ways – and in both senses of the term, included in the industrial process as well as heightened in visibility – musicians need to accept that they have elected for a place in an process that both precedes them and exceeds them in the power of its resources, regularities, routines and certainties. Furthermore, this is a process that devolves into limiting the likelihood that negative readings may be made of the symbolic good that the original text becomes. This can then mean that what those musicians have constructed as a text will be subject to modification beyond their control; to mishandling and caprice; to the negative impact of the exercise of company priorities that compromise their efforts and which they are unable to control. This is why musicians can be hostage to fortune, not because of the clichés about 'luck' and 'being in the right place at the right time', but because, in an industry which makes symbolic goods whose value lies in their idiomatic currency, the fact that, as the previous chapter argued, 'the position of "particular subjectivit(ies)"' (Bailey, 1994, p. 146) can be extremely volatile means that the notion of a preferred reading is itself hostage to fortune.

Taken as a whole, the objective position of musicians attempting to reach music markets, and to prosper and remain there is fraught with considerations that far exceed playing, singing or programming. Popular musicians of all kinds and at all career stages face powerfully established industrial practices that demand that they behave as businesses in order to be musicians, but their ability to behave as both is compromised by their simultaneous need to exist as commodities, and all of this within a system that is geared to produce profit rather than music, *per se*. Even so, none of these points, either separately or collectively, necessarily mean that music companies are always omnipotent and musicians always powerless. The essential points to remember are that musicians who work with companies want to become market successes. This does not mean that they are necessarily subservient; in fact acts can be assertive, dogmatic even, about what they regard as their particular qualities and may refuse all suggestions for 'improvement' towards market entry.

Where the process of music industry is concerned, the key issue facing all parties is how to realise potential without destroying it in the realisation. Decisions on the final configuration of the symbolic good emerge from processes of negotiation between music company personnel, the act and the act's manager. In such negotiations (which are always substantially informal) the likelihood is that the most coherent vision predominates, and there is no 'rule' which says that this cannot be generated by the act itself. The embedded problems facing acts are that the Music Industry as an institution appears to have a monopoly of knowledge about market entry. This appearance is continually reinforced because, periodically, big stars are produced. The problem for acts is that there is no way of verifying whether the individual personnel that acts encounter, or even the companies they represent, enjoy this knowledge and the expertise it is meant to underwrite. Consequently, acts must trust companies regardless if those companies are trustworthy or not.

To describe music companies as potentially untrustworthy is not to be antagonistic towards them; for example, as Chapter 5 will discuss, major record companies experience considerable turnover in staff. When an act signs a contract with such a company, what they truly sign to is the latest 'regime' inside that company, and staff change induces uncertainty: disruptions in working relations or changes in focus, priorities and strategy. This is 'untrustworthiness' because there are no guarantees of full, undivided, consistent and creative attention when acts ally with music companies of any description. There is a constant provisionality to music industry because there is constant turmoil in the Music Industry. There is constant turmoil because, if 'nobody knows' what goods will sell then those who appear to offer the best guesses can often be given the reins of power. The problem for acts is that they have to become very big stars before they gain access to those reins.

The nature of the Music Industry institution as a repository of tacit knowledge ensures that new recruits take on the gloss of being effective and efficient at market entry whether or not they possess the necessary attributes; there is little in the way of professionalisation in the Music Industry to ensure the standards that it imposes. In this way, entrepreneurialism is never fully reconciled with standardisation; music company personnel can be as capricious and mercurial as the markets they serve. Acts always need to recognise and keep pace with them but, as the following remarks are intended to demonstrate, musicians are 'set up' in ways that make it unlikely that this necessary alertness can ever be generated and sustained.

The four dimensions of musicians

Unlike hopefuls on the outskirts of other cultural industries, musicians are musicians almost by declaration and the continual sudden acceleration of outsiders to 'stars' is a testimony to the ways in which, unlike actors or film directors, there may be little or no career preparation for the role of successful musician. For this reason, it should be no surprise that young musicians across all of the popular music genres continue to look for investment in the form of 'deals', by which they continue to mean recording deals even as the power of record companies continues to falter: the lure of 'overnight success' is a powerful one, especially for individuals already convinced of the merits of their own material. This search for deals persists even now that deals are more scarce and, as Chapter 6 will explore, less attractive than ever. The fact that the tough trading conditions of record companies has not lessened the hunt, nor stemmed the flow of ambitious contenders, tells us a great deal about tensions between culture and industry; for example that they can unfold in disconnected ways at different rates. Even so, the hunt for deals tells us even more about the musician as they face a need but also a desire to reach a market and there transmute crowds into appreciative audiences.

In working to satisfy need and slake desire musicians can be tireless, but they can also find their energy drained – by being forced to react to the complexities of the production process for symbolic goods which, almost as an expression of quantum mechanics, has them inhabit different roles simultaneously in that production process. More than this, though, what can be argued is that the complexities of their positions in production exacerbate the already embedded complexities that define the role of musician. These complexities are in themselves constraining ahead of or, more accurately, in anticipation of entering alliances with investors in symbolic goods. Together they comprise four dimensions of practice common to popular musicians of all kinds.

Musicians who seek to enter markets in search of appreciative, and paying, audiences must face up to a set of potentially conflicting conditions that 'come with the territory'. It is their ability to reconcile these role conflicts that then influences how effectively they adjust to the further, contradictory demands placed on them in production. These conditions can be identified as the four, following dimensions of acting in the role of musician chasing successful market entry:

1. To play the role of the musician, individuals must be musicians of some kind; they must play instruments, sing, or programme, or perhaps all three. They do not necessarily have to do any of this very well, in fact in some genres of popular music, playing 'well' in a technical sense might be a barrier to popularity (consider Daniel Johnston as an example).

2. Musicians who make original music become the owners of property that is of potential value. It is potentially valuable because performances of the works they create can be exchanged for money, but only if customers can be found. This then raises the need for them to act as businesses if they are to make progress as musicians – either in their own right or in preparing to make, legally binding, working alliances with music companies.

3. Musicians are text-makers more than they are musicians. In choosing to look and behave in certain ways and in choosing to explain why they look, behave and sound musically as they do, musicians

present an entire text from which meanings can be generated and values affirmed. The entirety of the text offers itself for consumption, for use, and the symbolic good is created by attending to all the various aspects of the text as well as their inter-play. Musicians need to confront the idea of themselves as commodities as well as music-makers and businesses.

4. The fourth dimension musicians exist in is then a direct consequence of the other three. Even if they were to conduct all of their music making, business relations and market entry and commodity marketing practices themselves, musicians would find themselves preoccupied in these three ways, not just constantly, but simultaneously. It is this need to be simultaneously alert, and responsive, to these three demanding aspects of the general practice of being a musician seeking success that forms their fourth dimension of day-to-day 'career existence'. Further, it is in the need to constantly balance the demands of the other dimensions that musicians are so open to conflicts of control. Balancing competing demands is not an attribute that single-minded people may be adept at and it is this lack of balance that makes acts 'inefficient' from an industrial perspective, but also attractive from a textual, popular cultural one.

If the conditions of being a musician are potentially onerous, then the realities that are contingent on them are equally demanding. As previous remarks indicate, whether as music maker, music business organiser, or proto-commodity, the question of management is posed. Moreover, it is posed within each realm and across them as a whole. Essentially, for musicians to make the alliances they need to with companies that specialise in music market entry, they first need to convince those companies that what they signify in embryo can be translated into mass sales. For them to stand a chance of surviving those alliances, musicians must be in control of each of the dimensions they simultaneously inhabit but each dimension exerts a peculiarly specific set of demands. Even so, to fail to be in control of these different dimensions is to cede managerial responsibility over them to forces they cannot control. To understand this point, both for itself and for the study as a whole, we need to consider in turn the management of each of the four dimensions that define the musician chasing popular music success:

Dimension one – managing music

Whether they recognise it or not, self-management is a central issue for musicians because of the signifying nature of symbolic goods. To use a truism, we cannot not communicate; consequently, all aspects of a text must be constantly monitored in order that the messages created by the act are the ones intended. Furthermore, because meanings can be made from all aspects of the text, therefore all efforts made towards market entry are, in important senses, 'marketing'. These can extend to the way a musician holds their cigarette in photographs or discusses their choice to be vegan in interviews; because secondly, what 'sells' the work of the musician – the recording, the gig, the merchandise – is as much that pose, that concern for animal welfare, as it is the chords they play or the beats they programme.

Considered in this way, when musicians come to work with music companies whose aim and purpose is market entry, unless they are in conscious control of all the signifying systems they engage as the total of the act they have become, they can find that total re-formed and re-formulated and placed in contexts, expressed in ways, situated in jux- taposition to other texts that significantly alter the meanings that can be made of them as signifying wholes. Because this is the case then to concentrate on making music while ignoring the dimensions of being a business and creating themselves as a marketable commodity is short- sighted and reckless. Equally, though, because the commodity is the total of the musician then it is difficult to 'protect' the making of music from the opinions and actions of others with whom those musicians have elected to work on market entry.

Deciding if, how and what to defend about their total practice as a musician is emotionally draining. Musicians invest enormous amounts of energy and sometimes alternative life chances in chasing success or in sustaining it if it has been achieved. The emotional and often finan- cial turmoil this tension can create is what leads to so many musicians breaking up their bands or abandoning solo careers before the market proper is ever reached. Moreover, musicians do not exist in a vacuum; they must contend with a variety of distinct pressures while managing their immediate practice. The most notable of these could be argued to be:

a) Musicians make music but under conditions neither of their own choosing or making. For example, they do not choose the condi- tions of the production of symbolic goods. This is not to argue that the system is inflexible and unchanging. For example, punk rock in the UK and hip-hop in the USA initiated the rise of new record com- panies and new entrepreneurs to positions of power, thus making the Music Industry more receptive to those genres. Even so, acts operate through genre categories and networks and, beyond those, they face an entrenched industrial system as preoccupied and mostly isolated entities. Under these circumstances the likelihood is always that they will accede to the demands of industry for fear of alienating support if they should resist its demands.

b) Similarly, musicians do not choose who they are as people. Differences in gender, social class background, ethnicity, sexuality, age and even geographical point of origin can all have an impact on access to investment. There is a wide range of literature on how social and cultural circumstances play out in the lives of groups of musicians, but it is fair to say that there is little which explores their effect on the industrial fortunes of individual musicians. Further, whether the internet modifies or even obviates these factors as constraints demands to be researched. Taken as a whole, pop music is not a level playing field and all of the factors discussed as contributing to exert pressure on musicians seeking success are intensified and modified in their different ways by the differences in the starting points experienced by musicians and the acts they form or become.

c) Although this is difficult to evidence short of a dedicated study, it is remarkable how crowded the spaces of practising musicians are. Partners, friends, relatives, 'scenesters', local industry figures and generalised hangers-on are all eager sources of opinions on gigs, recordings, and the public profile of acts. The temptation for discussing events and to gauge 'progress' with these individuals is almost irresistible, but their reflection and advice is hugely difficult to evaluate and such figures can help to generate false doubts and entrench false certainties in ways that are the source or fuel for what can often be fatal conflicts within bands and between musicians and their representatives.

It is against these backgrounds, or within these sets of constraints, that musicians manage their music. It is musicians who choose the notes and the beats but they do not make their choices in isolation; in either 'romantic' or 'autonomous' spaces. Managing of music can be a fraught affair because that music and the way it is meshed with other textual dimensions of performance rely on the intangibilities of nuance to have their effect. To be fraught about nuance is almost a contradiction in terms and this is certainly a preoccupying contradiction: one that can re-channel vital energies away from other, equally important considerations, especially those concerning the practicalities and the protocols of market entry.

Dimension two – managing business

Unless they are simply the front-people for a production company, it is musicians who are the ultimate managers of their music. Even so, they manage that music in the face of the distracting pressures already identified. The question then is, 'distracting' from what? Clearly the answer could be a very general one, 'distracting from conducting the role of musicians effectively' but the more likely answer is that musicians can be distracted from the aspect of being a musician that listening to music and rehearsing material is no preparation for – the business of music and the need of this to be managed. Key constraints on managing the business dimension of music can also be summarised:

1. Musicians, especially young ones, face the major barrier of their own inexperience when confronted with the business dimension of being a musician. This business dimension will consist of all the aspects of the self-organisation required to seek and receive payments for performances – among them negotiating the tax and national insurance dimensions of becoming self-employed and, if a band member, identifying how to trade as a partnership; learning about intellectual property and the collection of revenues from rights ownership; as well as contending with contracts as legally binding agreements of varying kinds and types. It is little wonder that musicians seek managers. The problem then can be that, rather than working with the manager, musicians are liable to form dependencies on them and dependency is an unhealthy condition for managing what most musicians envisage as a career rather than an ongoing state of business.

2. Musicians can often behave badly. This is not to imply that all musicians are feckless, but when the culturally entrenched trope of the romantic and bohemian artist persists in the form of seductive role models such as Robert Johnson, Billie Holiday, Chet Baker, Jim Morrison, Steven Tyler and Amy Winehouse, the lure of excess is a strong one. Even when not living to excess, the simple fact that the work of a performing musician is to entertain audiences mostly at night militates against the traditional notion of 'business' as a '9–5' activity; if the demands of touring, rehearsal and recording are added to this then musicians don't so much refuse to engage with business as are forced to delegate these concerns. The problem here is that, normally, those who delegate know what it is they are delegating, and the combination of inexperience, preoccupation with music and the life of the musician, and absorption in

the demands of the role work against musicians developing this alertness.

3. Preoccupation is a general barrier to 'taking care of business'. This pre-occupation is in part the total of being absorbed in music making and in the role of musician and it is also an outcome of the previously discussed 'crowding' of the musician. More than this, musicians can be understood as, in varying proportions, unrealistic and idealistic people who want major changes to take place in their lives. Uncertain of how to make these changes happen (save for making 'great music') they seek a mixture of re-assurance that they are heading in the 'right direction' together with estimations of where they are in relation to the often hugely vague goals they have set. This encourages the constant checking on 'progress' referred to previously. As it is, musicians can become preoccupied by 'making it' without being able to articulate what 'it' is, and so have no reliable system of measuring how far away they are from 'it', and how quickly they are moving towards or away from that goal. Similarly, identifying their actions as a 'project' can be equally misleading. The notion of being involved in a project can give an organised and substantial gloss to what might be a chaotic practice. Worse, the term comes with its own reassurances, as if actions taken in the name of 'the project' give it a reality, focus and momentum that may well be lacking in practice. The most negative outcome of carrying all of these beliefs is that musicians can come to exist in a state of constant feverish anticipation. Inside this, the world is reduced to the day's events and to pouring over them for portents of acceleration and ground gained.

Dimension three – managing the commodity

Reference has already been made to what can be argued to be the self-generated marketing practices of musicians. These range from and encompass choosing performance names, becoming prominent in scenes as acts and courting 'contacts' and 'industry figures'. Furthermore, the argument has been made that what music users draw from is the entirety of the symbolic good derived originally from the text initiated by musicians ahead of their coming to engage with music companies. Becker (1963); Finnegan (1989); Cohen (1991); Straw (1991; Bayton (1998); Kirschner (1998); Leonard (2007), and Barna (2011) among others all discuss different aspects of the work that musicians do on themselves in the context of scenes and through different experiences of constraint associated with gender, ethnicity, sexuality, age, location and social class. What these writers tend not to do is to consider this work as a set of tactics within a strategy towards market entry. If we think of musicians working assiduously on their sound, look and story then it is reasonable to think of this as working on themselves as a commodity-in-waiting. The barrier to conceptualising musicians and their behaviour in these terms derives from the cultural resistance to the implication of musicians with industry discussed at the beginning of Chapter 1.

Clearly, this is a contentious judgement and it seems to fly in the face of, to choose only one example from a vast number, the tortured life of Kurt Cobain. Rather than represent all that Cobain did as a 'shtick' or contrivance, the point is more that, by configuring himself through a combination of expressive choices centred, but not exclusively, on musical ones, Cobain sought to enter the world of popular music – which is an industrial one and one geared to the production of commodities. That the text, Nirvana, offered the possibility of the sales of recordings, tickets, audio-visual performance licences and merchandise then encouraged all of the various companies he and his band engaged with to create out of Nirvana a set of symbolic goods. Cobain did not agree to this reluctantly; already in becoming part of the Punk scene of the Pacific North-West, he was (objectively) in competition with other bands in that scene for the attention of investors.

When faced with competition, the choices made in gaining competitive advantage over rivals help decide the next stages of the transformation of texts into symbolic goods. We cannot know the entirety of the impacts of the perspectives and actions of music companies on Nirvana, but their co-operation with a major label for the album *Nevermind* is testimony to a determination not just to make the best record possible but to be the most successful commodity possible. To this extent, Nirvana did not resist engaging in a set of production relations that resulted in an enormously successful album and career (cut short as it was by Cobain's suicide). Their background in Punk does not appear to have in any way modified the industrial practices they engaged with; save, perhaps, for their 'subversive' cover art representing innocents being led by, or chasing, dollars. In engaging with those unmodified relations, the members of Nirvana demonstrated their recognition of the need to cede control over market entry (and with this themselves as a commodity) to Geffen Records. In this way, Nirvana can be argued to have worked on themselves as proto-commodity but to have recognised their own inability to decide their market fate, unaided. This is typical of popular musicians generally: as commodities, they cannot govern how customers are accessed and in what ways customers are attracted to them, all they can do is prepare the text, co-operate in production of symbolic goods and trust in the abilities of those who take them to market.

Dimension four – managing three dimensions simultaneously

The fact that musicians must manage their music, manage themselves as a business and do what they can to manage themselves as commodities represents a set of needs that are inescapable. As inescapable dimensions of the role of a musician seeking market success these managerial imperatives can be argued to be active from the moment a musician begins to organise themselves for market entry. This demand to manage begins with striking the first chord and the first pose in earnest, often in the earliest years of adolescence. Further, it remains active throughout the entire period of addressing, entering and experiencing the market. The simultaneity of needing to address different regions and orders of self-management is, at the very least, a drain on energy, but its consequences can be argued to be defining for the act's progress, or otherwise.

The likelihood of each dimension of a musician's existence being addressed equally and effectively is slim indeed, as is the likelihood that the whole effort is harmonised by a singular, clear, realistic and responsive vision. Consequently, any musician will exist in what might best be referred to as a state of dynamic torsion. By 'torsion' I mean the shape the act finds itself in when discussing agreements with investors. All musicians need to cope with being simultaneously pulled in the direction of different aspects of the role of musician. When the act is a band then the demands on these coping skills can become severe, indeed. So it is that ambitious and talented people can seek the support of companies towards market entry while not necessarily being 'fit for purpose'. By this I mean that musicians are required by music industry to be business partners, workers and commodities and it can be the case that they never achieve a working version of themselves that allows them to exist in these three necessary states at once simply because it is so difficult to manage successfully all aspects of being a musician. Again, this is not a product of bad or even naïve behaviour; it is, in fact, an ontological issue.

The ontology of being 'industrial'

Musicians make music, but in seeking audiences they must enter markets. Because it continues to remain the case that musicians enter markets more productively in alliance with music companies they have to be more than musicians to attract audiences. All of these demands are challenging to rise to but the argument being made here is that there are constraints on making the effort to make meet challenges that derive from being an 'industrial' (market-seeking) musician, itself. In dimension one, managing their music, musicians can be said to be self-determining, they choose one note over another, one key over another, and so on. Whether deliberately or carelessly failing to manage themselves as businesses, musicians can be argued to be unself-determining. In being unable to manage themselves as commodities beyond the stage of preparing for market entry, musicians are non-self-determining.

All of these states of being are separately tense if not conflicting. For example, musicians are free to make 'artistic' choices, but when creative choices are made with the market in mind then references other than strictly musical ones can bear on compositional choices. Similarly, while they may do little practically to manage themselves as businesses (preferring instead to turn these responsibilities over to an artist manager), musicians can still choose to be fussy about details or to be challenging about some aspects of business while ignoring others. Focus is vital when entering an alliance as a means to entering a market in which competition is fierce, but the ontology of the role of musicians makes focus difficult to achieve and to sustain. Because it does, it severely problematises the 'industrial' positions expected of musicians. In turn, because these positions are always problematised but by different combinations of tensions on a case-by-case basis, then this demands to be read back in to the account of cultural production associated with the 'cultural industries approach' discussed in Chapter 1.

The objection to the 'cultural industries approach' was made in Chapter 1 that the idea that cultural production proceeds by 'throwing mud against the wall' fails to take account of how such 'throwing' is managed in terms of relations of production established between living human beings. If we understand musicians as inherently conflicted and as coming to alliances with music companies in individual conditions of torsion we begin to see cultural production for the human drama that it is. Musicians are ill-disposed to be 'efficient' not because they behave badly (although they may), but because their very being predisposes them to be inefficient from a business perspective. So it is that, when music companies contract with music acts to make symbolic goods, musicians are not clear-cut business partners; they are not clear-cut workers; they are not clear-cut commodities.

Each act has its own history, its own defining characteristics, idiosyncrasies, and plain bad habits. Each act is as coherent as it can be under the circumstances. As the previous chapter argued, the problem facing music companies is that acts demand bespoke solutions when what companies need are workable, winning formulas. In the struggle between unique and formulaic treatment companies have little leeway. The office walls of major record companies glitter with platinum and gold discs, but they are still offices with people doing office – routine and bureaucratic – work for all their casual appearance and custom sound-systems. Music companies live on an edge between the expansive drives of entrepreneurialism and the conservative forces of standardisation. The reason that they can 'square the circle' is because one success pays for many failures. So it is that acts, who recommend themselves for the idiomatic currency they promise to bring to symbolic goods, can still be made subject to routines of production: there is a permanent over-supply of acts; if one proves too difficult to deal with, even if their difficulties are not wilful ones, there are others waiting to fill their shoes. 'Mud' is not thrown at walls; talented, ambitious but ill-prepared acts tend to hit them in the form of companies who need to control investment at the expense of acts in which they invest.

Conclusion

When either the personnel of music companies or the main commentators on it (as in Chapter 1) refer to the Music Industry, they use the term more as a rhetorical device than as a clear descriptive term. It is a rhetorical device because it helps conveys a sense of weight and scale to the countless erratic encounters between structurally conflicted musicians being often crudely shoe-horned into production positions while the window of their cultural relevance appears to remain open. The encounters between musicians and music companies are 'erratic' because each musician, whether solo or a band member, will be in a distinct state of the torsion described previously. Further, acts will be re-assessing performances, cultural relevance and market chances constantly as new symbolic goods enter the market in pursuit of Bailey's 'unstable subjectivities'. Because they do, their morale will fluctuate with each event that has a significance sometimes only they register. Equally, though, the companies acts works with on market entry will also be making these continuous re-assessments and their fluctuations carry greater import: for example, acts can find that the contracts they signed because they appeared to guarantee certain types of investment, may not deliver on their apparent promise (this is the subject of Chapter 6).

The true penalties of attempting to make popular music are those associated with the inescapability of facing four intractable dimensions of practice while courting and anticipating what transpire to be three equally intractable positions in a production process that produces acclaim as almost a side-effect of profit. Musicians are forced to deal with four differently demanding dimensions of their practice; which, because they are so demanding, then problematises the management of each of these dimensions and further problematises their management as a whole. I write 'forced', not in the direct sense that they are made to act against their will – what is so notable about musicians is how much they will themselves into a position of marketability – rather they are 'forced' in the sense that there are limited opportunities to behave differently and still achieve recognition and acclaim which, at the very least, are goals that unite the diverse musical and cultural practices of popular musicians.

The reason that opportunities are limited is because the very form of popular music is industrial – 'professionalism' in music was established on and in the terms of market entry; consequently, in order to enter the market and to stand a chance of making an impact there musicians must first seem marketable to someone who has, or can access, the resources necessary to accomplish this objective. In seeking to convince others, in the face of enormous competition from equally ambitious acts, musicians are already conceding power to decide the final form of the symbolic good suggested by the texts they make. The struggle for power in music industry is the struggle to define outcomes. In such struggles, perfectly good texts can become lost, and for a vast array of reasons in the very specific instances of each act's particular journey to market.

Understood in these ways, musicians are never solely alone with their 'muse' and indifferent to 'discovery' as romantic conceptions have it; they work hard and against the odds to enter a market which is both mercurial and unforgiving; and they do this because they know that a refusal to engage with it promises only obscurity. On this basis, what needs to be explored is the condition of not being 'alone' for the bearing it can have on the attempt to escape obscurity. Towards this exploration, the next chapter will discuss the role of the artist manager followed by discussions of music companies and music contracts. Once this exploration is complete it will be easier to approach actual experiences of attempting to make symbolic goods in music to market in pursuit of outcomes that satisfy the desires of musicians and the desires of music companies.

4
Artist Managers

Introduction

Thus far, the argument has been that musicians must unite their efforts with those of various music companies if they are to succeed in markets for symbolic goods that have music at their centre. The notion of 'success' will vary from act to act, but what is certain is that success for a musician is not identical with success for a music company – companies must make profit and must grow, these are inescapable logics of capitalism. Musicians might want to make money but they can be motivated by other considerations, not least of them achieving the acclaim of their peers and of audiences whom they feel appreciate and value the music they make and the performances they give.

The reason that musicians work with music companies is because there are certain aspects of their existence as musicians that, potentially, can be enhanced and improved by being supported by companies whose expertise lies in entering markets for symbolic goods. The problem here is that musicians did not create these markets so, inevitably, in taking actions to enter markets they take actions that favour the industrial configurations of market address. These 'configurations' involve the creation of production relations – music companies, as all companies, seek to produce commodities they deem appropriate towards maximum sales, and they expect these to be produced on time, on budget and in a condition that is likely to survive competition from rival and (implicitly) similar commodities. As such a conception is far-removed from any notions of musicians as 'artists', then conflict is to be expected in the production of symbolic goods if musicians want to be treated as artists while companies want them to comply with production processes. As the previous chapter argued, the roots of conflict and tension are not restricted to relations between musicians and music companies, they can be argued to characterise the very role of the musician with the strategies that musicians adopt to attract the resources to themselves that they feel they require to become market-successes.

Musicians not only have to enter markets, they must remain and develop within them if they are to build and sustain careers. What militates against this aim is a set of intractable dimensions that all musicians can be argued to exist within. These different dimensions come with their own demands but they come with the further penalty that the distraction induced by one can create problems in others. In this context, the appointment of a manager (referred to tradition-ally as an 'artist manager') seems an immediate solution to both a more efficiently organised market entrance and to the tension and conflict musicians can experience in working, simultaneously, on themselves as music makers, businesses and commodities. As will be explored in this chapter, rather than a solution to problems, the appointment of an artist manager can witness the introduction of further layers of tension and conflict.

In Chapter 2, once they come to work with music companies in ded-icated ways, musicians were argued to enter three, new simultaneous states – as workers in the production of symbolic goods; as business partners with music companies; and as commodities to be bought and sold. By taking on an artist manager to broker relations with music companies, musicians transfer much operational responsibility to them. I write 'much' because one of the central points of tension between musicians and artist managers is that boundaries are almost impossi-ble to set between where and how in their practice musicians expect to be managed. Furthermore, and especially where bands are concerned, becoming 'workers-with-representation' and 'business-partners-under-guidance' makes even more complicated what is already a complex set of role positions played by musicians in their pursuit of market entry – four dimensions of the role; three states in united effort with compa-nies; and two modifications to those states under management. In these ways, when artist managers enter relations with musicians those musi-cians can be understood as experiencing a degree of torsion in their professional lives. While they may be unconscious of this, or at least unable to isolate its points of origin, the expectation in the manager is likely to be that, not only will they be able to reduce this torsion by man-aging it in some unexplained way, but they will also deliver what the act might regard as not just its promise by its deserved status as a market-successful act. Both are challenging goals and there are no clear ways in which they can be met or, more accurately, of re-assuring musicians that they are being or will be met.

'Challenging' is a key term in defining the role of artist manage-ment: because musicians find themselves in competing conditions, artist managers are therefore forced to deal with dynamics between (and, even, 'within') musicians that are neither necessarily transparent nor amenable to influence or direction. Moreover, any actions taken or sug-gested by an artist manager will be filtered through these conditions and responses to any suggestion will only be as focused and coherent as their nature allows. Further still, such are the challenges of making symbolic goods that, at any one time, the musician might be preoccupied with one role while the manager needs to address them in another. More than this, a manager might have knowledge or supposition about one region of the musician's practice that, if discussed, might impact nega-tively on another. Deciding how to address the musician is a decision about whether it is possible to address them as being fully integrated in their role and not preoccupied by one or more of the dimensions discussed in Chapter 3. If not, the manager needs to estimate which particular aspect of the musician's multi-role reality to address, and in what terms. When nuance and timing are at such a premium in the production of symbolic goods, working environments can be intense; under these conditions each decision can be a 'judgement call' because the repercussions of decisions can be exaggerated by the conditions in and under which they are made.

Whilst artist managers can face challenges in relation to the musicians they manage, the industrial environment they enter and must work within also presents its tests and predicaments. As Chapter 1 argued, they must operate in different music industries; but alongside this they must also learn the protocols of the Music Industry (how business is done; through what perspectives; in what ways); while paying atten-tion always to music industry itself – what is the outcome of joint work; how does the operation of joint-working relations impact on their clients (and themselves); where does power lie in working rela-tions and how might it be seized on behalf of those clients; is progress being made or not; is it lasting; could it be happening more quickly, effectively, efficiently? Added to all of these considerations, there is the stark reality to face that considerable change is taking place within and across the music industries which can mean that old and new business practices will co-exist but in different measures and under different cir-cumstances. Large-scale change further problematises the formation and implementation of business strategy and it exerts pressure on managed relationships with musicians. In all of this, the artist manager faces the ongoing problem of trying to understand 'the big picture'; trying to keep track of its currents and flows; trying to find ways of readjusting the practice and expectations of musicians without overly disturbing them; while trying to survive and make a living in their own right and mostly without support systems of any obvious kind.

All of this accepted, it would be wrong to create the impression at the outset of the study that only the artist manager experiences challenges: artist management can be a source of challenge for musicians too, because their investment in the manager is substantially an emotional one. This is because young and inexperienced people can become dependent on a manager as a symbol of hope as much as of authority. Moreover, inexperience can be a poor guide in deciding what to delegate to a manager so that some degree of autonomy is retained in working on the texts that become symbolic goods. As such it is the source of the 'boundary disputes' that characterise musician–artist manager relations (see Chapter 7). More than this, and for reasons discussed in greater detail below, musicians are apt to invest heavily in the idea of a manager and can be led to ignore the reality that they often place their entire but indeterminate future in the hands of an individual they might barely know; one whose experience (should it exist) they cannot evaluate and whose actions they cannot monitor.

What all parties involved in the production of symbolic goods require is a clear-headed address to the market but if musicians are, for whatever reason, unable to do this, there is no automatic reason that an artist manager should be able to clarify this address. This is true even if this is the premise on which he is appointed and on which he may have advertised himself to the act. Musicians may well not want to enter the industrial process 'alone', as the last chapter has it, but this then raises the question of the nature and qualifications of the person or persons with which they enter that process. As this chapter will argue, the role of the artist manager comes with no 'rule book'; no professional framework to ease creation of strategies for market entry that involve contributing strategies for satisfying the sometimes contrary demands of musicians and of music companies. Managers learn 'on the job'; it is the quality of their experience on which the aspirations of musicians depend and what problematises this is that there is no mechanism for facilitating it and, in fact, no real source of compulsion that it should happen at all. Artist managers tend to be self-appointed individuals and the *ad hoc* nature of their appointment can lead to an *ad hoc* performance of the role. To understand why this is the case, we need first to consider the historical background to the emergence of the artist manager.

The artist manager and the music industry

Expresso Bongo is a remarkable film for many reasons, a number of which are pertinent to this study. The film was released in December 1959. It was directed by Val Guest and was based on a satirical musical first performed in London in 1957. The musical was written by Wolf Mankowitz and Julian Moore; Mankowitz also wrote the screenplay and then published a novelised version of both play and film in 1960. The film stars Cliff Richard. This was Richard's second film appearance but his first in a leading role. Unusually, and perhaps unwisely from a marketing perspective, it occurred in an X–rated movie, which thereby disallowed what was likely to be the vast bulk of his following from actually enjoying the performance. Despite this, Richard was inspired casting; he had enjoyed his first hit single in the previous year and, in the months before the release of *Expresso Bongo*, his first number one, *Living Doll*, which remained at number one for six weeks. More than this, Richard was exactly the type of figure satirised by Mankowitz (accepting, here, that Moore worked as a lyricist rather than dramatist on the original musical).

What Mankowitz chose to satirise was the coming of rock and roll and, with it, the version of the Music Industry which is only now beginning to pass. The film involves the transformation of young and inexperienced singer from a working-class background and employed in a menial role at an amusement arcade into a transatlantic star. The film is set in London's Soho district and is substantially a satire of the rise of Tommy Steele; Mankowitz makes this clear in his novel. Steele had been 'discovered' playing at the *2 i's* coffee bar and became the UK's first rock and roll star two years before Richard emerged. In a wide variety of ways Mankowitz signalled his contempt for this new phenomenon and, again, it is the novel which makes this absolutely clear; for example calling the Richard character 'Herbert Rudge', a composite, a 'Herbert' or a 'nobody' with an echo of 'drudge'. What is most telling from the perspective of this study is that the film's co-star, and the novel's protagonist, is an artist manager, 'Johnny Jackson'. Played in the film version by Laurence Harvey, Jackson is a drummer in a dance band in exactly the period when dance bands were giving way to rock and roll groups. In the film, because his girlfriend insists on an espresso, Jackson is seen reluctantly entering the coffee bar where he encounters Rudge. Once in the bar he laments how amateurish the players are until, upon seeing how Rudge's performance electrifies the crowd, his antipathy to the new pop music vanishes; he approaches Rudge, charms him, and, in the course of a single conversation becomes his manager, at an extortionate commission of 50 per cent.

Jackson's 'conversion' is an inspired piece of acting by Harvey, and it can be argued that it vividly captures the full flush of an entrepreneurial 'moment'. To this point Jackson has been shown to be someone who is alert to moneymaking opportunities, and following his capture of Rudge (whom he duly re-names 'Bongo Herbert') he sets about doing 'deals'. He begins by persuading the proprietor of a rival café to hold a show to which he invites a record company and a television company. He is then able to complete a deal with Rudge himself in the form of what transpires to be an unenforceable contract, a plot device that is identical to the Elvis Presley film of the same period, *Jailhouse Rock*. The satirical nature of the film carries with it a barely veiled contempt for this new pop music. This can be considered to be the contempt of a show business 'old guard'. Another way of understanding this would be as 'The Entertainment Industry'. This consisted of several constituencies. One such example would be Variety agents and theatre owners (the successors to Music Hall) who feared the loss of audiences to the new phenomenon. Then there would be also dance band and jazz players who were likely to despise what they perceived to be the limited musicality and musicianship of pop players. Also, although only temporarily, the record companies could be seen to be part of this tide of resistance to rock and roll. They will have feared that an apparently musically uninformed mass of teenagers would come to constitute an unstable market that would lack discrimination. Even so, as the film makes clear, 'business is business' and what is of particular relevance here is not simply Jackson's opportunism (though this needs to be kept in view) but the fact that, in becoming Rudge's manager rather than his agent, *Expresso Bongo* bears fictional witness to the birth of a new form of music industry, an industry that would be dominated by *recording artists*.

Music Hall was supplanted by cinema as the principal site of paying audiences for symbolic goods. The arrival of 'talking pictures' witnessed the rise of the 'Hollywood Musical' which made good much of the audience's loss of Music Hall. The live music component of the halls was then dispersed into four realms. Firstly, musical theatre in the form of revues and 'musicals'. Secondly, dance venues which ranged from ballrooms and dance halls to church halls and 'co-op' halls. Thirdly, Variety which was essentially an adapted form of Music Hall concentrated mainly, but not solely, in holiday resorts and holiday periods; for example, 'end of the pier' shows and pantomime but also broadened to include private member's clubs; where the 'working man's club' would be its last bastion. Fourthly, recording and broadcast of acts from these sectors. These developments allowed the live performance industry to continue to be the dominant music-industrial sector, acting in many ways as a 'tutor' to the emergent recording industry (see Chapter 5). While this industry remained dominant, a period from roughly 1920 to 1960, the role of artist manager was differently and perhaps less-deeply inscribed. In these years managerial functions were distributed across two main specialisms – the agent and the publicist. Alongside them, the functions of 'book-keeper' and 'diary keeper' were then either contracted out to specialists or subordinated as 'secretarial' duties.

The live performance industry revolved around the interactions of agents, promoters and publicists. Agencies signed 'talent'; in the first instance bandleaders and latterly their singers as these became important in their own right. This talent was then offered to promoters at the highest fee the agent could win, where the agent's interest was the commission of 10 per cent for securing the 'booking'. In this arrangement, the singers and bandleaders signed directly to the agency which then 'represented' them to the 'market' formed by the network of promoters. It was the individual musician's responsibility to work on their music which, even so, is only 'creative autonomy' to the extent that, firstly, they fitted the requirements of agents and promoters and, secondly, they absorbed the need to be the same as, but different from, their competitors. Under this system, singers, referred to as 'crooners', sought to establish a 'unique selling point' through a slogan about them created by publicists. In turn, bandleaders tended to commission the independent earnings of their singers, on the basis that they were known because the band or orchestra was, while subordinating the 'career management' of those singers to their own needs. In all of this, the role of the publicist was exactly what the term suggests, to publicise a band in order to justify a higher fee based on the band's track record in guaranteeing paying customers for the promoter.

Perhaps the principal beneficiary, and best exemplar, of this mode of management was Frank Sinatra. Sinatra broke from being managed as a singer by Tommy Dorsey in Dorsey's orchestra, and replaced his management with a joint arrangement between an agent, Music Corporation of America (MCA), and a publicist, George Evans. Evans is credited with the stratagem of paying young women to scream and swoon at Sinatra's performances, thus raising Sinatra's profile. With his profile raised, Sinatra not only commanded higher performance fees, he attracted the attention of record companies (he signed with Columbia as a solo artist in 1943) and Hollywood film studios (he signed with RKO Pictures, also in 1943). In all of this, the negotiation of live performance, film and recording contracts would be done by MCA. Given that MCA's fee would always be the industry standard 10 per cent, it is not clear whether Sinatra took advice from Evans or how Evans was paid. The fact that Sinatra was dropped by MCA, Columbia and RKO later in the 1940s then raises the question of the extent to which he was managed at all; even Evans broke with him in 1950, shortly before his (Evans') death.

Considered in these terms, when the fictional Johnny Jackson makes his transition from drummer to manager, he does not entirely start from scratch. This will have been true of the real artist managers of the period such as 'Colonel' Tom Parker, the manager of Elvis Presley, and Larry Parnes, the manager of many of the original UK rock and roll stars. But if these managers did not entirely invent artist management, what they were required to do was to radically re-think the role, as the coming of rock and roll saw the record industry begin to create its *own* stars rather than simply make records with musicians whose fame was an outcome of their live appearances. In this way, while the recording industry became powerful in its own right it remained comparatively secondary to the live performance industry in the creation of recording artists. Until the mid-1950s the movement tended to be in one direction only: from live performance, dancehall, ballroom or Broadway/West End, to recording and to film. If the domination of music, film, theatre and recording by artists signed to MCA and to William Morris is factored in to this structure then the soubriquet, the 'Entertainment Industry', becomes a compelling one. With the coming of rock and roll and the impact, especially, of Elvis Presley, in a very real sense the recording industry began to extract music from the Entertainment Industry, dragging live performance and publishing in its wake and reshaping the Music Industry around its own needs and imperatives. It is in servicing these imperatives or, at least, in organising musicians to fit them, that the practice of artist management is located.

The emergence of artist management

The consolidation of the recording industry as the dominant force in a music industry that was distinct from the entertainment industry was not accomplished over-night. It took the success, and the emulation of the success, of The Beatles, more so than even Elvis Presley, to create the

concentration of capital that was the true power of the recording industry or, more accurately, of the 'major' record companies at its centre.
Major record companies were companies which owned their own means
of distribution and they consolidated themselves in the years following
the Depression. Gillett (1970/1983) gives the best account of how difficult their adjustment to the new opportunities presented by a teenage
market in the post-war years was, where what was new and different
about this market was not simply its increasing scale and spending
power, but the fact that alcohol licensing laws precluded it from engaging directly with the most lucrative forms of live music. In turn, this lack
of direct access to the 'sophisticated' spaces inhabited and celebrated
by, for example, the rejuvenated Frank Sinatra, provoked a need for
music that reflected their specific experience and desires. In the UK, the
importation of jukeboxes and their installation in cafés serving espres-
sos was the bridge to a new cultural experience complete with a new
soundtrack.

In truth, jukeboxes and espresso were never ubiquitous throughout
the UK; rather it was the new phenomenon of television in the form
of shows such as *6-5 Special* and *Oh Boy!* that brought the music associated with them to a new, young, national audience. In contrast, what
were ubiquitous were spaces that could be adapted to 'teenage dances'
and in these spaces the groups of the skiffle, and beat booms flourished.
Amplification meant fewer players were needed to make enough of a
sound for dancers to move to and, in any case, the new music which
bypassed the nightclub chic of Sinatra was based on the formula established by the stripped down 'rhythm and blues' music that was the
inspiration for rock and roll. The problem from both a business and
an industrial perspective was the kind of market teenagers were considered to represent – by definition they aged rapidly and the supposition
was that their demand was likely to be for 'fads' (Hirsch, 1969). This
appeared to mean that only short-term gains might be possible so the
immediate response of the existing industry was to be as exploitative
as possible. This tendency was exemplified in Tom Parker's 50 per cent
commission for managing Elvis Presley to The Beatles' recording royalty
of one farthing per disc side from Parlophone. Such exploitation could
go on because acts were not expected to last and because it seemed that
only by transforming them into 'adults' could any career-longevity be
secured. This perspective led to the 'inappropriate' first film roles for
Cliff Richard together with the rapid transition of Tommy Steele into
films and musicals and, in the USA, the lengthy and poorly conceived
film contract for Elvis Presley.

Brian Epstein's contract with The Beatles embodies the dilemma facing the early artist manager. The document established that his commission was to be less than Parker but still an exceptionally high 25 per cent (even today the 'industry standard' is 20 per cent). It established also that his control over them was intended to be total: the contract expresses his role as,

> to advise the Artists on all matters concerning clothes make-up and the presentation and construction of the Artists' acts and also on all music to be performed of or in connection with such acts

Alongside this, the document reveals that his confusion about their future was also total:

The Artists are desirous of performing as a group of musicians to be known as 'THE BEATLES' and pursuant thereto of taking engagements in the following branches of the entertainment industry:

(a) Vaudeville and revue
(b) Motion Pictures
(c) Balls and Dances whether of a private or public nature
(d) Radio and Television broadcasting
(e) Concerts, private parties, cabarets
(f) Phonographic and tape recording
(g) Sponsorship projects

The fact that making records is sixth in the list of 'engagements' to be taken in 'the entertainment industry' demonstrates better than any other document could just how new the world of managing this type of act was. There was no live music infrastructure appropriate and specific to rock and roll through which The Beatles might progress. The arena of live music was divided in the ways the contract reflects: between 'vaudeville and revue', both 'non-teenage' worlds and ones in decline, and the small-scale club and/or church hall appearances they had experienced in Liverpool and Hamburg. As far as Epstein could understand it, The Beatles' route to market needed to take place through recording, but recording would not be an end in itself; because, presumably, audiences would dissolve rapidly as they aged. Consequently, it was to 'motion pictures', 'Balls' and 'cabarets' that he looked as opportunities for making money. How long this might last could not be anticipated but the expectation inside the group was that they, too, should make hay while the sun shone. As George Harrison expressed in 1963 after a handful of hit records, and in response to a question about exactly the issue of how long The Beatles would last:

> I hope to have enough money to go into a business of my own by the time we do...ummm...flop. I mean, we don't know. It may be next week, it may be two or three years.

As Harrison's honest assessment attests, no one can anticipate that they will be at the very centre of cultural and cultural-industrial change; yet somehow the coincidence of what The Beatles seemed to represent and express, inside and beyond popular music, helped to re-invent the Music Industry. Singles that sold in mass quantities became the norm by the mid-1960s but more lucrative still was the rise of the album as the main object of consumption. The Beatles were instrumental in the creation of this phenomenon as they left behind live appearances to concentrate solely on recording.

By generating enormous wealth in a market that rapidly mutated from one that was considered capricious to one that became the bedrock of an industry, the major record companies eased away from the entertainment industry to cater for the demand for music from a demographic that, while initially young, grew up and developed with 'its' music. In being driven by the enormous success of The Beatles and the album-focused precedent they set, the record industry then became concerned to sign 'album artists' where the effect of this was defining. Firstly, by offering recording contracts with multiple options, even when these were entirely in the gift of record companies, those companies established the notion that any act could enjoy a recording career. Secondly, because 'nobody knows' what records will sell then all acts, 'signed' or 'unsigned', were encouraged, or encouraged themselves, to believe that they were in for the 'long haul', and towards this hugely indeterminate 'goal', it became essential to appoint a manager (after all, The Beatles had had one and look what had happened to them).

The dilemmas of artist management

Considered against this background, the rise of the recording industry created a new context for the practice of a newly inflected form of artist management. Essentially, all of the new rock and roll, pop, and 'beat boom' acts were experiments in a new order of cultural production. Continuing tensions surrounding the act–artist manager relationship derive from the effects of comparatively 'sudden' appearance in an industry that then underwent two seismic upheavals in barely a decade. The first of these was that managers needed to learn to operate in an arguably re-constituted music industry focused on recording artists. They also needed to adjust to the idea that these recording artists could have 'career's *within* recording'. While the latter did not mean that musicians might not extend their practices into other forms of cultural production – for example, The Beatles signed a film contract as did Mick Jagger with and without the Rolling Stones as too did David Bowie – the emergent 'mind-set' of musicians and managers alike was that there was a future, an uncertain one, but one that promised to stretch out almost indefinitely, and it lay in making and touring albums. In this way, the new configuration of the Music Industry had recording at its centre with the live performance and publishing industries serving substantially in supporting roles; as sites to market albums and to husband the royalties of album-focused, performing songwriters. The imperatives of the recording industry therefore predominated over popular music generally and, effectively, artist managers had the content if not exactly the form of their roles determined for them by the sheer weight and scale of events. For example there was an enormous new market for record albums; this market needed album artists; album artists were likely to sign contracts for the production of up to ten albums and so they required to be organised to deliver these albums.

The problem with this determination of the role of artist manager was not so much that it was imposed externally by large-scale industrial changes; the previous form of artist management had, after all, developed in response to the centrality of live performance to the entertainment industry. What had changed was that what artist managers were expected to do was to 'square' the industrial 'circle'. The point has already been made that the definition of success for music companies and musicians are not identical, but as the go-between between musician and music companies, artist managers are expected by both parties to fulfil their separate, although over-lapping, aims. In trying to pull off not just this balancing act, but this blending of distinct polarities, artist managers come to almost embody or to 'live' irreconcilable tensions; tensions that are exacerbated by other irresolvable dilemmas that 'come with the job'. In turn, the experience of embodying tensions, if it is not handled with sufficient dexterity and resilience, can intensify rather than reduce tensions that they meet in their address to musicians.

So it is that artist managers can be identified as facing competing logics in attempting to deliver two ultimately incongruent goals. These logics derive from four different regions of their practice: there are dilemmas embodied in the nature of management itself which impact on their role performance; dilemmas which derive from their objective position in relation to musicians as clients; dilemmas which derive from the industrial position of musicians in general; and dilemmas which derive from their relationship to the needs of the companies they inter-act with and the industries within which they operate. How managers respond to all of these pressing demands results in their own version of the 'torsion' discussed in the previous chapter. Just like musicians, artist managers do as well as they can under the circumstances. This then leaves their acts to exist through the cumulative impact of the man-ager's address to these challenges. Their own state of torsion and modes of coping with it then decide how well, if at all, they contend with the decisions taken by their managers.

To consider more closely the defining pressures associated with artist management identified previously:

1. Williams (1983) is a useful guide to a contradiction deeply rooted in the concept of management itself; one that, in a form of industrial production that tends to be light on rule-bound behaviour, can be an unrecognised source of irritation and tension. In his excavation of the etymology of the term, Williams indicates two, contradictory usages that, while these have merged, can still be seen to persist in practice. The first route, traced from the Latin *manus* (hand) and identified as entering the English language from medieval Italian, is 'maneggiare' (1983, p. 189), a term derived from handling horses and driving horse drawn vehicles (from which we get the terms 'taking the reins of power' and 'being in the driving seat'). Along-side this, also from Latin but in this case deriving from *mansionem* (a large dwelling or early form of hotel) and entering from medieval French (*ménage, ménager* – household) (1983, p. 190), is a sense of management that is restricted to housekeeping; a 'hands off', attention-to-detail, form of management and one very much in con-trast to the 'hands on' and leading-from-the-front sense with which it co-exists. Considered in this way, playing the role is not a clear-cut undertaking: an artist manager may well be expected to be a leader (see below), while checking constantly that there are always guitar strings, valid passports; and that there is always money in the bank

2. A source of contradiction more specific to artist management derives from the nature of contractual relations between musicians and artist managers. For example, as Bagehot and Kanaar express it (1998),

'The usual legal structure is for the artist to employ the manager' (1998, p. 1); to this extent, the manager can be understood as a service provider to musicians. In this way, the manager, as well as the musician, faces the dilemma that a servant is hired to effectively be a leader ('organise...all aspects of an artist's career'). Perhaps this recognition should not be over-dramatised, and also 'leadership' can take several forms, but at the very least the construction raises issues of power and authority in a working relationship. Even if we substitute 'operational responsibility' for 'leadership', the anomaly does not go away. It refuses to because someone must 'take charge'; someone must exert control over effort, and because this is the role of the manager, it can be the case that the led might not appreciate the transference of power the appointment entails even as they are anxious for what they imagine the appointment will bring. At the same time, the manager is faced with this possible resistance and also with the dilemma of how to play roles they may not be prepared for, in the sense of being sometimes or always an autocrat, a democrat or other places in between as occasions present themselves.

3. To manage effectively, a manager needs access to the total of the act, but, as Chapter 3 sought to demonstrate, the 'total of the act' is likely to always be in a state of conflict and the consequent torsion this produces. At its very worst, 'access' can become read as 'intrusion' and the need for the manager to be able to act with authority can be resisted in struggles over artistic integrity that are misconceived and can impact negatively on the joint effort made between musician and manager, and between and music companies. In this way, managers can end up fighting battles with musicians who do not necessarily derive from the specific set or conduct of relations the two parties have created between each other. Instead, this tension can be traced to the contradictions associated with the strength of the recording industry during the years of rock music: put plainly, musicians are not 'artists', they are individuals who contribute specific abilities to the formation of industrial commodities. These 'specific abilities' may be substantially distinctive when compared with those of other musicians and may be praiseworthy for this reason, but, in industrial production, the pressing need is to complete the commodity in good order. Managing musicians who believe they should be afforded the privileges of artists is extremely challenging. Similarly, managing musicians who expect to have 'careers' is also challenging because, again, the expectation is not one created within the managed relationship, but one induced in both parties by a strongly influential

model of industry associated with a specific historical period in the production of symbolic goods.

4. Artist managers occupy the only position in the Music Industry which interacts with all other areas of activity and the individuals involved in them. This is of particular significance and will be returned to; here what needs to be recognised is that the manager cannot but help become immersed in the perspectives of those with whom he interacts. This is because all parties have their needs and priorities, and compelling reasons why certain actions needed to be taken in certain time frames. The question then is, 'what is the manager managing'? Is it the musicians' interests in the final outcome or the musicians' contribution to the final outcome? In this, what becomes all-important is the definition of the final outcome, who makes it and how? Even when this is not intended, when so much time is spent dealing with music companies, what is difficult for the manager to resist is the temptation to see the needs and perspectives of those companies as their own, which can mean that what begins as an artist manager representing his clients to the industry can subtly shift to his representing the industry to those clients.

Ultimately artist managers are individuals who have ambitions of their own. The significance of specifying 'Johnny Jackson's' awakening to the market potential of 'Herbert Rudge' is that this is Jackson's awakening, not Rudge's. In the film, Rudge has to be persuaded of his potential, while in reality, musicians, especially young ones, are filled with a strong sense of their own potential and tend to be ambitious for management – where the difference is that an 'entrepreneurial moment' is one that at the very least encompasses business ambitions even, if it cannot entirely be reduced to them. The problem, especially for musicians, is, as Chapters 1 and 2 have both argued, that the 'risk taking' associated with, even defining of, entrepreneurialism is risk-taking with the aspirations, ambitions and potential of living human beings. This is why the dilemmas of artist management, and the solutions created for them, on a case-by-case basis, have such substantial impacts on musicians making music that they hope becomes successful.

The dilemmas of being managed

'Johnny Jackson's' moment of realisation that 'Herbert Rudge' had what it took to become a star is important to this study for three reasons. Firstly, because it illustrates the historic transition from one industrial form to another. Secondly, it illustrates that this transition is a cumulative effect of what would have been thousands of human encounters; of a single individual's capitalisation of a moment. Thirdly, in capturing a moment of prescient cultural calculation, Jackson's actions raise the issue of the qualifications of artist managers, particularly at the outset of their embrace of the role. In Jackson's case this consisted of little more than being alert to potential cultural purchase in musicians. To an extent, this notion maps onto Brian Epstein's decision to manage The Beatles but, crucially, shorn of Jackson's cynicism and it is also present in accounts of Rob Gretton's management of Joy Division and, after them, New Order.

Gretton first encountered Joy Division under their first name 'Warsaw' and he believed them to be 'the best band I'd ever seen'.[1] He had had some involvement with another Manchester band, Slaughter and the Dogs, and had begun to manage The Panik. As it transpired, Joy Division and its successor band New Order became hugely influential bands. This status is attributed to the special qualities of the musicians in those bands, especially to Ian Curtis of Joy Division. In all accounts of those bands and the Manchester music scene of the 1980s more widely, Gretton is also consistently praised for his contribution to them. The problem with this praise is that Gretton's contribution is never specified. Gretton died in 1999 at the age of 45 and his obituaries are revealing in this respect: both the *Independent* and the *Guardian* cite him as being of instrumental importance to the success of both Joy Division and New Order ('as important to his charges as Brian Epstein was to the Beatles'[2]) but neither is able to specify why this is the case. Instead both offer potted histories of Joy Division, Factory Records and post-punk Manchester generally, as if Gretton's centrality explains itself.

To begin to appreciate this centrality we need to consider the limited edition of parts of a collection of materials associated with his management of Joy Division and New Order that Gretton had kept stored. Published as *1 Top Class Manager* (2008), the work takes the form of a series of photographed pages of his notebooks. At first sight the publication is mundane; typical entries are:

> Sort out at rehearsals about sound at Band on the Wall (...); Phone Joly about badges; Phone Rough Trade (...); Contract to Solicitor. (2008, pages unnumbered)

The minutiae are compelling – not necessarily individually but cumulatively. As Joy Division became better known, played gigs beyond

Manchester, at larger venues and higher up the bill, began touring Europe, signed recording contracts and made records, the scale
of Gretton's interactions with music companies and their personnel
increased exponentially. This increasing, and ever-more consolidated,
network of contacts transformed Gretton along with his band from a
marginal figure in a provincial city to an increasingly central figure
in the national and international music industry. For all practical purposes, and from the perspective of market entry and those who organise
it, Gretton was Joy Division – he was the person who cajoled, pleaded,
explained, deferred, demured, haggled and delivered. In this way, while
Joy Division was its songs and performances; its grey overcoats and the
flailing arms of its singer; Gretton and his actions became the environment of the band. By this I mean the unseen but strongly sensed
membrane that helps to transform into a popular cultural force what,
simultaneously, it helps protect and grow as a musician or group of
musicians.

The explanation for Gretton's contribution to how he became instrumental to Joy Division, and through them post-punk Manchester and
eventually the history of UK pop music, lies in what tasks he considered necessary to undertake, how he prioritised them and in how he
accomplished them. The point here is that there was no guarantee that
he would do any of them well; and if he had done any badly then all of
those histories, all of those comfortably nested narratives, would have
been different. If we go on to consider that for every Joy Division there
are countless numbers of 'The Paniks', then, to some extent at least, the
performance of the managerial role becomes the pivotal variable in the
success, or otherwise, of market-aspirant musicians and their pursuit of
competitive advantage. The problem then is that a pivotal variable is
not necessarily a strong and reliable one.

There are very few studies of artist managers and their practices. The
principal example is Rogan's *Starmakers and Svengalis* (1989). Despite
its attempt to establish a taxonomy of managerial styles in its conclusion, in the very title of the work, Rogan deflects attention away from
the lived reality of managerial practice to reposition the actions of successful managers as an outcome of some kind of supernatural ability
that the success of their clients seems to suggest they possess. Notably,
Gretton is one of Rogan's subjects and, equally notably, the discussion
of Gretton is far more an account of the life and tragic death of Ian
Curtis. Yet as Gretton's notebooks indicate, he was not a Svengali, rather
he was someone who identified tasks and followed them through. It is
the 'following through' that can be argued to create the conditions for

successful joint working with music companies and successful market entry.

As Chapter 2 argued, what musicians need is to create idiomatic currency in and through the texts they fashion so that these texts engage with and animate structures of feeling exhibited by collections of people they can transform into audiences. Structures of feeling can change and some symbolic goods pitched towards them can quickly seem irrelevant. As a consequence, currency only remains current when signifying materials signify currency. The artist manager has to be able to organise the act so that its claim to currency is demonstrable, but can also be maintained while he organises his own efforts to persuade music companies that this act can constitute audiences from crowds; customers from potential buyers. Ultimately, where managers are concerned, all of this takes place in one-to-one encounters: in face-to-face meetings, by telephone or email, as well as in multitudes of informal encounters when, somehow, business is always being done. Music industry management is not 'rule-bound' so that the conduct of these encounters, and the actions they stimulate, is entirely the province of the personality and the understanding of the artist manager involved. Artist managers are not the direct employees of musicians. This means that while contracts abound, contracts of employment with their associated framework of employment law do not apply. In turn, the familiar conditions of employment – job descriptions; induction and training; regimes of continuing professional development – equally do not apply. In many ways, all of this allows music, as a cultural industry, the degree of latitude required to respond to changes in expressive demands on symbolic goods, but the downside of this, especially for musicians, is exactly the issue of managerial latitude.

What Gretton's list does not show is how he addressed his tasks; but the success of Joy Division suggests that he addressed them successfully. In line with other bands and solo musicians, such is the scale but also the intimate nature of exchanges between artist managers and music companies, that individual musicians have no real way of accessing, let alone monitoring or evaluating, the actions of their manager; consequently they would have no way of judging whether a course of action was a necessary one or the only one available because others had been botched. When we then consider the spiralling outwards of the managerial field of action as success takes hold, where none of the manager's actions and decisions might ever have clearly been agreed, then the true source of tension and conflict between managers and musicians is revealed. In turn, this tension and conflict then reveal and arguably induce the vulnerabilities of texts undergoing transformation into symbolic goods.

As has already been noted, Bagehot and Kanaar (1998) express the musician–artist manager relationship as one in which the manager can be understood as a service provider to musicians: 'The usual legal structure is for the artist to employ the manager' (1998, p. 1). What complicates the matter is that, as the same authors continue,

> Essentially a manager will advise upon, organise and administer all aspects of an artist's career, including seeking out and creating contracts and opportunities. The manager may well also play an important part in the creative and artistic elements.
>
> (1998, p. 1)

This observation is made in a publication that post-dates Brian Epstein's contract with The Beatles by almost 40 years, by which time, apparently, the idea that the manager should be accepted as competent to 'advise the Artists on all matters' (Epstein, ibid.) was taken for granted; but this still begs the question of where this authority and where this ability comes from. Even if we accept that not all 'Johnny Jacksons' are only interested in themselves and any money they might make from their clients, being passionate about music made by particular musicians is not a qualification as such. While a shared sensibility between musician and artist manager can be gratifying for both, the construction of that sensibility might not be congruent between the two and, arguably, the manager's construction can be skewed and solidified as skewed the more they have to deal with the organisation of the act in relation to music companies in the pursuit of the former's translation into symbolic goods. Further, there is no guide or template by which passion can be converted into ability – the only real course is trial and error. So it is that, and certainly at the outset of a relationship between a new act and a new manager, artist management can only be a hit-and-miss affair.

In the absence of what might best be called 'professionalising' mechanisms in the formation and recruitment of artist managers and the relationships they form with musicians, boundaries are difficult to perceive, easy to breach and extremely hard to restore; take this example from Rob Gretton's notebooks:

> Synthesiser – My idea is to introduce it at the end of the set in the form of a jam – Ian suggests he talks over but who is going to play it?
>
> (2008)

The question here is how can a self-selected individual with little or no previous experience and no preparation for the role extend their remit to cover making suggestions about the music that was being played before they happened on the scene; especially when their involvement with the musicians in question may well be based on the extra they believe they could add to what already exists in their practice? The problem this represents is then a compound one: the manager's first enthusiasm is for the text the musicians already are. Inspired by such a text, they are unlikely to be able to restrict their belief in their ability to facilitate its development to its infrastructural needs. On the other hand, by pursuing the vague but extremely urgent goal of 'making it', musicians offer, effectively, a 'blank cheque' to a manager where issues of competence and authority are concerned because their desires and expectations are often a lethal cocktail of the lavish and the hazy.

Conclusion: The dilemmas of artist management as a relationship

Making symbolic goods begins with musicians. Musicians create texts from music and from their performance of music, but because so many musicians do this then, in order to gain the attention they believe they deserve (and need if they are to remain musicians), they find themselves in competition with each other as music acts. One way of gaining competitive advantage over other acts is for musicians to appoint managers whom, they believe, will facilitate their entry into music markets, mainly by brokering relations with music companies who specialise in such activity. If, in these terms, the motivation of musicians to seek to appoint artist managers is driven by the nature of music markets, the motivation of artist managers to become artist managers is less clear cut – they lack impulsion and so can only be seen as self-selecting in their choice. This recognition brings two further ones into play. Artist managers at the very least must be self-motivated individuals who, equally, have to be self-tutored. In becoming an artist manager, individuals lock themselves into a relationship with a specific set of musicians. This relationship represents a combined torsion: the product of the manager's adjustment to the role and to the musicians' adjustment to being musicians. Artist–act relations are not more 'business-like' simply by declaration; the degree of business success depends on how coherent their collaboration can be made as a platform for entering further alliances with music companies. For these reasons, an artist manager is unlike a 'conventional' manager – he does not so much learn about the workings of the retail or pharmaceutical sector and so is enabled to take on a managerial role in any firm in that sector – rather, he learns his client or clients as well as he can and tries to figure out, in the face of immense competition, how this client can be made or allowed to progress to market entry and from there to market success.

Considered in this way, it is reasonable to argue that artist managers come up with individual solutions to the challenges posed to them by musicians, on one side, and 'the industry', on the other. In each case, such is the pressure and intensity of making symbolic goods, these solutions are likely to be pragmatic and *ad hoc*; in the sense of being 'tailor-made' for a specific contingency. Furthermore, the impact of any decision made in relation to any contingency will then produce its own effect or effects that are likely to induce more solutions of these kinds. As decisions accumulate, so the fortunes of acts take shape. What makes artist management such a problematic resource for musicians is not simply the tendency towards pragmatism and the *ad hoc*, it is that there is no mechanism for evaluating the nature and quality of decisions and their effects – management relations are private affairs; the Music Industry does not encourage the sharing of information; there are no institutes of learning; no professional bodies to maintain and develop standards. In this way, each and every manager begins as a 'Johnny Jackson' and those who survive come to be the 'elders' amongst a turbulent constellation of similar individuals who do not necessarily create and manage knowledge, but accumulate and pass on a 'commonsense' understanding of market address that might not always bear scrutiny; yet this is still a commonsense that musicians are hungry to hear.

The often-indiscriminate hunger of musicians brings its own reward, which tends to be that few of them become market successes. That this is the case is only partially attributable to deficiencies in the formation of artist managers and their relationships with those musicians; mostly it is because this is how the cultural-industrial system has always worked – idiomatic currency is mercurial and structures of feeling are erratic, consequently music companies manage risk by creating relations with as many likely candidates for market success as they can and by offsetting as much of the production costs of making symbolic goods onto musicians. Even so, musicians are still tempted into joint endeavours with music companies on the substantially erroneous basis that 'careers' are on offer when, for the most part, they are not. Under these circumstances, artist managers work with the imperatives that command them – musicians' desire for 'deals' (truly contracts that describe working conditions) and music companies desire for musicians to fit processes established for the conversion of texts into symbolic goods from which they profit should those goods sell.

Where music is concerned, the processes of the production of symbolic goods featuring music are in enormous flux – to the extent that new music industries are emerging and the relations between existing ones are changing – yet core tensions and contradictions persist. Some artist managers are successful and some musicians enjoy careers (so there is much to learn from those who 'get it right'), but all artist managers act as lightning rods for collisions between the substantially incongruent goals of musicians and music companies. Whether the changes in and among the music industries are sufficient to re-inscribe the role of artist manager remains to be seen, but the defining volatility of musician–artist manager relations can tell us much about how, more generally, symbolic goods are produced. In turning to consider more closely what tends to be regarded as the Music Industry it is essential to keep in mind that much industrial work is done in the intense and ongoing interactions between musicians and artist managers.

5
Music Companies and Music Industry

Musicians need paying audiences; only paying audiences allow them to be just musicians and not workers of some other kind who play music in their 'spare time'. Paying audiences, though, do not occur naturally and can only be constituted through market practices. In Chapter 1, the argument was made that it is impossible to separate musicians who make music for markets from the industrial process of making music commodities. Essentially, the only things that can be admitted to music markets are music commodities, tradable experiences of music making. Musicians are not bound to rely on the intervention of others to enter markets and to exchange the experiences of music they offer, but they cannot escape the logic of organising those experiences as commodities, or the logics associated with market competition. Musicians compete with each other and those of them who achieve market success, and sustainable 'careers' as musicians, are those who find and go on sustaining competitive advantage over other musicians. In this way, 'competitive advantage' is not solely an outcome of music; it is an outcome of a combination of factors which involve the 'non-musical' effort associated with entering markets.

Ultimately, while it is not necessary for musicians to come to rely on others when entering markets, the vast majority become embroiled with those 'others' because what the latter offer (although in a complicated way) is a range of market entry services that may possibly, when combined with the offers made by musicians, result in market success. The reasoning behind this tentative expression of the working relations between musicians and market entry companies will be referred to below; what needs to be recognised is that such relationships always involve two defining sets of conditions. Firstly, when working with others, musicians must concede that others investing in their market entry

99

will expect a return on their investment. Secondly, if outcomes are to be achieved, 'working relations' need to be organised in ways that allow decisions to be made that are adhered to by all. Companies want profit but they do not want to lose invested capital. As previous chapters have indicated, music companies always need to balance risk. If the market success of any specific symbolic good can never be guaranteed, what makes life easiest for music companies is when the conversion of the text into the symbolic good proceeds with limited equivocation. Equivocation is the nemesis of cultural production, because once all parties attempt to 'second guess' the market, the chances of a coherent symbolic good emerging from production by a dysfunctional 'committee' of stakeholders is low indeed. Consequently, whether it is acknowledged openly or not, the issue of who determines specific courses of actions is always posed and always active in these alliances.

To put this last point another way, in collaborative endeavours there is always a question of who exercises control over effort towards a specific goal. As management is, broadly, a systematic attempt to exert 'control over effort' towards goals or outcomes, then the questions of who manages what aspects of that process, together with how they do it, is the clue to the industrial process of music. As the two previous chapters should have made clear, a great deal of management goes on before musicians come to form the decisive joint endeavours with music companies that can bring them market success. So it is that the management of the industrial process of music is pre-disposed to be a tense and inherently conflictual affair as three different parties, musicians, artist managers and music companies, can all make strong cases as to why they should be the ones to decide the finished article and its mode of 'delivery'. When it is considered that what frames all actions and all opinions (articulated or not) are the deep uncertainties of popular cultural production, then this frame can only aggravate latent friction.

To develop observations about 'music companies' made in Chapter 1, in Business Studies and Management Studies, when discussing industries, the term 'firms' is usually used to identify their constituent elements; conversely studies of the Music Industry tend to refer to 'music businesses'. In this study the comparatively non-standard term 'music companies' is preferred. Firstly because the term 'music business' is an over-familiar one which, especially in the substitution of 'the music business' for 'the Music Industry', tends to draw attention away from music industry as an active industrialisation of music. Secondly, use of 'companies' can be argued to offer the advantage of 'equalising' both very large and very small businesses or firms as organised attempts to achieve market success for some music and some musicians. In addition, companies in and of themselves suggest joint effort; to be 'in company' is to be, purposively, with other people. Essentially, in preferring this term, what can be argued to count most where notions of 'industry' are concerned is that companies, whether great or small, exist as concentrations of capital investment in an organised effort to achieve market success. Because they do, and because they involve the collaborative efforts of numbers of people, the need to manage the people involved in pursuing market success so that a return on investment is achieved is, arguably, more clearly suggested by 'company' than it is by its cognate alternatives.

The tentative construction of the working relationship between musicians and companies offering market entry services as one that 'might, just possibly, ... result in market success' is deliberate in that it refers to previous references to Caves' observation that 'nobody knows' which symbolic goods are likely to find buyers in sufficient quantities to provide a worthwhile return on investment. Because 'nobody knows', then music companies have needed to develop coping strategies for the deep uncertainties of the markets they compete in. In turn, it is inattention not so much to the logic of this coping but to its management that excited so much comment about Hesmondhalgh's work in Chapter 1.

Hesmondhalgh's main point is that cultural-industrial production is a risky business in general, but he does not explain what makes it so risky. The argument in Chapter 2 was intended to broach the context and content of this riskiness, where the context would be that individuals came to expect the existence of products, and a subsequent supply of individual commodities that facilitated leisure and, more importantly, identities that were not defined and confined by work-roles. The content of such products and such commodities is that they are intended to offer pleasurable, affirmative meanings to those individuals. The problem facing individual companies is twofold. Firstly, there are so many originators of symbolic goods who appear to have the ability to supply such pleasurable meanings. Secondly, pleasurable meanings are fragile and fleeting, making it impossible to predict what (potential) offers of meaning will resonate and be taken up.

To clarify this last point, the connection between the symbolic good produced by a company and the intended recipient is that the symbolic good 'speaks' in a familiar, or at least an intelligible, idiom and that the signifying materials animate specific structures of feeling that bring individuals into states of connection with other users for the duration of the event. Very few symbolic goods make these connections – the failure rate for new product launches is, as Hesmondhalgh indicates, extremely high: for example, only one in ten acts signed to major record companies makes back the costs of production of the symbolic goods that bear its name. They fail to for a combination of reasons: symbolic goods are delicate to construct because their idiom can easily be misconfigured and their currency is also equally unstable. Furthermore, market competition is intense. In addition, music companies are reliant on channels of access to the market that they cannot entirely control. All of these factors put symbolic goods at risk and, therefore, the 'coping strategies' employed by cultural companies devolve into managing market risk. The question remains of how such strategies are effected when the performances of people are central to the symbolic nature of the goods produced.

In the context of the above, the problem for musicians and their managers is that, even though they are likely to be welcomed with open arms by the companies that intend to take the symbolic goods they help to produce to market, those companies are practising risk management strategies that can easily have negative effects on their experience of joint work with the company. The issue then is how musicians, together with their own managers, manage their experience of the alliance with a music company whose strategy is, essentially, to spread risk across all such alliances. For example, the key risk-management strategy of major record companies is to over-sign, to take on more acts than they can market in the hope that signals from the market will indicate which of the acts to prioritise. Music publishers and live agencies also work in these ways, although historically, they have been dependent on the major record companies to do much of the work of sifting through acts for them.

As the rise of the internet phenomenon MySpace, and before it Vitaminic, so convincingly and graphically demonstrated, from the perspective of generating a profit from market competition there is an over-supply of musicians. The over-arching industrial question then is 'how to manage an over-supply when nobody knows which musicians will make market-successful symbolic goods?' For music companies almost any musicians might offer the possibility of return on investment but, at the same time, arguably all musicians believe they are worthy to be heard. From the perspective of the musician, the alliance with a music company is there to make them market successes, but from the perspective of the music company, the alliance is there because they need commodities to sell. Because which specific symbolic goods will sell cannot be predicted, there can be no loyalty to any particular alliance. Further, companies need maximum control over the conditions and content of any alliance they form in order to be able to respond quickly and effectively to market information.

Taken as a whole, relations between musicians and music companies are structurally and therefore inescapably tense, and, because they are, who manages this tension and how goes to the heart of the industrial process of music. It goes to the heart of it because, in enough cases that make it economically sensible to invest in cultural production, market successes happen in music that produce enormous profits and glamorous stars. This in turn indicates that some companies get market entry of some commodities right, on their terms, as profit yielding symbolic goods. On this basis, we find music industry in the realisation of effective market address. 'Realisation' is an outcome of solving the managerial tensions inherent in creating cultural commodities. These managerial tensions can be identified, broadly as 'horizontal' and 'vertical' ones. They are 'horizontal' because companies must manage relations with all the acts they work with in terms of their own need to manage risk, but they are 'vertical' because risk must be managed on a case-by-case basis with each and every musician or musicians and their respective artist managers. It is for this latter reason that every musician's experience of the Music Industry is a distinct one, but even so is generated by the same sets of considerations and conflicts. Several such experiences will be discussed in Chapter 7; here we need to consider specifically how music companies perceive and experience the processes of market entry as an industrial one of investment in, and organisation of, production.

Music companies and management: fixity, fluidity and hybridity

If we consider that music is an industrial product when it takes the form of a symbolic good then this poses the question, 'when does music *become* a symbolic good?'. This question can only be answered by considering market entry and the activities that bear on music which prepare it for market entry. These 'activities' can be regarded as ones that 'add value' to the original work of the musicians. 'Adding value' to music occurs in three main ways: firstly, by configuring 'raw' texts so that they can enter markets; secondly, by alerting possible users to the existence of those texts; thirdly, by enabling those users to enjoy them, for a price. Music, as a text, becomes a symbolic good when additional dimensions have been added that can connect that music with audiences. Audiences for the purposes of this study are to be assembled through taking music into markets. Audiences access symbolic goods in music through the efforts, now or in the past, of value-adding music companies. This is the *raison d'être* of those companies and the focus of their activities is the generation of profit through configuring texts, alerting potential users to their existence and enabling access to them for a price. Each one of these dimensions needs to be managed, as does their co-ordination. It should therefore be no surprise that the exercise of such control collides with existing and on-going managerial effort expended by the originators of the texts that become the symbolic goods produced for sale in markets.

Musicians can manage themselves; the problem with self-management though, is that it is essentially non-musical activity. As 'non-musical activity', the organisation of market entry poses exactly the same sets of challenges to musicians as it does to music companies: how to configure a text in such a way that it connects with a target market in the face of permanently fierce market competition; then how to deal with a dependency on channels of access that lie outside their direct control; and how to meet these challenges while nursing goods that are inherently unstable. Each of these aspects of market entry poses the need for control to be taken at all stages of the configuration and delivery of the symbolic good. If the text-originating musicians are a band and are, nominally at least, 'equals', then that one of them should assume control over what is effectively all of the actions of the rest can make the practice of self-management so contentious that it is a very rare one indeed. Instead, and as we have seen, musicians seek out artist managers to 'take care of business' so that they can focus on creating the music texts from which symbolic goods emerge. The issue that will not go away though, is that of control: who decides when the text is finished? Who controls the value-adding so that it does not compromise the text during its journey to market as a symbolic good? These questions become even harder to answer when musicians meet the decisive 'value adders' in the form of music companies from the main music industries.

Symbolic goods have to enter markets. They are brought there by music companies whose specialist work this is. On this basis, it may seem unequivocal that musicians and their managers should cede their managerial stake in the texts they have produced to those who know best how to accomplish market entry. The fact remains, however, that 'nobody knows' what symbolic goods will succeed in the market place and the problem is that if nobody knows, anyone might be right about how best to enter the market. Viewed purely from the perspective of music companies, there is an urgent and insistent need to address this dilemma and to resolve it in their own favour; they are the investors in value-adding; their existence depends on adding value effectively; they need latitude in order to adjust the angle and velocity of market entry up to the very last moment. In order to ensure that they are not subordinate to the combination of the musicians and artist managers that they work with in production alliances, music companies need to assert control over the production process. They do this through a combination of strategies I have identified as Fixity, Fluidity and Hybridity. The configuration of these strategies will vary on a case-by-case basis, even as their total represents a 'global' strategy for dealing with the embedded managerial tensions associated with a production system variant wherein key contributors to the production process are not under the direct control of the music company.

Before beginning this analysis, it is necessary to deal with two thorny issues. What has already been implied is that there is an industrial process in music which derives from the implementation of control strategies by music companies, yet there is no 'Music Industry' as such. In addition, remarks to this point have either directly cited, or implied, relationships between musicians, together with their managers, and record companies rather than with some kind of standard 'music company'. The potentially severe limitations on this analysis are, therefore, twofold: firstly, at a time when the power of the major record companies is uncertain and possibly in decline, record companies will be made to stand for 'the Music Industry'. Secondly, the existence of such a music industry has yet to be fully specified. Towards addressing both these problems, the following remarks apply.

The recording industry and music industrialisation

In Chapter 1, the argument was made that, given the shared perspectives, purposes and interdependencies of companies across the music industries, the term 'the Music Industry' can be a legitimate one if used carefully and consciously and it will be so used here, but with certain caveats. Arguments made in Chapters 2 and 4 suggest an additional dimension to the interactions and inter-dependencies of the three main music industries – which is that different music industries have predominated at different times in music industry history. Clearly to detail and to justify this claim is beyond the scope of this study, but obviously, before the recording industry emerged and became consolidated, the live music industry and music publishing vied for dominance; wherein rival industries, as rival companies, compete for market share. Subsequently, it took recording a considerable period to become the main music industry. In the early part of the 21st century, while the recording industry has lost what gave it its dominance as a music industry in the form of its virtual monopoly of recording and the distribution of records, the major record companies remain the dominant music-industrial forces because they represent the primary concentrations of capital in the commodification of music. What, then, a 50-year period of predominance has given the recording industry is a power of inflection: even if the live performance and music publishing industries are no longer as beholden as they once were to a business model predicated on selling albums, the imperatives and working habits associated with the recording industry are proving slow to subside.

One of the primary reasons for beginning a discussion of the industrialisation of music with an albeit brief account of the rise of Music Hall was to draw attention to an historic change in social and cultural conditions which led to the formation of a generalised, rather than localised, market relationship between musicians and audiences. Because this process entailed the creation of a recognisable industrial infrastructure for entering music markets, it was argued that once such an infrastructure consolidated itself as an institution, two key factors followed. Firstly, musicians would henceforth be subservient to this infrastructure and so would need to shape their efforts to win its personnel's approval. Secondly, those who populated the music-industrial infrastructure would continue to justify their fitness to participate in the revenues generated by music commodities on the basis of a specific market entry expertise. This was, and remains, an expertise they not only believed they enjoyed but embodied.

The points have already been made that, as an institution, the Music Industry is characterised by being a body of knowledge that is almost entirely tacit rather than explicit. Tacit knowledge is difficult to contest; it also allows for contradictory beliefs to go unrecognised and unresolved. So it is that, with no associated infrastructure of standardised professional qualifications, the induction of new personnel into music companies tends to happen on an informal basis. What allows this happen, and what substitutes for professional induction, is the persistence of what might be referred to as a 'culture of practice'; a working commonsense that has accumulated over time to underwrite typical types of decisions made to address recurring categories of contingencies. By the beginning of the 20th century, when recording first became used to create profit from music performances; profit making in symbolic goods in music had enjoyed something in the order of a 60-year history. As gramophone records began to grow in popularity, the existing music-industrial infrastructure was not supplanted by the rise of the recording industry, rather the recording industry adapted to the already accumulated, substantially tacit, norms and values of industrialising music. For example, as Jones (1985) shows, what became the UK's major record company, EMI, proceeded from a speculative investment by a solicitor, Trevor Williams, who, with two friends, invested £15,000 'to work Berliner's British and European gramophone patents under a royalty agreement' (Jones, 1985, p. 80). Berliner was the American inventor of the flat gramophone disc who, in a tense relationship with another inventor, Eldridge Johnson, created the Victor Talking Machine Company in 1901. Between them, Berliner, with his flat disc, and Johnson, with his governor that allowed gramophones turntables to revolve at a constant speed, helped to create the recording industry as the, for a considerable period, dominant music industry as described here.

The purpose of citing the example of the origins of EMI is to indicate that recording's origins as, effectively, an engineering industry, meant that it emerged in isolation from the other two industries – the recording industry's focus was not music, at least at its immediate outset. Furthermore, it was separately capitalised. What both these conditions meant was that when the commercial exploitation of popular songs and singers became an attractive business proposition, the recording companies were forced to enter new fields – negotiating and creating contracts with publishers for the use of songs, together with the representatives of singers for the use of their services and, when applicable, with musicians under the terms and conditions of their union agreements. In addition, these new types of music companies needed to respect intellectual property laws in their use of those songs and to make royalty payments to the owners of their copyrights.

This need for negotiation and compliance with existing regimes meant that the managers of record companies, who, in their initial phase, tended to come from outside the existing music industry, needed to become not just fluent in the practices but, far more importantly, the perspectives and the prejudices of those already in that industry. In this way, the recording industry's technological distinctiveness did not lead the music industry to be immediately re-cast in its image and around its imperatives, rather it was the existing culture of practice of the collaborative industry of live performance and publishing that dictated the norms of the record industry's transformation into a music industry. So it is, and so it will be argued, that, at watersheds in music industry history, existing norms and practices may be modified and inflected to serve cultural, social and technological change, but are not necessarily uprooted and entirely remade at every such juncture, however profound conjunctural effects may be across the relations that constitute music industry.

These points acknowledged, the examples drawn on in this discussion of tensions between musicians and music companies derive from the recording industry and there is a danger in taking record companies to stand for all music companies. The music industries are different, they produce different commodities not so much for different audiences but for audiences at different 'removes'. For example, a record company supplies recordings to music users but will need to work through offline and online media to bring those recordings to the attention of potential users. Music publishers supply songs to media companies to use in addition to other 'messages', and so their immediate users are those companies. Live performance agencies, promoters and venues enjoy far more direct relationships with music users. They can reach them through 'fliers', posters and databases. These are forms of advertising that, in most respects, are not dependent on the additional filters of media businesses. The media dependency of much music company activity will also need to be returned to; here the issue is that, while the recording industry is not the entirety of the Music Industry it has been its core for so long that the values of key operatives can be argued to be reasonably representative of the thinking of the industry as whole. In this way, while the recording industry is only one of the music industries, how its personnel conceive the market entry of music can be used in this instance, as a general set of predispositions.

Fixity

To return to the discussion of how music companies solve the 'production control' problem they face when working with key personnel who are not their direct employees, three strategies can be identified – Fixity, Fluidity and Hybridity. The first of these derives from the fact that, whether as private or public entities of great or small size, companies are 'fixed' entities in the sense that they are required to obey company law. While not an onerous obligation in itself, the very fact that companies need to be constituted legally can be argued to bring a certain focus to their activities. Companies are not 'casual' undertakings, and when individuals sink their wealth into a company it is reasonable to imagine that they do this with the intention of, at the very least, not losing their investment. Further, there is a logic to capital investment that cannot be evaded. Companies are expected to make a profit and expected to grow: legally no company can trade as insolvent and it would be unlikely, should a company offer shares to the public, that share holders would remain loyal if dividends from profits were not forthcoming. In reality, companies are created with specific and related goals in mind; namely, to enter specific markets and to achieve competitive advantage in them with the intention of generating a profit. Obviously, not all companies achieve these broad goals and many fail but without a goal there is no reason for a company to exist and it is reasonable to imagine that all individuals who form companies believe, at least at the outset, that they know 'their' market and believe that they can prosper in that market. Additionally, new companies inevitably come to trade with established companies and so will be drawn into the comparative fixity of the cultures of practice associated with different forms of company interaction, as well as with the legal requirement to accept and to comply with trading standards of various types and kinds.

Where music industries are concerned, one of the reasons that music, as a sector, is difficult to identify as uniformly industrial is the co-existence of huge, globally active music companies with an immense number of tiny ones. Both types seem to happily exist in the same environment. At the very least this makes music unlike, for example, the automobile or pharmaceutical industries where there is little room for small companies and, what there is, is only for highly specialised ones. In music, record companies can be vast or tiny, as can publishers and live agencies. This will be argued to have its consequences for the industrial process in terms of the fluidity of 'the Music Industry' but here what needs to be considered is that, whether great or small, a music company faces a vast over-supply of musicians. Because of this, and because musicians both compete with each other and are variously inclined to cede aspects of control over aspects of their effort, then what a company has to offer those musicians is their belief, sometimes supported by an often very heavily censored 'track record', that they can take them to market and have them succeed there.

When 'nobody knows' what symbolic goods will succeed in the market, then any company which exhibits an apparent expertise allied with belief in them as talented people is an attractive proposition to a hungry musician. In turn, this is the first step in such a company exerting the control it needs over the symbolic good it takes to market. Musicians are inclined to accede to the expertise of companies, whether this exists or not. Musicians are liable to do this at the outset of their careers as they have no prior experience and because idiomatic currency is only idiomatic when it is current, so they always operate, or feel that they do, under a sense of great urgency. Eventually musicians and their managers might be more circumspect, but as so few musicians genuinely enjoy careers, this scenario tends to repeat itself continuously. So it is that, once musicians and music companies are 'matched', the music company will offer those musicians a contract for the provision of its services where such offers are based on the tacit agreement that the company 'knows best' with regard to market entry.

Contracts are the subject of the following chapter, but the point needs to be made here that these are invariably 'standard' ones. As Chapter 2 argued, standardisation in popular music developed through Music Hall. The standard contract, whether recording, publishing or live agency, can be argued to be a powerful component of the regularisation, and with it the 'fixing', of musician-music company alliances. Where contracts are concerned, the fact that they are 'standard' can be reassuring. Firstly, the notion of an industry standard conveys an air of legitimacy. Secondly, the idea that a contract is 'non-standard' tends to convey the notion that it may be in some way harmful and so should be rejected. 'Standards' imply the tried and the tested; they imply that adherence to them creates the positive results that musicians so want. The problem is that the forces that created these standards were those of companies making profit, and it is reasonable to imagine that the composition of a standard contract reflects the precepts and objectives of companies, rather than the musicians who come to work with those companies. Contracts can be argued to act almost as an extension of the legal nature of the company beyond its immediate environs. In this way, even the smallest and newest music company is likely to offer its own version of a 'standard' contract, thus sealing their nascent relationship with musicians on its terms.

The nascent relationship begins substantially on the terms of the company because, by signing the contract, musicians are implicitly agreeing to a particular process of market address; one that they are legally bound to comply with, even though the contract which seals the relationship is, at best, an imperfect instrument for joint work. The weaknesses of contracts are many. For example, they cannot specify contingencies; which means they offer no clear guidance when problems arise. Contracts are costly and challenging to dispute if those problems become severe and, certainly in the case of recording contracts, they tend to be far easier for the company to walk away from than for musicians. All of this underscores the ironies of 'unsigned' musicians who are defined by the idea that they deserve the recognition of tying themselves into a legally binding agreements that do not necessarily favour their interests and that rarely lead to market success. In these ways, the role of the contract is to ensure a certain degree of fixity in the relationship between music company and musician. This is a fixity that enjoys the force of law and with it the force of custom, but it is also a fixity that only truly becomes useful to the music company when the role of the artist manager in 'activating' the fixed agreement is considered.

Fixity and artist managers

As the previous chapter argued, the role of artist manager is a highly complex and demanding one. What is most striking about it where the relationship between musicians and music companies is concerned is the fundamental fact that, while they will be instrumental in brokering agreements between the musicians they represent and the companies those musicians come to work with, artist managers do not actually sign any of the contracts themselves. At first, this may seem of little or no significance, but consider again the points made in that chapter: that artist managers 'live' the 'irreconcilable tensions' of, what this chapter argues, is the dispute over the management of the text as it becomes the symbolic good. What must be factored into the understanding of musician–artist management relations is that artist managers are self-employed 'third parties' in the industrial process of music whose stake in the working relationship between musicians and music companies is, ultimately, in the success of the commodity. It is because only if the symbolic good (the record, the tour, the song) sells will it generate the income that pays their commission. How artist managers conceive and perform their role is pivotal in determining the outcome of the industrial process, because it is the artist manager who interacts with all those who add value to the act. All of these interactions need to be 'productive' in the sense that the client's interests are protected and advanced in and through each encounter, but the immensely challenging, and ever present, dilemma is a dual one: firstly, of being able to identify what those interests are and, secondly, of distinguishing between protecting and advancing those interests.

Viewed from the perspective of the artist manager, the artist gains if the commodity sells in the market; therefore it may seem best that the artist complies with the industrial process on the terms and conditions *of* that process. Conversely, how companies sell symbolic goods can be in ways unsympathetic to their originators; or else, how companies organise production and market access of the symbolic good might be counter to the wishes of the originating musicians. This is an insistent dilemma and the position of artist manager is an invidious one; if they side with the artist at the expense of the company's perception of its own needs then the act can be harmed; but if they appear to side with the company against the perceived needs of their clients then they are not doing their job. Truly, if cultural production was identical to factory production then the artist manager must always choose between two roles: they are either the 'shop steward', the often feisty advocate of the workforce; or they are the 'foreman', the representative of capital inside that workforce.

When most acts fail to have hit records and do not go on to earn publishing income and enjoy lucrative live appearances, it may seem reasonable to allow companies to decide best how to conduct their business. Yet when the conduct of that business involves prioritising some acts over others, then the manager has every reason to fight for his client's interests. Conversely, if the artist manager is to take this militant stance, it means that the act must trust the manager's analysis of the company's strategy; they must support that strategy unequivocally and must play their role in its implementation. This will involve a relinquishment of their own managerial capacity (their 'creative autonomy' in Hesmondhalgh's phrase) to that of the manager and given that the manager might not be equipped for such power, then the act might harm its own interests by supporting its own manager! Effectively, acts which enjoy the best chance of succeeding are those who have managers that understand the company's strategy and current thinking at any one time, and can persuade the act to comply with the industrial process in ways that minimise harm and maximise advantage. Clearly, this is a tall order. Managers may never enjoy the degree of data they might need to make what can become an endless succession of judgement calls, nor might they enjoy the stamina to go on implementing such judgements. Even so, however the manager calls it is the way in which the industrial process proceeds, in specific cases with all their narrative particularities.

Companies, especially very big ones, are reluctant to proceed with truculent acts but passive acts can be easily damaged, neglected or discarded. Equally, an artist manager is not managing if he encourages the act to slavishly obey every whim of the company. Yet having the act comply with his strategy for dealing with the company's strategy involves negotiating the place of the act in the formation of their joint 'policy', something that the intensity of the industrial process is rarely willing or able to allow, let alone the effect of the musicians' collective distractions as discussed in Chapter 4. 'Fixity' then succeeds as a strategy for companies because it can be experienced, especially by new acts and their managers, as a set of undeniable and even inscrutable logics. These 'logics' involve the legal form and concomitant focus of a company as a *fait accompli*. As a company, a body of people with interests in producing symbolic goods gives every appearance of embodying expertise. More, a contract is a legally binding and comparatively inflexible form of agreement. Faced with these intangible but comparatively inflexible realities of business, and given the complexities of their own role, a manager is forced into seeking a way forward that might rarely result in his securing the act's place as an equal partner in a joint enterprise. That neither the musician nor the artist manager is a direct employee of a music company is therefore 'solved' from the company's perspective by winning their compliance to company-determined market entry procedures either willingly or by default. In turn, music is secured as an industrial process through the subordination of textual creators to the routines of commodity production, however haphazard and wasteful this process of subordination might be.

Fluidity

In an ideal world, musicians would manage the production of the text and artist managers would manage their co-operation in a process of the transformation of texts into symbolic goods managed by companies. This would be a realisation of a 'stable' cultural-industrial process in which all parties understood and performed their separate roles and there was mutual co-operation and trust in all quarters. Unfortunately the reality of music-industrial production can be far from this. It can be far from it for the reasons already discussed: music companies need to guarantee a profit on their investment; this can mean switching attention away from some signed musicians to others as signals from the marketplace are received and acted upon. Furthermore, the market for symbolic goods is highly volatile while the goods themselves are individually highly fragile. As Hesmondhalgh argues, cultural producers employ a suite of strategies to cope with this volatility and the consequent fragility of their commodities, but what is interesting is how these conditions also demand that companies, however 'fixed' they may in regard to their relationship to musicians and managers, be fluid in how they deal with contingencies. Because the creation of new music and new texts is ceaseless, these 'contingencies' are also ceaseless.

When upheaval is the norm, the very large companies which define 'the Music Industry' have learned to cope with it as a defining condition of their operating context. Music companies have learned to cope with continuous upheaval, thus strengthening the industrial process that defines them.

Text-creators are entirely self-selecting, but this does not mean that the creation of new texts is a random affair. It is reasonable to assume that new text creators have recipients in mind as they fashion their texts, but recipients have to be reached and the defining mode of reaching recipients, even as the internet facilitates this as never before, is still to encounter them in markets. As soon as new text-creators begin to seek audiences they become publicly accessible and, because the 'public' they desire is an appreciative, paying audience, new entrepreneurs will be called into being to offer additional services in constituting these audiences through market-focused practices. These new entrepreneurs will be individuals who, at a price to be met sooner or later by the musicians they come to work with, are willing to take the risks involved in entering markets with what might be, at any particular time, radically new texts. While the dominant music companies persist, and with them the dominant form of music industry, then they will need to be able to withstand the impacts made on them as constant 'new waves' in music and in popular culture generally crash against the infrastructure they represent and maintain. Thus far, they have survived; most record companies and music publishers can trace their roots to times before dubstep, hip-hop, punk rock and even rock and roll itself. This is less true of live agencies but even some of these companies will have lengthy histories. In turn, the fact that music companies, generally, continue to survive suggests that the constancy of 'new waves' might reinforce rather than destabilise the music industrial process.

The reason that new text-creators and new texts are ceaselessly produced is because audiences are ceaselessly recomposed. Not only do individuals age and die, but the very fabric of sense-making practice is constantly rippled and remade as social and political events impact understanding and as cultural producers maintain their constant flow of nuanced commodities in response to those events and to their own need for profit. In popular music, the term 'scene' is used to identify pools of new sense-making, expressive practices centred on or involving music.[1] Popular music's past is a tumult of different scenes. Each scene then throws up its managers, its record company founders and its myriad service providers. Not all of these will prosper and build companies that take their place in the Music Industry, though some of course do, and the array of powerful figures and powerful companies is re-ordered to admit them. The crux of this is that, even after a scene as seismic as hip-hop deeply impacted the US recording industry, its main 'players' have reproduced and reaffirmed 'the Music Industry' far more than they have radicalised and reshaped it to make it more open to those who would follow them. This is the source and measure of 'Fluidity' as a strategy.

With upheaval a norm, it is almost as if the new entrants behave as the 'research and design' departments of the major companies. This is Negus's point in *Music Genres and Corporate Cultures* and, as he argues, major companies have become used to hiring and firing staff. Such staff seem stoically to accept such practices; there have been no strikes by music company personnel in music industry history. 'Hiring' and 'firing' takes place comparatively smoothly, not just because of the constant interaction between new and established companies, so that new entrants learn the existing practices and values of music industry on a day-to-day basis, but because established companies need exactly what new entrants offer them; notably their immersion in an idiom that might prove profitable. Symbolic goods only sell if they connect, and they only become profitable if such connections are extensive. Music companies need research and design because they need to connect to structures of feeling in convincing ways. Research and design is done 'in house' to the extent that all major companies across the music industries employ staff who are alert to the fine nuances of popular cultural expression and to change in those nuances but there is no substitute for fresh blood. It is the constant injection of fresh blood into the Music Industry, its metaphorically 'fluid' nature that preserves the industrial process. It accomplishes this in four main ways:

1. While the industry has a need for stability, the limits of tolerance of the music-industrial process are equipped for extremities: any industry which can survive a 90 per cent new product failure rate can survive the sudden appearance of punk rock (in the 1970s) of R&B (in the 1990s) or the rise of TV talent shows (in the 2000s).
2. The 'limits of tolerance' of music industry can be extremely flexible and robust because induction of new entrants into the industry proceeds informally. Entrepreneurs and outsiders become insiders and respected members of the establishment in very short spaces of time. They do so because the culture of practice of music industry is not open to verification: the only qualification required for admittance to the inner sanctum is a hit act.

3. Once a new company becomes powerful, or a new entrant becomes a powerful figure in an existing company, they then speak with the authority of the industrial process they now implement. They enjoy this power not so much for itself, but because it is a necessity if they are to continue to attract the latest texts and text-creators to them now that they have left the immediacy of the scenes that spawned them. New 'players' come to obey the logic of industry because they are tied to the logic of profit.

4. The experience of new entrepreneurs is absorbed into existing industry commonsense because experience is made sense of informally; in ways that are not transparent and open to scrutiny. On this basis, successive new waves accumulate (as the 'expertise' that emerging text-creators seek and believe they need in order to constitute the new audiences their new texts need. Fluidity underwrites the authority of fixity by continuously refreshing 'expertise' through constantly reaffirming what is already 'known'.

This last point bears closer examination: the question of what music industry expertise consists of has been raised at different points in this and previous chapters. Music industry knowledge has been described as overwhelmingly 'tacit' in character. In an operating environment where upheaval is the norm, while the 'fixed' nature of companies allows them advantages in dealing with managerial conflicts of authority over the text during the conversion process into symbolic goods, the essential informality of music industry lends even the largest companies mercuriality. Staff turnover can be extremely high and replacement staff are drawn in constantly from the constantly churning pool of new, scene-based 'movers and shakers'. One of the deepest contradictions of 'the Music Industry' (and probably of cultural industries more generally) is that music companies represent themselves as bodies of knowledge in an operating environment in which 'nobody knows'. What music companies must then 'know' is how to survive when 'nobody knows', and how they survive is by constantly recruiting those with the latest versions of knowledge, with the latest sense of 'certainty'. This, however, is only a viable strategy for two further reasons: firstly, under conditions of over-supply, the limits of tolerance of bad guesses allow companies to, mostly, survive their mistakes; secondly, incoming entrepreneurs rarely seem to want to 'remake' the Music Industry so that it operates in some more sympathetic manner whether to entrepreneurs, musicians, or both; rather they want 'a piece of the action' and they want to hold on to it as a career. For example, there are likely to be more UK 'executives' who can trace their entrance to the Music Industry from the days of punk rock than there are punk bands still meaningfully extant, and the same may well apply in the USA in regard to hip-hop.

Taken together 'fixity' and 'fluidity' complement each other, because both devolve onto questions of authority; the authority of music company managers over musicians and artist managers. For music to be an industry, musicians must comply with how companies see their needs in the market. 'Hybridity', as a strategy of ensuring this compliance, is then the application of the general dimensions of fixity and fluidity on a case-by-case basis under the specific, market-entry constraints experienced by companies from specific music industries. Again, though, as a general approach to conducting music industry, the example of the recording industry will stand for the Music Industry as a whole.

Hybridity

In 2009, Island Records (once one of the UK's biggest and most influential record companies but a label inside what is now Universal Music Group for 20 years) released a series of 'educational' DVDs aimed at giving young people a sense of how a record company operates. For the purposes of this argument, the most telling sequence involves the presentations made by two 'product managers'; the role most directly charged with taking musicians into the market. It is by evaluating these presentations that some final observations about the work of music companies and its centrality to music industry can be made. In abbreviated versions they are:

> A product manager is kind of . . . its official department is Marketing and that is kind of the core role of it is taking records to market (sic), turning them from pieces of lovely music, giving it an identity and something that is visually able to be sellable, giving it a brand, make a package, but beyond just the advertising and the getting it into shops side of things is the entire building up of an act and managing a successful campaign . . . From day one when an artist signs . . . it's determining what they are gonna look like, how they're gonna be presented to the people, finding a good team of PRs and press people to be able to take the artist to their relevant media and make a success of them, get them on Radio 1, get them in the right magazines, get them on the right web-sites [. . .] and from there, trying to hold together a team that pushes the artist into success.
>
> (Chris Scott, Music College interviews, DVD, unnumbered, Island Records, Island 50, 1959–2009: Marketing)

And,

> It's different for each act but in a nut-shell work out what the band wears, who styles them, how you launch them [...] You've got to work out, make sure that's all being done right, it's all happening in the right places [...] You've got to completely over-see a full campaign and make sure that you're getting people motivated, that people want to work for you, but you make sure you're getting the best out of the artist [...] I think it's a good role, it's an extremely creative role and, um, it's very, very hands on [...] You've got to keep your eye on every other act, every other label, absolutely every form of marketing and you've gotta know exactly, you've got to keep an eye on absolutely everything ... it's quite an all-encompassing job and you do that for nine acts at a time.
>
> (Tom Marsh, Island, ibid)

'Fixity' is in evidence in these two examples in three main ways. Firstly, the two men work for a 'major' company, where the expression itself conveys authority through reference to the scale of the company which is currently the largest of the four remaining major record companies. Secondly, they both carry the title 'manager' and one of them refers to other 'director(s)' and 'heads' which has the effect of indicating the formal hierarchy of the company with its lines of power and authority. Thirdly, the certainty with which they speak conveys their company's sense of knowing its own business and its expertise. What is additionally significant about how they describe what they do is that the 'products' they manage are not aimed directly at the public – the market for music goods is only accessed indirectly through 'the right magazines', the 'relevant media'. This is the true challenge of the Music Industry as an industrial process because, to a greater or lesser extent, personnel from companies in each of the industries have to convince representatives of media companies that the acts they have signed will lend those companies exactly the degree of idiomatic currency they need to maintain their market share, and so maintain their advertising rates; or licence fee where the BBC is concerned.

What the DVD reveals, which a print account of it cannot, is that both Island product managers are very young men who are both casually dressed; that they speak casually is then evident from the quoted sections of their presentations. Simply in these terms, the combination of formality and informality indicates that they bring a certain fluidity to a fixed role. In turn, that such comparatively young and 'casual' people are entrusted with such roles then speaks to the constant 'churn' of scenes and their associated idioms. What is pivotal here is that those who represent the symbolic goods produced by record companies to the intermediary market represented by the media, both online and offline, do so in ways to which those intermediaries can recognise and respond. The message is that the commodities their efforts help to produce have the necessary currency to satisfy media audiences because they themselves are the living embodiment of the tastes of that audience.

The search for idiomatic currency in music performance is the driving force of the Music Industry. That industry's answer to the question of how to manage an over-supply when nobody knows which musicians will make market-successful symbolic goods is to constantly recruit or admit young people who demonstrate or at least seem to suggest that they have a sensibility for 'the right places' and for their protocols. These 'right places' are the hubs of communication that specific swathes of the population use to confirm their tastes and the lifestyles associated with those tastes. The work of product managers is to 'read' popular cultural patterns; to read forms of collective expression; to identify how these collectives reproduce themselves through affiliations to specific forms and sites of cultural expression, and then to configure a specific symbolic commodity to those values and codes and angle them towards those collectives as markets. Because they cannot do this alone, they need to constitute 'teams', 'a good team of PRs and press people' (Scott ibid.), where the reliance on, and management of, such teams completes the industrial process of music.

Conclusion

'Hybridity' is a combined strategy in two senses. It is a combination of 'fixity' and 'fluidity' with regard to the management of internal considerations of exerting industrial discipline over originators of texts who are not direct employees of a company (musicians and artist managers), but companies also need to control external interactions with media companies as far as this is possible. Outside of the three major music industries there is an industry of public relations (PR). For example, the *Music Week* directory[2] lists over 300 such firms in London, alone. Essentially, it is PR firms, alongside artist management, that stitch together the three industries into a single 'music industry' and also attach the music industry to media industries. PR firms and 'press' people are constantly active in the networks of 'taste makers' and power brokers of the 'old' and 'new' media industries; the offline TV and radio producers and magazine editors; the online bloggers and aggregators. The thrust of their constant activity is to work the story and look of a client as a platform to have the sound they make received as favourably as possible by the guardians of access to the users of a particular TV show, website or magazine. These 'gate-keepers' though are equally hungry for music and musicians who validate their claims to be the most appropriate source of information, interaction and so social reproduction for their specific users.

In the frantic search for constant currency, media 'gates' swing both ways. Consequently, the teams assembled by product managers must be teams of people who can not only guarantee access to media gate-keepers, but are ones who have the power to have those gates open to them, willingly. This 'power' derives from their being associated with hit acts and with 'happening' scenes which means that individuals can be as capricious as the idiomatic currency and the structures of feeling they seek to connect. In this way, teams of PR agents, press people and the networks they access and reproduce are enormously volatile, far more so than even (cultural) markets themselves. They are extremely volatile because they seek, almost minute-by-minute, to promote individual symbolic goods in line with, and in the face of, how they read the constantly shifting patterns of self-expression of target markets and the allegiances of individuals to particular cultural commodities at any one time and in any combination. In this way, the market fate of an individual symbolic good can be determined in a single encounter between a single PR agent and a single magazine editor. In this, the company hiring that PR agent (or employing them) can only hope that the product manager is ensuring that, as Tom Marsh expresses it, those people are 'motivated, that people want to work for you'. All of this then raises a series of questions about how such teams are managed; about the nature and quality of their management; about the relationship of musicians and their managers to the actions of these teams and their management and about the symbolic good itself. What is certain, though, is that musicians and their managers rarely get to ask these questions; as Chris Scott puts it:

> There is a regular forecast meeting and, um, in those meetings every act that's on the label is looked at and they decide between the finance director and the heads and directors of every department in the company decide (sic) at what stage an act is, how hard they need

to be pushed financially and what they reckon the results will be and the budget is set according to that.

(Scott, ibid)

Hybridity means that, on a case-by-case basis, a major record company switches resources between its signed acts. The act which receives the biggest 'push' is not guaranteed to succeed but, conversely, the market chances of an act which receives no 'push' at all will be slim indeed. Without such a push, live performance agencies are unlikely to seek the tours and the prestigious live appearances that they can offer and music publishers will be less inclined to seek the covers and 'synchs' that raise profile and earn extra income for an act's songwriters. Popular music is a world in which many are called, and one in which many 'call' themselves, but few are chosen because the choosers are, first, foremost and decisively, music companies whose aim is to profit from a specific set of 'value-adding' activities. Because these value-adding activities need to be made in the face of the fact that 'nobody knows' what symbolic goods will succeed in the market for them, companies attempt to maximise their control over their production and promotion in order to protect their own investment in them.

The assertion of managerial control in value-adding creates the industrial process in music, but this is such an imperfect science that inevitably texts fail to convert into symbolic goods and most symbolic goods fail on market entry. All of this means that most musicians, together with their managers, never reach the audiences they imagine they deserve to find. The decisive point is that this is an outcome that is not entirely traceable and solely to the music they make. It is an outcome of an industrial process that succeeds not just in the face of majority market failure, but because of it. Industry succeeds because over-supply allows music companies the leeway they require to find the hits that keep the music industries in business. To echo the observation made in Chapter 1, the 'mud' thrown against 'the wall' by music companies and by cultural industries, generally, consists of real, living human beings who have hopes, dreams, ambitions and a measure of ability to bring pleasure to music users. For the conversion of so many contenders into so few 'winners', the industrial process of music has to be robust enough to withstand its tendency to produce failure and sophisticated enough for it to go on producing profit in the face of that failure. The Music Industry has existed, and profited, thus far because the unceasing passage of time means that its 'solutions' to its own contradictions are permanently provisional: it goes on tumbling into the future, always finding texts able to resonate as symbolic goods, now for increasingly short periods of time. While music remains useful to its users; and while market entry implies value-adding, then musicians need not always be at the mercy of the value-adders, but only those who can check the excesses of the value-adders are likely to find sustainable audiences and the careers that come with them.

6
Music Contracts and Music Industry

The processes through which musicians pass before they sign their first recording contract can encompass a lifetime's effort. When writers write and players play they draw on every aspect of themselves that led to a particular point in their personal history. They do this because they elect to go in search of audiences and the acclaim they offer. There are no real blueprints for any of this activity; the autobiographies and biographies of musicians tend to treat industrial interactions as of marginal relevance and, in any case, audiences constitute themselves through ceaselessly changing signifying materials drawn into ever-shifting structures of feeling. Effectively every musician, at least at the outset of what are too loosely referred to as their 'careers', reinvents the wheel; the wheel, they hope, will roll them into public consciousness and through this to the acclaim of discerning audiences. But as every chapter has so far argued, this 'wheel-rolling' is, in fact, an industrial process: audiences can only be found through market practices and, consequently, how markets are entered, in the face of enormous competition and with an offer of enormously fragile symbolic goods, decides the fate of all musicians, established or otherwise. In turn, because it is an industrial process and because new musicians can be so unprepared for its industrial nature then the process tends to favour music companies as investors in the production of symbolic goods, rather than musicians. Considered in these terms, musicians mostly come and go and music companies usually survive, but so far in popular cultural history, what outlasts both is the industrial process of cultural production itself.

The previous chapter discussed the music-industrial process as an outcome of three strategies adopted more-or-less consciously by music companies. In this analysis, the term 'music companies' stood for the continuing centrality of record companies to that process. These strategies, identified as ones of 'Fixity', 'Fluidity' and 'Hybridity', devolve into the need for music companies to form joint endeavours and, through them, working alliances with musicians. The music-industrial predominance of the recording industry persists for the reasons argued in the previous chapter: the recording industry held unchallenged sway between roughly 1955 and 2005, but its influ-ence persists not just because the major record companies remain as formidable concentrations of capital, but because the perspectives on how symbolic goods should be prepared for market entry and how and for what reasons they should be supported in music markets can be argued to be diffused throughout the music industries generally.

The perspectives of the major record companies, together with the judgements and actions they inform, can themselves be traced to the rise of a music industry centred on Music Hall and can be tracked through subsequent reorderings of music's place in cultural production. These would include the development of a subsequent Entertainment Industry formed through close alliances of record companies, music publishers and live performance agencies around the new media of broadcasting, film and mass circulation periodicals. This was followed by a new incarnation of the Music Industry produced by the enormous strides taken by the recording industry during the 1950s and 1960s. What needs to be confronted is that these same perspectives and pre-cepts continue to be exercised in an epoch in which much of what defined cultural-industrial production, especially laws governing intel-lectual property, is now substantially unviable. What this means is that, while musicians continue to require investment towards market entry and market performance, the chance of a return on that investment is more uncertain than it has ever been. As this chapter seeks to demon-strate, in the immediate term these uncertainties are being dealt with not in the market, but in relations between investors and musicians in their pre-market phase. In this phase, the signing of contracts is central and pivotal.

Taken as a whole, when confronting an industrial sector which is characterised by standardising works of culture as symbolic goods, what needs to be accepted is that the key tension driving the specific form of that sector's industrial process is the way in which it deals with inordi-nately high levels of market risk. While this has been cited throughout this study so far, there has been little opportunity to explore the ten-sion between the entrepreneurial embrace of risk and the inbuilt need of investors to minimise risk. Intense risk is characteristic of cultural production generally, because 'nobody knows' what goods will sell on release into their relevant markets. Consequently, cultural production 'lives with' very high rates of new product failure. The thrust of the previous chapter was to extend this recognition and to argue that not only do cultural producers live with these high rates of new product failure; they can be argued to live through them.

Music companies live 'through' failure in the sense that they consciously spread risk as far as is possible because they know that, if this risk-spreading can be achieved, they will survive the caprices of the market. The spreading of risk makes strategic sense, but does not allow companies to escape dealing with musicians on a case-by-case basis and because they must, they require an elaborate, combinatory strategy to allow them to accomplish what are two incompatible ends; to maintain the loyalty of musicians so that they produce the texts that become symbolic goods, but to show no true reciprocal loyalty to those musicians. This is evidenced in their failure to guarantee those musicians either access to the market or support in the market. From a company perspective, this balancing act between embrace and non-support is a managerial challenge of the highest order and the work of the last chapter was to specify and explore the strategies that, together, accomplish this deeply contradictory practice. It is contradictory because it is both counter-productive, in the sense that companies can easily alienate the musicians they work with, and 'productive' in the sense that some musicians have 'hits', and hits keep the Music Industry in profit. The work of this chapter then is to explore the centrality of contracts to this process.

Contracts and contradictions

In the absence of legally enforceable agreements, joint work between musicians and music companies could not be undertaken. Yet, equally, because of the anomalies inherent in the contract form, those binding agreements are still loose enough to allow companies offering contracts to define their performance; at least in the sense that they fail to prosecute them in ways imagined, envisaged or expected by the parties with whom they contract. Greenfield and Osborn have probed this area of anomaly. They begin with the classical interpretations of contract law and they find it severely wanting. In its place they propose what they refer to (after Macneil) as,

> the idea of relational contracting, that places the context to the relationship ahead of narrow doctrinal rules.

> (2007, p. 1)

Greenfield and Osborn utilise Atiyah's summary of classical contract theory to suggest that 'commercial music contracts' (by which they mean recording contracts) diverge so substantially from classical theory that a new theory of contracts needs to be formulated; one that allows for the fact that:

> All contracts are borne out of some sort of social relation and are based around relational patterns...relational contracts are incremental and unable to be fully articulated at the beginning of the contractual relationship.
>
> (2007, p. 15)

As they put it:

> A record contract may appear, at least from its form that expresses longevity, to be broadly relational. The record company hopes that it will be a continuing relationship as this will be an indicator of commercial success. At the outset it should be seen as a relationship and not simply as a contractual transaction. The initial signing of the contract injects capital to finance the recording and distribution of the sound recording itself, and over that period the relationship between the parties should be a close and cooperative one. However the contract will contain a series of options exercisable solely at the behest of the company that permits termination. Effectively, we have an example of a relational contract with a get-out clause for the party with the superior bargaining power.
>
> (2007, p. 17)

Greenfield and Osborn liken this kind of contract to a 'rheostat' (2007, p. 16, an analogy is taken, by attribution, from Macneil), by which they mean that the joint relationship between the musician and the record company is not suddenly 'switched on' when the contract is signed, but varies in intensity from the moment of first contact between musicians and record company until it is terminated. There is some value in this analogy, at least in the way that it construes the relationship forming through a courtship of musicians by record companies, but the effect is to make the theory serve the analogy rather than vice versa. What Greenfield and Osborn explore is how asymmetrical relationships, relationships in which one contracting party has far more power than another, might still be encompassed by a theory of contracts. They are alert to several of the dimensions of the argument made in this study so far. Firstly, to the inequality of bargaining power between musicians and music companies and the 'take it or leave it' approach this has inculcated in the latter. Secondly, to the standardisation of contracts and how this expresses and enshrines this inequality. And thirdly, to the tendency of the desire of musicians for investment, when coupled with their inexperience, to override caution when signing such contracts. Even so, though they recognise 'mass failure' as the majority outcome of the relationships formed in and through the negotiation of contracts, what they do not acknowledge is the role the contract plays in the management of this failure.

As Greenfield and Osborn argue, there is a tension between the 'real and the paper deal' (Macaulay, 2003 in 2007, p. 6) and it is there because a paper deal is meant to obey classical principles of offer and acceptance made between parties who 'know their own minds' (Atiyah, 1995, pp. 402–3, in 2007, p. 8), while the reality of a deal is that it is an expression of a relationship which exists beyond, rather than within the contract and that develops over time. There is much to agree with in this recognition, but the problem is that while 'there is … far more to the recording contract than the paper expression', it does not necessarily follow that,

> the contract operates at a largely symbolic level. The paper contract is symbolic in the sense that it is an indicator of a relationship that operates beyond the boundaries of the formal legal one. The contract is unimportant when contrasted to the context of its formation and its subsequent relationship.
>
> (2007, p. 6)

Rather, Greenfield and Osborn should follow their own logic: if the relationship begins before the contract, then it has begun asymmetrically. Musicians are indeed desirous and inexperienced and, as they acknowledge, signing a contract does indeed act as a 'badge of honour' (2007, p. 5) for musicians. The objection to this is that the symbolic transformation does not entail a material one in the sense that musicians are no less desirous and inexperienced after signing. Consequently, the 'paper deal' becomes the condition of 'the real deal' (it is what allows the relationship to proceed), but this proceeding can only happen on the terms and conditions favoured by the contracting company. It cannot happen otherwise for all the reasons argued in the previous chapter: because companies are expressions of an industrial process that both precedes and exceeds them. This does not mean that the industrial process of music is unchanging or cannot be impacted and modified by the actions of a single company or the philosophy of new companies. For example, consider the '50/50' deal emblematic of the punk rock record companies of the 1970s and 1980s in these terms; or by the market changes that characterise the current era. Further, as the recording industry business model falters in the face of increasing transformations in digitisation, then new ways of enacting and ensuring relationships between musicians and companies beyond the recording industry are coming into play (see Chapter 8). But the point remains that this is a relationship, first and foremost, between capital and a form of labour.

On the above basis, what is instantiated when capital and labour come together is not so much a 'relationship' or simply a 'social relation' (as Greenfield and Osborn have it) but a set of production relations. In turn, these relations have to be managed because investment requires management. Whether this is managed efficiently from the perspective of capital is a separate issue and, interestingly, the one that triggered the emergence of the contractual theory (as a challenge to the classical theory of contracts) that they cite in their article's title. But what counts for this argument is that capital cannot be managed in ways that are simultaneously sympathetic to the interests of labour; this would be a contradiction in terms. Clearly, to conceive of musicians as sellers of labour flies in the face of notions of musicians as 'artists' and invokes the positions rehearsed in the introduction to Chapter 1, but this is a 'nettle' that demands to be grasped, and it can best be grasped by considering what contracts achieve and how they achieve it for the form of capital embodied as the music company.

Recording contracts – then and now

When Greenfield and Osborn observe that 'relational contracts are incremental and unable to be fully articulated at the beginning of the contractual relationship' (2007, p. 15), what they miss is what is able to be fully articulated at the beginning of the contractual relationship and arguably this is not only substantial, but definitive. Throughout this study the terms 'joint endeavour', 'alliance' and 'working alliance' have been used to describe what is formed when musicians come to work with music companies. In the previous chapter, the root of the joint endeavour or working alliance was specified as musicians' collective recognition (but always on a case-by-case basis) that they cannot enter markets and survive within them without assistance. In the history of music-industrial production, this 'assistance' has so far come in the form of the 'value-adding' activities of various types of music company. In all cases, the music company not only expects but needs to make a profit from the services it offers, thus ensuring that it looks to its own interests before those of any musician or group of musicians, regardless of the relationships they form with those musicians.

Relationships can be argued to characterise all areas of business and all types of industry for the simple, but also highly charged reason that a market economy is characterised by competition, and that the pursuit of competitive advantage will involve companies seeking reliable, even favoured, relationships with companies they engage with across all of their activities; from the gathering of raw materials to the retailing of their goods or services. Relationships in popular music can be particularly intense because the product is pleasure and because that pleasure can often be first encountered by an individual 'value adder', such as an actual or potential manager or a 'scout' from a record company, in the obscurity from which all musicians emerge. In this way, the conditions of first encounter can very often encourage a distracting and distorting intimacy between company representatives and the musicians in question. In turn, the restriction of such encounters to only pleasure and intimacy, and with these positive feelings their insulation from any consideration of industry, is the root of the sentimental myth-making that is so potent in 'reality' music television shows, but also present in the passionate narratives of various types of 'independent' music. Yet, whatever the pleasure-driven intensity of relations formed by artist managers, record company A&R personnel, music publishers, promoters and live agents with particular musicians, the primary directive of 'value adders' is to achieve market success and so generate profit. Consequently, despite their apparent interchangeability, there needs to be a distinction drawn between a 'joint endeavour' between musicians and music companies and a 'working alliance'.

A 'joint endeavour' can be better understood as an initial intention to enter a market, where this intention is expressed in and through increasingly focused interactions between musicians and specific individuals representing music companies. In contrast, a 'working alliance' is the actual, day-to-day, enactment of that intention. This 'enactment' is 'music industry' in the sense outlined in Chapter 1: the actual 'activity' of the production of symbolic goods as a managed process. It is then reasonable to argue that 'industry', in the wider sense, is not reinvented on a case-by-case basis; that, in fact, it derives from existing practices and forms of justification for those practices. This does not of course preclude modification and innovation within, and to, either those practices or their associated justifications. As the enactment of the intention can only proceed on the basis of legally binding agreements between musicians and a 'value-adding' music company, it is also reasonable to imagine that much of any individual company's conception of how the working alliance should proceed will underpin and drive the form of agreement it will be willing to make in order to pursue a working alliance with specific musicians. Furthermore, as companies are in the habit of not so much 'drawing up' agreements, but of offering them, what musicians then face when entering into joint endeavours with music companies is a standard form of contract which, by its very nature, exerts a standardising force on the working alliance generated between them and the company.

This is not to say that 'standard' contracts are the sole standardising force in music industry or the sole resource to ensure that music companies enjoy the control in the production process that their capital investment insists that they must. Rather, as the previous chapter argued, music companies use a combination of strategies to subordinate musicians to routines that generate profit. What will be argued here is that standard contracts are the adhesive that not only brings the fixing force to the strategy of 'fixity', but which bonds the various strategies together. In this way, contracts do not have an irresistible logic in and of themselves, but their place in the mix of strategies helps to make that mix the intractable force that is the industrial process of music. To illustrate how they can be argued to act as this adhesive force, and to remain with the recording industry as the principal music industry, two contracts will be compared. These contracts derive from 1997 and 2011 respectively, and so from before and after the onset of the impact of digitisation on the recording industry. They are contracts from the same major record company and so invite comparison far more substantially than would two contracts from different companies. There are clear and substantial differences between them, but also they exhibit clear and substantial consistencies. Identifying and understanding both, and how both are connected, then indicates the extent to which contracts are far from 'symbolic' and far from being 'unimportant' in regard to 'a relationship ... beyond (their) boundaries' (Greenfield and Osborn, 2007, p. 6).

Organisation and layout

The contracts will be referred to from this point onwards as '97' and '11', respectively. Both contracts consist of the same five elements: firstly, a 'disclaimer'; secondly, an identification of the parties to the agreement and a space for their signatures; thirdly, a set of definitions of terms used in the body of the contract; fourthly, a set of agreed terms (organised as separate clauses); fifthly, a set of 'schedules' which are identified differently between the two documents. The layout and organisation of these elements is substantially different; in 97, following the identification of the contracting parties, the document begins with a series of definitions of which there are 17 in total. In 11, the definitions are placed after the agreed terms, with 60 terms defined. In contrast to 97 they are arranged alphabetically, but what is interesting is that, while what is defined has increased substantially, this increase is not directly attributable to a need to specify new contingencies associated with digitisation. For example, only 21 per cent of the expanded definitions of 11 are derived in this way; to include, among others, 'database', 'limited download' and 'mobile applications'. Instead, it appears that 97 is deficient in regard to what needed to be defined, in the sense that possibly contentious terms are either addressed within relevant clauses or are ignored. Presumably, then, trial and error has led to a natural process of refinement of the organisation and layout of the contract, but what needs to be noted are four points: firstly, what definitions appear to insist on themselves across the two contracts; secondly, what modifications and omissions there are between 97 and 11; thirdly, what significantly new terms appear; finally, what important terms continue to go undefined. To discuss each of these dimensions in turn:

1. As these are recording contracts then, substantially, what they are concerned with is the following: establishing what a recording is from the perspective of the recording company; when it should be delivered to them; how much it will be sold for; where; by whom; and with what financial rewards for both parties. Consequently key terms defined include 'performance', 'album', 'masters', 'recording', 'dealer price' or 'published price to dealer' (PPD), along with the 'term' and 'territory' during which and in which the agreement applies where 'territory' is expanded from 'the world, including extraterrestrial satellites' to 'the world and the solar system'. To risk a cliché, the devil is in the detail and this detail will be returned to below.

2. The modifications made to key definitions are substantial and significant – in 97 an 'album' is defined as 'not less than forty-five (45) minutes playing time and comprising a minimum of eight (8) separate masters' (97, 1). In 11 an album has become 'Masters sufficient and suitable to comprise a Record of not less than 45 minutes

playing time when played at the correct speed and not less than twelve tracks' (11, 44). So, by 11 a musician is expected to provide four more compositions than in 97. This is a noteworthy increase in the 'minimum commitment' which is a term defined in 11 but open to negotiation in 97. Further, the definition of a single is substantially transformed – in 97 it was defined principally by dealer price, 'fifty per cent (50%) or less of the dealer price of a full price Compact Disc Album' (97, 1) (although there is a reference to 'a single record' under 'Masters'). As of 11, a single has become defined as 'a Record containing not more than 4 tracks' (11, 58) where a 'track' is defined as 'a Recording which reproduces 1 Title whose playing time is not less than 2½ minutes when played at its correct speed' (11, 59); in 97 it was three minutes. In this way, the musician is also expected to provide more material for essentially the same remuneration. Instructively, a key omission would seem to be the definition of a 'live album', indicating a shift away from rock music and towards forms of music (pop, R&B, hip-hop) in which 'live' performance has no distinctive cachet.

3. The key post-digitisation term to be defined in 11 is 'EMD'. Actually, this is misleading, as 'EMD' (Electronic Music Distribution) is not defined. Instead, the abbreviation is used and EMD is defined in an open-ended way as 'dissemination … of recordings … excluding the manufacture, distribution and sale of records' (11, 47). Clearly, though, EMD articulates all of the other digitally derived definitions and indicates the new environment record companies are forced to operate within, where their response is then captured in changes to the 'agreed terms', as will be discussed subsequently. The second major innovation is the extensive, and arguably onerous, definition of 'delivery materials'. In 97 'delivery' was, simply, 'the date of tape to disc transfer of the relevant record' (97, 2). By 11, materials to be delivered are grouped into nine categories making this the second longest entry in the section. To an extent, each category could be taken to indicate the increased autonomy of the musician: they are now (apparently) in charge of not just delivering 'the original masters and multi track tapes and all computer software applicable thereto', but 'a radio mix and one other mix of each track', 'an acoustic version (and if possible and practical a "live" version) of a minimum of four tracks (to be released as the A-side or lead track of singles)' (11, 46). Even so, this is a 'compromised' autonomy for not only does the company spell out its expectations with regard to recording in the 'agreed terms', but allows itself generous leeway with regard to

its commitment to release such recordings. More, as the next point discusses, there is nothing in the 'Definitions' section which identifies how the company defines its own obligations with regard to the marketing and promotion of potential releases.

4. What is striking about both sets of definitions is the omission of key terms and, indeed, key regions of the agreement between musicians and record company. To an extent this is because, historically, a recording contract was exactly that, an agreement that a record company would pay for a recording to be made by musicians, and no more. Considered in this very restricted sense the actual processes of taking any subsequent recording to market did not form part of the agreement. In this omission, alone, something of the scale of the power of the record company inside the industrial process is indicated. If the company is not obliged by the agreement to market and promote any recording, then the joint venture is not an exercise in market entry. Instead it is an exercise in which a record company gains the rights to recordings that it may, at its discretion, promote and market. One of the main variations between 97 and 11 is what 11 refers to as the company's 'release obligations', but even these were absent from recording contracts for many decades. On these bases, it is difficult to identify what is 'joint' about the 'joint venture'; and 'allied' about the 'alliance'. Further, the term 'recoupment' is used in both contracts, but is defined in neither which means only that (rather than how) the record company will recover its costs from the sales of recordings is brought to the attention of the musician. In turn, this has the effect of masking how fundamentally small a proportion of total costs the record company actually bears should a record become a hit. This masking is, then, compounded in 11 by the introduction of what are now commonly referred to as '360°' elements to the contract, discussed below but meaning that the record company now expects to earn income from streams beyond the sale of recordings. Further still, the practice of 'cross-collateralisation' is not mentioned, but the certainty is that the record company will meet unrecouped advances and budgetary shortfalls deriving from one album out of income accrued by another, should that other album be successful. Again, there is a lack of transparency even as 'transparency' is apparently being practised in the form of a compendium of definitions.

Taken as a whole, while the section of definitions referred to as a 'schedule' in 11 but not 97 is not the 'meat' of the contract, they should not be ignored. For example, both contracts seem to bear out much of Theodor Adorno's condemnation of popular music – that it is standardised and pre-digested – albums must be not less than 45 minutes long and consist of a minimum of 12 tracks where each track must not be shorter than 2½ minutes and, by this equation, not longer than three minutes and seven seconds. What 'art' there is in popular music would seem to be confined to constructing a text idiomatically, so that its sonic dimensions impact in three minutes or less in the face of all those other texts that are attempting exactly the same outcome. In 97 the musician would find themselves very tightly restricted to what recording costs the record company would be willing to meet. In 11 this is less the case where both restriction and comparative lack of restriction speak to the ways in which record companies need to respond to changing tides in technology and in the expectations of musicians. For example, by 97 the recording industry was no longer indulging exorbitant studio bills for albums that might take sometimes years to make in studios situated in exotic locations; by 11 record companies recognise that musicians are recording much of their work on home systems. Again though, the degree of 'creative autonomy' associated with the latter is compromised partly by the 'delivery' requirement, partly by the definitions of 'album' and 'track' and mostly by the unspoken sway the company will have over market entry itself. When we factor in identification of the periods to which new recording is confined (in 11, no new period can commence until five months after the date of the company's eventual release of the previous album); the restriction on re-recording songs should the contract be terminated (five years in 97, three years in 11); claims to control releases on formats and devices 'now known or devised in the future'; together with the grant of rights for 'the world and the solar system', any autonomy allowed under the recording contract in question is a crowded and confined one indeed.

Agreed terms

To define a term is not to apply it; the application of the defined terms is, ostensibly, an outcome of negotiation, but what is so striking about both documents is how little about them seems open to negotiation. This is the true force of the 'standard contract' – it is the gateway to 'the world and the solar system' for mainly young, hugely aspirant musicians. Such musicians have no incentive to contest the gateway: they simply want to pass through it as quickly as possible. Greenfield and Osborn make the point that, in his decision on a landmark UK music industry dispute between Schroeder and Macaulay in 1974, Lord Diplock argued that there were two types of standard contract: those 'of very ancient origin' (where incessant negotiation in early history eventually produced an agreed form) and those that lack the 'presumption of fairness' –

> If you want these goods or services at all, these are the only terms on which they are available. Take it or leave it.
> > (*Schroeder* (1974) All ER 616 at 624 in Greenfield and Osborn, 2007, p. 7)

The lack of fairness Diplock attributed to 'the result of the concentration of particular kinds of business in relatively few hands' (Diplock, ibid.) and he traces the rise of such businesses, and their attendant contracts, to the social and commercial changes of the 19th century. Certainly, both 97 and 11 show how recording contracts are flexibly 'standard' in the sense of being able to 'move with the times' and to insist on the retention of advantages. Considered in this way, and to use Greenfield and Osborn's expression, the various historical challenges to music contracts have, in part, driven their redrafting as, increasingly, 'judge-proof' (2007, p. 15). For example, 97 specifies that 'the entire term of this agreement may not exceed ten (10) years duration' (97, 23) which it is reasonable to imagine is an adjustment made following George Michael's challenge to his Sony contract in 1991. Similarly, both contracts are headed by an identical disclaimer, almost as one that hangs over the forbidding gateways of history and literature, which itself is likely to have been instituted following successful challenges to contracts in the late 1980s and early 1990s:

THIS DOCUMENT CONTAINS AN IMPORTANT AGREEMENT WHICH IS LIKELY TO AFFECT YOU IN YOUR CAREER ON A LONG TERM BASIS. BEFORE SIGNING YOU SHOULD BE SURE THAT YOU UNDERSTAND ITS CONTENTS AND THAT YOU WISH TO BE BOUND BY IT. YOU SHOULD TAKE INDEPENDENT LEGAL ADVICE FROM AN EXPERT IN RECORDING AGREEMENTS BEFORE COMMITTING YOURSELF. YOU CONFIRM THAT YOU ARE OVER EIGHTEEN YEARS OF AGE (capitalised and emboldened in the original).

In these ways, whatever the vicissitudes of individual court cases, major record companies remain that 'concentration' of a 'particular . . . business in very few hands' and, while this continues it continues to reinforce a mind-set which that expresses itself throughout 97; one that drives individual clauses to read more as declaratory statements rather than terms open to negotiation and where each appears designed to contribute to a concerted effort to maximise control and minimise risk in every dimension of their joint working with musicians. For example, in section two, 'Recording/Release', clause (a) reads: 'Artists will perform record and deliver... newly recorded performances... acceptable to company' (2(a), 5). Under section three 'Grant of Rights', 'the artists... grant and assign to company':

> the sole exclusive and perpetual rights throughout the Territory in respect of the Masters to manufacture Records therefrom and to sell release and otherwise deal with the same *or to refrain therefrom as company shall think fit*.
>
> [emphasis added] (3 a, 8)

Further, under section six 'Royalties', while the actual royalty rates and the advances to the musicians in question made against them are indeed subject to negotiation, what clearly aren't are the fact and scale of deductions. For example, deductions for packaging are up to 25 per cent for 'Compact Discs in deluxe packaging' (6. (iv), C, 14); records sold in the form of 'a "New Technology", 25 per cent deduction (6. (b), 14); and records sold through 'mail order' 50 per cent reduction (6. (d)(ii), 15). 1997 was around the time that record companies briefly flirted with releases of pre-recorded minidiscs. If an act signed under the terms of this agreement released on this format, in deluxe packaging, and discs were sold by mail order, then by these formulae, their artist royalty income would be zero; the company's income would, of course, be unaffected.

If statements determining the company's power over recordings and their power to determine what musicians will earn are clear and incontestable, their obligations to the musicians are made of less stern stuff: for example, again under Recording/Release:

> After delivery... Company shall use its best commercial endeavours to release and exploit Records (2(c), 6)

But what are 'best commercial endeavours' and how is a musician to know whether the company is expending those endeavours? What does 'exploit' involve and will the exploiting actions be appropriate to the musician or crudely subservient to profit? Musicians have no reliable mechanism (save the problematic efforts of their managers) to monitor or to audit the actions of companies. This was an essential part of George Michael's case against Sony and one that the judge in the case, Justice Parker, dismissed on the basis that he found it unthinkable that a company would fail to exercise such endeavours. Yet because 'nobody knows' what symbolic goods will succeed and consequently, record companies switch resources constantly between their signed acts. There is an absence of accountability in, and transparency to, company actions because contracts between musicians and music companies evolved this way.

When the first Music Hall entrepreneur took the first contract to the first Music Hall act, the former knew what they wanted and expected from the 'deal'; the latter simply knew that they were to be paid, perhaps regularly and perhaps reliably, to sing. Singers wish to sing and to be acclaimed for their talent and it is likely they would enjoy being paid for giving performances; music entrepreneurs take the risk that a singer might be 'better than' others. For taking this risk, the entrepreneur expects to be rewarded, but the longer the entrepreneur is in the business of taking singers into markets, the more they find ways to minimise risk and maximise return. So it is that this experience becomes codified in the form of the agreements that the entrepreneur, now formally constituted as a company, offers to an unending supply of new singers. No more stark confirmation of the accumulated power of a record company is there than the clause, in 97, covering 'Breach and Suspension' which refers to:

> any wilful default or substantial breach by Artists in the performance of any of Artist's material obligations hereunder (12(a), 22)

The first objection might be that there is no such clause which addresses a similar breach on the company's part. The principal expression of power, though, comes in the assertion that

> breach by Artists of any provision of this agreement will cause Company great and irreparable injury and damage Accordingly Artists hereby expressly agree that Company shall be entitled to injunction ... to prevent a breach of this Agreement by Artists (12(b), 23)

It would easily be possible to fill a book with chapter after chapter of case studies of acts who feel aggrieved that their 'careers' were cut short by breaches made by the company, if not to the letter of the agreement, then always to its spirit. One of the key problems to be faced when writing about popular music is that its history tends to be one of popular musicians, those who enjoyed market success. The entire thrust of this particular work is to explore the central theme that market success is an outcome of industry and not music alone. Consequently, when market success fails to manifest, as it does in the vast majority of cases, then this lack of success must be traceable to failings in the industrial process rather than to the abilities of musicians as musicians, *per se*. If contracts are one of the principal implements for managing failure then they can be seen to contribute to this management in and through a robust assertion of the rights of the company and the absence of such an assertion on the part of the musician. This assertion of rights reaches its apogee in the company's claim that it will be caused 'irreparable injury' if musicians are in breach of the agreement when in fact, no major company has ever experienced 'irreparable' injury at the hands of a musician; or else where is the evidence of such a failure? Sadly, the reverse of this is true many, many times over. Certainly, badly behaved musicians can fail to deliver records on time or can deliver recordings of poor quality, but the core strategies of major record companies is to allow for this as only one of the many risks they face where what counts is that they do so with so brutal a mechanism, that even records delivered on time and to a very high standard enjoy no guaranteed chance of being released or supported by the 'best endeavours' of the company.

Agreed terms and the crisis of the recording industry

Turning to the consideration of 11, there are both striking consistencies and striking changes to the agreed terms specified in the contract. Further to those already discussed, changes to the layout and organisation of the contract are manifest in the sequencing of the agreed terms. While the overall number of terms is comparable (25 in 97; 27 in 11) no agreed term appears in the same place between the contracts; 11 contains five entirely new terms and is 24 pages longer. While the extra length of 11 is partially attributable to the narrowing of margins in the 'Definitions' section, the additional length is substantially the result of the introduction of new terms and the greatly increased length of sections that were comparatively concise in 97; notably but not solely those dealing with 'Royalties', 'Provisions Applicable Where The Artist Is A Group', and (at first sight, surprisingly) 'Representations, Warranties And Undertakings By The Artist'.

The re-sequencing of the 'Agreed Terms' could be attributed to an 'in-house' redesign of the company's standard contract, but it is difficult to resist the sense that it also derives from changes in company priorities. If we return to Diplock's distinction between contracts of 'ancient' origin and those of more recent origin, then it is worth observing that, for example, contracts to buy and sell staple food goods (a wagon of wheat, for example) have their roots in the replacement of hunting and gathering by agriculture in the remote past, whereas the rise of cultural industries is, historically, a comparatively recent phenomenon. Given cultural production's implication with technology, and the impact on it of technological change, cultural contracts can never 'settle down', never take on the familiarities of contracts to buy and sell wheat. Under these circumstances, the only 'settled' elements are those that reinforce their 'take it or leave it' nature – no company can know the future, but what it does know is its defining need to secure and to further its own interests. So it is with 11. Some of the differences between 11 and 97 are astonishing – notably in regard to the introduction of a clause headed 'Provision Of Services' and in the tone rather than the extent of the 'Grant Of Rights'. Added to these are further types of change that it is important not to confuse or to make inter-changeable with each other, in the sense that there are new terms and formulae that appear out of an inevitable need to respond to the impact of digitisation on the making, the use and the nature of symbolic goods in music. Instructively, there are others which do not simply reflect the new technologically changed environment, but attempt to ensure that profit can still be made under its conditions, the 360° dimensions. To take these consistencies and changes in turn:

1. In 97 the 'Grant of Rights' is the second of the 'agreed terms'; in 11 it is, or can only seem, 'relegated' to thirteenth. While the relocation of this term should not be over-dramatised (just for itself), the location of a new term, 'Provision of Services' to first position draws attention to itself. The reason this term is 'astonishing' is because what it asserts is that:

    > In consideration of the payments made by the Company to and on behalf of the Artist, the Artist agrees … to perform as a recording artist exclusively for the Company during the Term, and to perform *the other services* [emphasis added] provided for in this agreement (1, 1)

On this basis and in these terms, the 'Company' is repositioned from a service provider (a 'market entry specialist') to, effectively, the employer of a specialised form of contractor. In turn, the musician is relocated from a partner willing to give up part of their income for services rendered to hired service-provider (perhaps a musical labourer?). In this way, the 'social relation' (Greenfield and Osborn (2007, p. 15) so formed is all too clearly a social relation of production. The 'Grant of Rights by the Artist', supplemented by a new term, 'Further Grant of Rights by the Artist', then reads as assertively as in 97; with the additional provisions that:

> The Company is entitled to call for delivery of *all* [emphasis added] Recordings embodying performance by the Artist made during the term whether or not those Recordings constitute Masters (12.1, 17/18) (and) The Artist unconditionally and irrevocably waives... any and all moral and like rights that the Artist has in Recordings (12.3, 18)

In both of these instances, the power of the company as a form of employer seems total: what these terms and their clauses all but 'say' is, 'we will give you money, and you will give us everything you have, exclusively, with no recourse to forms of protection that exist for the type of effort you make'. In an age of their instability, record companies here appear to be construing a stability through terms expressed more obviously one-sidedly than before the digital upheaval.

2. The observations made above are borne out in terms that are standard and yet significantly modified in 11, or else are entirely new additions to existing standard terms. For example, the 'Recording Commitment' modifies 97's 'Artists will... deliver... newly recorded performances of Artists *acceptable* [emphasis added] to Company' (2(a), 5) to 'During each Period of the Term the Artist must record and Deliver (3.1, 2) (performances that) are artistically, technically and *commercially satisfactory* [emphasis added] to the Company'. (3.2.8, 3). In addition, the 'Recording Commitment' includes the stipulation that 'the Company, may, if it chooses, designate 3 Titles to be recorded for each Album' (4.1, 3). In this way, and in addition to the entirely new dimensions discussed below, the company appears to want to not only register its power to arbitrate the activities of its signed musicians, it wants to reach into the sphere normally given to them (their 'creative autonomy') to ensure that their presence is registered and their bidding is done.

3. Where the 'new dimensions' are concerned, these are of enormous, defining significance and require contextualisation before these innovations and their implications can be fully appreciated.

The 360° record contract

The '360°' concept was introduced by Sanctuary Music Group (although perhaps Motown might be understood in these terms). Beginning as the management company for Iron Maiden, Andy Taylor and Rod Smallwood experimented with the melding of diverse music business interests from the early 1980s onwards. With the rise of 'grunge' music in the early 1990s and the consequent passing of the dominance of heavy metal acts inside rock music, Taylor and Smallwood created Sanctuary as a company that acquired broad swathes of intellectual property rights in publishing, recording and merchandising. Given their experience with Iron Maiden, Taylor and Smallwood understood that acts could retain large fan-bases even after being dropped from their contracts by record companies. Beginning with heavy metal acts and then expanding to encompass acts from other genres, Sanctuary's formula was to organise, in some instances, every aspect of the continuing careers of 'big names' that had lost their major deals. Despite the obvious conflict of interest that can occur when a company is both management and record company (as well as, in some instances, publisher, live agent and merchandiser), Sanctuary appeared to work so well for names such as the Pet Shop Boys and Dolly Parton that, by the early 2000s, the company was able to rapidly expand, though ultimately disastrously. In this way, while Sanctuary itself was a failure, its business model became hugely influential.

At the same time as Sanctuary began to expand, EMI completed an agreement with Robbie Williams. Williams, a former member of the successful boy-band Take That, was considered by EMI to have the potential to become a worldwide solo star. Because both he and the company wanted and anticipated success in the USA, they reached what was then a unique deal. This was one considered, as it briefly transpired, to be a 'one-off', by the record company and the Music Industry more generally. It was an exceptional contract, allowed only by the already high degree of success Williams enjoyed. The thrust of the agreement was that, because supporting an act in and through entry into the US market involves heavy investment, the company should participate in the revenues generated not just by the sale of Williams' records, but from income streams until then separate, even inviolate, from the sale of recordings; among them live concerts, merchandising and sponsorship. As it transpired, Williams was 'globally' successful for several years, but made no impression in the USA. Oddly, while both Sanctuary and EMI failed in their ultimate objectives, these different models created an irresistible chemistry as record sales and revenues continued their precipitous decline.

The 360° deal went from exception to rule very quickly with, perhaps, the emergence of Live Nation as, if not the catalyst for the transformation, then certainly both its accelerant and its legitimation. Live Nation began as a subsidiary of US company Clear Channel Communications. Clear Channel originated from a single radio station in 1972. It added billboard advertising to radio station ownership and rapidly expanded following the deregulation of media, a facet of the ideological project of Neoliberalism pursued by right-wing governments in the USA and UK from the early 1980s onwards. The company continued to expand horizontally and vertically, acquiring the live promotion and venue-owning company, SFX in 2000. The object here was to create synergies between radio advertising and concert promotion. As it transpired, because further opportunities in live promotion presented themselves, notably in merchandising and then ticketing, it proved prudent for Clear Channel to 'spin off' these new activities as a separate company, Live Nation, in 2005. The new company then 'ran with the ball' and announced that they were pursuing 360° deals with some of the biggest acts in popular music, among them Madonna, Jay-Z and U2. These deals are not identical (for example U2 continue to make records with Universal Music Group), but they have proved hugely influential, to the extent that such deals are now commonplace throughout the Music Industry. It is against this complex background that the innovative clauses in 11 need to be read.

Agreed terms and the crisis of the recording industry (continued)

To return to the contract, as previous remarks indicated, it is important to distinguish in 11 between material that has needed to be included to respond to the rise of digitised forms of music delivery, and that which reflects the record company's profoundly altered perception of what it is due, and why, from the records it invests in.

1. Where the direct effects of a profound movement away from physical sound carriers is concerned, then considerable changes over 97

are evident. Digitisation's impact is registered especially in terms of the ubiquity of moving image materials. Moving image, and music's centrality to it, is everywhere in evidence, from multi-channel satellite television and its dedicated music channels to the ease of access of video material through websites and applications such as YouTube and through increasing availability of smart phones and tablet computers, whose selling point is their ease of use for watching films and music videos and for gaming. Specific applications are not named but, clearly record companies want, expect and have a right to earn if copyrights they own are being used, by other companies, to generate revenue. In turn, they must pass some of their share of the revenue to the musicians with whom they have contracted. Specifying types and usages of recorded materials and share of revenue generated from them greatly extends 11 over 97, making the document far longer and more demanding to read.

2. The impact of digitisation is already registered in 97. Even though Napster in 1999 can be considered to be the key digital music watershed, the Internet Underground Music Archive had emerged as early as 1993 and had pioneered music file sharing through MPEG compression. By 97, the record company already had its own website and expected 'Artists' to have 'registered an internet domain name within one (1) month of signature' (20, 33). 11, then, reflects how far digitisation has come since the days of 14 and 28K modems. The contract is longer and more detailed because the company, among other objectives, needs to establish who has 'the right to compile databases' (13.1.4, 18); must control 'performances...by way of...webcast and/or simulcast' (15.2.2, 22); and needs to be sure that 'Controlled Compositions...will be available...for use in connection with Records EMD and Mobile Applications' (22.1.1, 31).

3. That comparatively 'technical' inclusions with regard to digitisation are, and by a great distance, not the only distinguishing innovations in 11. The first appears within the section 'Further Grant Of Rights By Artist' and concerns 'the right...to incorporate into the Artist Website and administer a virtual shopping mall' (13.1.5.2, 19) involving a 'link to (or from) a Website undertaking sales of merchandise or concert tickets' where 'the company shall be entitled to make a commission...on the sale...("Link Commission")'. (13.1.5.2.1, 19). This is the first indication that the company believes itself entitled to participate in the live merchandising and performance revenues of its signed musicians, where both sets of expectations are then

articulated and codified under subsequent terms: 21/23 and 24/25 respectively.

4. Where earnings from artist merchandise are concerned, the core point is that the company seeks the right to create what it refers to as 'three (3) separate original designs' ('the Exclusive Designs') from which it intends to 'manufacture, distribute, promote, advertise and sell Products incorporating or utilising the Exclusive Designs' (21.3.1, 28). These 'products' are then the expected gamut of goods ranging from 'T-shirts' to 'calendars'. In return for granting these rights, 'The Company shall account to the Artist for an amount equal to fifty per cent (50%) of its Merchandising Net Receipts'. In this way, not only does the record company gain half of an act's merchandising income, it controls that merchandising: the power of this 360° element is not so much in the former, but in the latter.

5. Where live performance is concerned, the impact of the 360° is equally profound. Here, the company makes the provision that 'In consideration of the Company's payment of Tour Support...the Artist hereby agrees to pay Company 20% of Tour Revenue' (24.4, 37) – where this means all revenues (merchandising, sponsorship, advertising and endorsement as well as ticket sales). Yet earning from live appearances (something unimaginable in 97) is not the full extent of this particular 360° element. Rather it is the further stipulation (25) that 'the Artist shall render services and performances...for at least ten (10) live concerts...which shall be co-produced by Artist and Company (for which) profit shall be distributed as to 50% to the Company and 50% to the Artist' (25.1, 39). This is the true extent of the changed relation between a record company and an act. Nothing demonstrates the crisis in the recording industry more than a contract clause that secures revenue from sources other than the sales of recordings in this pro-active way. By commissioning web commerce and merchandise, the record company's revenue sources are extended beyond the sale of recordings, but this particular insistence takes the record company effectively beyond the recording industry and begins to usher in a new type of music company, and with it, a new inflection of the industrial process.

Taken together, the 360° elements of 11 are not, in strict terms, completely 360° – there is no claim made against the act's publishing income. Even so, 11 is a markedly different document from 97, because record companies are now in a markedly different position from that of 1997. Because they are, then recording contracts are constructed differently for 'different' times but they continue to devolve upon, and revolve around, the same core position, which is that they ensure that the record company is able to protect itself as effectively as it possibly can from the punishing uncertainties of the market.

Conclusion

The great changes in the standard recording contract can be interpreted as an attempt to deal with 'downstream' problems, notably the seeming constant volatility of music markets, far earlier in the pre-market entry phase than hitherto. When record companies were prosperous they were able to be cavalier in the production process. As previous remarks have indicated, they always signed more acts than they could process, but this was primarily for strategic reasons; the compensation (or perhaps consolation) for a proportion of those acts was that they might be retained by the company even while not selling albums. Further, major record companies could also indulge those acts by paying exorbitant recording costs incurred both by lengthy spells of recording and by permitting recording to take place in exotic locations. Those days are long gone; now, even before that process begins, contracts are being offered that spell out in no uncertain terms that production will not begin unless the act is willing to concede an even larger degree of control to the company than previously, and for a far larger price than formerly.

Record companies are fighting a desperate rearguard action, because very few people now want a physical 'product', but they continue to want 'tracks'. Shorn of the protections of intellectual property, except where business-to-business transactions are concerned, the record companies have decided collectively that what they 'produce' is, in fact, not recordings but a 'brand' and, therefore, they deserve to earn from all the ways in which the brand generates revenue. This substantially spurious notion will be returned to in Chapter 8 (and it is notable that 'Brand Rights' forms a further 360° dimension of 11), but the point remains that record company advances are what keeps acts alive; what makes the difference between the 'signed' and the 'unsigned' act. Furthermore, it was the investment made by record companies that mobilised and focused the actions of companies across the music industries in the sense that promotional and marketing campaigns provide work for live agencies and promoters; for publishers; for promotions companies; and even for managers. In this way, the music industries continue to need the recording companies because, thus far, there is no replacement for them, but the problem for musicians is that the record companies appear to be surviving increasingly at their expense.

Record companies can attempt to survive at the expense of musicians because, essentially, they always did. Record contracts have always been constructed in such a way that companies not only recouped advances to make recordings, but also clawed back the money they spent to promote and market them; by far the 'lion's share' of profit on the sale of recordings are accrued to the record company. The way in which those companies hedged against market risk was, effectively, to take controlled risks with the acts they signed; 'controlled' because the act and not the company bore the ultimate brunt of market failure. Considered in this way, the 'asymmetry' of the initial relationship was always operable and could only be corrected in the act's favour if and when the act became a substantial force in its own right. For these reasons, the contract was always far more real than symbolic. This is not to deny that relationships were, and are, important in music industry, but the cruel truth is that, as Chapter 3 discussed, in the intimacy of first encounters, the expectations of musicians are the outcomes of the incoherencies of their formation as musicians. Consequently, they, rather than companies, are the party most invested in the relationship and, therefore, the one least alert to the constraints and strictures of the 'paper deal'. Musicians are invested in the 'spirit' of the deal because, in part, their expectations are driven by degrees of inexperience and, because they are, then musicians can easily construct a fantasy of the relationship with the record company, rather than consistently evaluate its actual condition and adjust accordingly.

The anomaly inside music contracts is not that they are 'relational', but that they are constructed to a standardised and standardising formula that, so far, has allowed record companies advantages over those with whom they make such contracts. As the operating conditions of those companies worsen, so their agreements continue to function as a hedge against the contraction of the market for recordings, at least in their physical form. What none of this should obviate is the vital necessity that both parties should be able to trust the agreement. The fact that musicians mostly suffer them is not testimony to some fundamental untrustworthiness of record companies and music companies more generally. Rather it is testimony to the fact that, constructed as they are as music users, in and through the consumption of symbolic goods, musicians do not know their own minds in industrial terms, to the extent that music companies understand their own business needs. If, as it appears from transformations in their contracts, digitisation is driving record companies to become more general music companies then, clearly, a new industrial process is consolidating itself. This possibility will be explored in the final chapter. Before continuing that discussion it is necessary to understand how musicians experience their contracts and their relationships with music companies, both in terms of the preceding analysis, and as a further guide to what place they might come to enjoy in the emergent music industry.

7
Music Industry: Working Alliances

The previous four chapters could be read in any order. They are comparatively freestanding because they each deal with an aspect of a whole and no aspect is necessarily precedent to any other. Their purpose was to specify the four key constituencies involved in the production of symbolic goods. These are musicians together with the texts they originate, artist managers, music companies and contracts. As the analysis contained in those chapters should have shown, working alliances between musicians and music companies are the pivotal component of the Music Industry. They are pivotal because, working together, these constituencies form the production and supply process created to satisfy the demand for a particular type of good – a symbolic good with music at its core.

The uses made of symbolic goods all derive from the meanings that can be made from them, such as how they make us feel and what they allow us to communicate about ourselves and our understandings of who we are and where we consider we 'belong' in terms of our values and beliefs. There are many important respects in which this problematises symbolic goods as commodities, not the least being that they are a type of good which is not used up by consumption. What this means is that encouraging buyers to purchase more music when they already have music is a particular challenge. Part of the argument in Chapter 2 was that, in the face of intense competition, users can be attracted to specific, new symbolic goods should those goods exhibit what that chapter referred to as 'idiomatic currency'. Idiomatic currency is an ability particular goods have to 'speak to' or connect with specific 'structures of feeling'. In turn, a 'structure of feeling' is a state of living out values and beliefs we hold; a condition we communicate through our behaviour in all its aspects.

From a music-industrial perspective, what is absolutely pivotal is that both 'people' and 'structures of feeling' go on being continuously remade. For example, I may be a morose, male member of the baby-boom generation and, consequently, will be habitually drawn to the work of introspective singer-songwriters. Whilst I am that morose baby-boomer, if I feel a need for new music, then I can supplement my habitual listening to Bob Dylan, Joni Mitchell and Neil Young with, at the time of writing, purchases of materials by Bon Iver, Joanna Newsome and Midlake; although, of course, I no longer need to restrict that purchase to buying an album, or even make a purchase at all, which are topics for Chapter 8. In this way, while structures of feeling are composed from a palette of familiar sentiments read through a kaleidoscope of occasions and roles, who holds those sentiments on what occasions and how music helps them express themselves is in constant flux.

What it is important to recognise about the key constituencies involved in the production of symbolic goods with music at their core, is that they service uses they cannot control or determine. As Chapter 1 argued, 'nobody knows' which if any will prove useful to enough people to make investment in their production financially rewarding. In the face of social and cultural formations that are in continuous flux, music companies look for texts that they consider appropriate to continuously reforming ranges of expressive needs and sensibilities. At the same time, musicians originate texts including their own performance of themselves as a dimension of them in ways that can encapsulate the emergent and novel reformations of sensibilities which music companies seek to supply. These overlapping, if not strictly complementary processes are what keep both in business. The actions of music companies are driven by the search for idiomatic currency in music texts, whilst what drives the actions of musicians is that they believe the texts they originate have such currency. In turn, both act to connect with 'people' who are, individually and collectively, incessantly recast.

People are recast continuously because social and cultural contexts are neither still nor stable. Social and cultural change is continuous and so what meanings are made, how and from what materials is also subject to change. Clearly, the degree and pace of change can fluctuate dramatically over time and, in all of this, it is not so much that the texts of previous swathes of people are rejected wholesale because they are 'old' and therefore already 'used', it is because, as social and cultural patterns are continuously remade, the signifying capacity of older texts can become depleted or even exhausted as culturally and temporally specific referents melt away or become reinscribed. This is not to say that new uses cannot be found for old texts or aspects of them. The idiomatic currency of new texts is, to a degree, a product of the deftness of their construction in regard to their own inter-textual dimensions. For example, a rock recording might be identified by its structure, performance and instrumentation, a post-rock recording or performance would display many of these traits, but would be distinguished by variations in time signatures that would not be found in 'mainstream' rock music.

The work of this chapter is to look more closely at ways in which musicians, artist managers and companies ally and interact with each other in the making of symbolic goods, but in ways mindful of existing attempts to understand that process – notably but not solely those associated with the 'cultural industries approach' discussed in Chapter 1. With comments made in that chapter in mind then, the following is a summary of remarks made so far with regard to why, how, on what terms, and with what arguable results alliances between musicians, artist managers and music companies are experienced.

The essential music industry equation is a simple one, musicians have what music companies need, fresh texts; and musicians want what companies have – access to markets and the expertise to create an impact within them. The problems which flow from this equation are, though, far from simple:

1. Music companies are driven to pursue interactions with musicians on their own terms because of the basic logic of businesses: they cannot endure periods of dormancy; they must always make a profit; they must always grow. While musicians are also always seeking contacts with music companies, their need and desire to enter music markets is always oriented towards, or is at least mindful of, the market-entry frameworks and practices provided, by music companies. In turn, this is why the notion of the Music Industry as a separate and cohesive entity is such a compelling and persistent one.
2. The work of music companies consists of 'adding value' to what already exists in the work of the musicians with whom they contract. 'Adding value' consists of combinations of different sets of actions taken across the music industries. All such actions devolve into winning the compliance of musicians with the plans and therefore the perspectives of such companies. The problem for both parties is that these plans might conflict with musicians' own sense of who they are, whom they might appeal to and how this appeal might be realised. Furthermore, this compliance is not easily

achieved – musicians are not direct employees of music companies; they are partners with them in joint ventures and so cannot be compelled to 'follow orders'. Consequently, as Chapter 5 discussed, the musicians in question must either be won to courses of action decided by music companies or, if not, then subsumed to them through combinations of strategies more-or-less consciously pursued by companies in their own interests.

3. Music industry must obey basic logics of industry as well as of business: production must be carried on 'efficiently', in the sense that targets must be met and outcomes achieved on time and on budget towards maximum market impact. Because they are not direct employees of music companies, musicians are not susceptible to managed work roles, even so their inputs must be managed. What problematises the management of musicians inside the production of symbolic goods is a host of impediments – notably (but not solely), as Chapters 3 and 4 argued, that the role of musician is inherently conflicted and that their employment of their own managers does not always bring clarity and focus. In addition, 'adding value' can easily be registered by musicians as intrusive; as unwanted impacts on texts that they may feel are already complete.

4. Music companies conduct their business knowing that 'nobody knows' what symbolic goods will sell and also in the face of a massive and unbidden surplus of musicians. These twin intractable operating conditions produce two equally intractable impacts on their conduct of working relations with musicians. Firstly, they work with them knowing that most goods produced will be market failures. Secondly, companies habitually practice risk-reduction strategies in all aspects of the making and selling of symbolic goods as a hedge against this inevitability. Consequently, not only do such companies face the challenge that they cannot directly prescribe the actions of musicians, who are, nominally at least, their partners and not their employees, they risk antagonising those musicians through the 'value-adding' actions they undertake. Additionally, they also know that they cannot expect success with all of the musicians with whom they work. The greatest challenge of all is to manage the efforts and retain the loyalty of working partners in the face of the recognition that few joint projects will be intended for completion, and many will produce unwanted and therefore unhappy outcomes for those partners.

5. In seeking to manage alliances they form with musicians, music companies prioritise their own needs. They do this because their key

need is to stay alert to cultural change. In order to remain alert there can be considerable staff 'churn' in music companies both large and small. This 'churn' consists of replacing figures associated with music that is losing its currency with others associated with emergent music and musicians. In recruiting individuals for their alertness, no necessary attention is paid to their managerial skills and no necessary provision is made for inculcating these. Furthermore, in terms of the composition of particular markets, such individuals can be energetic and dogmatic about what 'works' and what does not in and for those markets. In the face of markets alive with rival goods, intensely self-confident employees interacting with conflicted musicians who can be represented by differently conflicted managers, when all are working within the constraints of contracts sympathetic more to one party than the other is a recipe for continuous and often overwhelming tension.

Taken together, the actions of music companies cannot fail to have impacts on the musicians with whom they work where this recognition problematises the notions of the musician as 'Romantic Artist' and the musician enjoying 'creative autonomy'. Ultimately, deciding that value can be added to a text to transform it into a symbolic good is a matter of judgement, but a matter of judgement that companies reserve for themselves. On this basis, companies and musicians have interests in common: both want and need market success, but they do not necessarily and automatically share common opinions about how texts should be configured for market entry as symbolic goods. In this way, the thrust of the argument thus far has been that, in vital respects, it is not the quality of the texts that musicians produce which decide their fate, it is the quality of the management of the conversion of the text into the symbolic good that counts. As Hesmondhalgh and many others imply rather than explore, the majority product of the Music Industry is indeed market failure – where this recognition is the subtext of the 'throwing mud against a wall' metaphor Hesmondhalgh quotes. The subtext of the metaphor is that very little 'mud' sticks to that 'wall' where the implication is that this lack of adhesion derives, not from any characteristic of the 'wall' or from how that mud is handled and thrown, but from the quality of the 'mud' itself. Ultimately, if musicians fail to become market successes, or to sustain market success should it arise, then this is entirely down to them and their efforts. Curiously, then, the Music Industry is somehow sacrosanct from its own outcomes: the industrial process 'works' but most musicians do not. This is an odd conclusion to draw from majority market failure of the goods that industry produces, yet, as Chapter 1 argues, this sentiment was rehearsed, by implication, repeatedly throughout the 1990s and early 2000s while the notion of 'creative industries', and the centrality of music industry to them, was in vogue in government policy making. At the very least this anomaly needs to be explored and it can only be explored if we recognise that 'mud' for what it is, the lives of creative, ambitious and optimistic human beings who believe, rightly or wrongly, that paying audiences can be assembled for the music they make.

The experience of music industry

The deepest contradiction associated with the industrial process of music is that symbolic goods are delicate to construct but tend to be constructed in indelicate environments. Their key ingredients – idiom and its currency – are both fragile and easy to misconfigure, so it should come as no surprise that three comparatively incoherent constituencies with differently constructed goals (musicians, managers and companies) should more often than not produce goods that find no buyers, or else too few to justify the investment made in them. Again, though, this is a highly abstract conclusion: the real question is how an alliance under pressure towards often hugely subtle and nuanced goods is experienced by those involved – where the sum of this experience is the reality of music industry.

Thus far, the actual experience of real, living musicians, save for mentions of a handful of 'stars', has been absent from an analysis that, as remarks in Chapter 1 testify, is made in their name. The reason for this is because this argument is an abstraction of years of close encounters with musicians and music industry and, rather than begin with the acts and extrapolate the industrial process from their experience, the extrapolation has been done prior to encountering acts and their fates. This analytical choice was made because, to introduce even one set of musicians who have, more or less, negatively experienced the music-industrial process would demand discussing all of the variables and dynamics that their particular experience was created from and animated by. Instead, the attempt has been made to identify those general variables and dynamics in order to explore how the particular fates of specific musicians are still the outcomes of general, industrial processes.

There is a significant body of literature on aspects of musicians' negotiation of cultural-economic spaces, notably Becker (1963),

Stokes (1977), Finnegan (1989), Cohen (1991), Kirschner (1998), Bayton (1998), Toynbee (2000) and Zwaan (2009) together with the unpublished work of Robson (2006) and Barna (2011). These can be added to studies of the music industry, cultural work and cultural economy more generally, among them, Becker (1982), Negus (1992, 1999) Davis and Scase, (2000), du Gay and Pryke (2002), Ross (2004), Bilton (2006), Banks (2007) and Currid (2007). Even so, none of these could be argued to theorise music industry as it was defined in Chapter 1. Towards this, arguably the most useful of these works remains Cohen's *Rock Culture in Liverpool*. In this work, Sara Cohen provides a model account of the day-to-day interactions of two 'unsigned' bands. As an anthropologist, her interest was in the 'complexity of social relationships involved' in the 'process of music making' (1991, p. 7) where, instructively, her focus is not so much on the music made, but the lives made by the musicians she studied. In turn, these lives are given shape and meaning by pursuing 'making it', the attempt to become market successes (1991, p. 39). This notion will need to be returned to for the reason that musicians' habitual and common use of the term can be argued to contribute to what disables them in the industrial process. Here, the point is that Cohen was able to conduct a sustained ethnographic encounter with two bands that, in turn, allowed her access to many more bands and, through them all, access to the local, music-industrial infrastructure. This infrastructure was, then, not simply economic and social in its nature, but cultural, a source of data and perspectives through which the musicians she studied formulated their plans for attracting the attention of record companies to their efforts.

Cohen's study remains a landmark in popular music studies. It is a thorough and comprehensive account of the daily reproduction of the role of musician. The study shows this reproduction to be inflected as much, if not more, by the pursuit of a 'deal' than by any absorption into the creative dimensions of making new music. In this way, business and industry are far from incidental to the musical lives of her subjects. Clearly, Cohen's study is one undertaken a long time before the rise of the internet and the impact of the digital distribution on music. More recently, in an unpublished work, Barna has revisited Cohen's study and 'territory', both metaphorically and literally. Barna also conducted an ethnographic study of bands in Liverpool but, in her case, the focus was more on their use of social networking tools and applications than rehearsal and performance practices, a concentration on online rather than offline behaviour.

For the purposes of this argument, what is striking about Barna's study is that, with the exception that one of her five bands seemed absorbed in an 'art for art's sake' project, the musicians in question were still preoccupied by the pursuit of 'making it', two of these quite consciously and determinedly. To an extent this should be no revelation – Liverpool is no more prosperous today than it was in 1985, many of the musicians she studied were unemployed (as Cohen's were), and all anticipated the transformations an external investor could bring. Furthermore, from Barna's research and, coincidentally, my own into some of the same bands, what is apparent is that the dynamics of 'making it' appear to be unchanged. 'Contacts' are coveted, managers are appointed in the hope that they can bring those contacts to the band and consolidate them as 'deals', careers are sought and the same careless metrics of 'making it' continue to apply. To this extent, very little has changed for aspirant pop musicians since the digital watershed, but from the perspective of this study, this conclusion is still of limited worth. It is limited because what is required to evaluate the industrial process of music are ethnographies of signed acts, especially now that the internet is having such profound, transformative effects on music use, musicians, music companies and, perhaps, on music itself. As it is, the outstanding example of a sustained encounter (rather than a determinate ethnography) between an 'outsider' and a band comes from several decades ago.

Geoffrey Stokes' *Star-Making Machinery* stands as a fascinating encounter with a music act as it experiences the industrial process of alliance with a record company and with the agents and publishers that batten onto 'signed' acts. Stokes enjoyed extraordinary access to the band he studied, Commander Cody and his Lost Planet Airmen. Additionally, he began his close association with them at a pivotal moment in their career, at a time when, due to an oversight, their record company had failed to take up their next album option. This just happened to coincide with the takeover of that company by a larger one. Understandably, the company conducting the takeover had factored in this particular band as one of its potential income generators and so attempted to prevent Commander Cody from seeking a new record contract. Stokes is able to quote from the disputed contract and from the contracts offered by two suitors (the major companies WEA – now Warner Music, and CBS – now Sony Music); he has access to the opinions of the band's manager, their lawyer, and their agent as well as to those of the band members; he sits in on recording sessions and attends gigs and promotional events. More than this, and quite remarkably, possibly because of the novelty of his role and the 'glow' of first contact, he also comes to enjoy access to executives from WEA to whom Commander Cody eventually signed.

What Stokes does not do is to theorise any of his encounters. Furthermore, despite his ability to quote contract clauses and the often quite brutal opinions of individuals involved in different aspects of the industrial process, Stokes' journalistic approach, intelligent, informed and sensitive as this is, tends to be a work of 'smoke and mirrors'. In much the way that Ondi Timoner in her film *Dig!* constructs a compelling but also distorted account of The Brian Jonestown Massacre and The Dandy Warhols, what Stokes accomplishes is to make an apparently unlimited access to key figures involved in the industrial process stand for access to its totality, when the latter is an impossibility. What I mean by this is that the industrial process is primarily a dispersed one. For example, while Stokes was interviewing a record company executive, the band's manager was likely to have been making policy and effecting either change or stasis in relation to the companies to which his clients were contracted. Similarly, the band, or cabals within the band, would be digesting the latest packet of information they had garnered from the manager and from their own impressions and would be adjusting degrees of optimism and pessimism, and with them degrees of openness to any 'value-adding' actions of companies, accordingly. Moreover, members of the Press and Promotions department of WEA in Los Angeles, where these events took place, but also around the country and 'the world', would be determining exactly how far they would be prepared to grant and to call in favours to and from media contacts on behalf of Commander Cody, given the roster of new album releases they needed to factor in to their work schedules.

Taken in the aforementioned manner, there would seem to be a methodological contradiction – I am, simultaneously, calling for ethnographies of signed acts and denying that such ethnographies can be mounted. Before discussing the solution to this apparent contradiction, or as a way of identifying one, what needs to be understood about this 'dispersal' of the industrial process is what counts is how its co-ordination is effected – how a dispersed set of inter-relations is impelled to cohere as an industrial process. We can begin to appreciate this if we understand that when a musician or musicians sign to major record companies, as well as to live agencies and to publishers, they do not work with any of these companies in a necessarily open and transparent way, as one business to others. Instead, they are signed as text-makers and are expected to open their text-making to value-adding.

This value-adding is then conducted on behalf of the contracting companies by individual representatives of those companies. Companies reach their particular states of consensus on how to enter a music market with what they infer is a specific symbolic good separately from musicians and their managers. They then charge individual staff members with bringing these decisions to bear on the musicians they will be working with, and on (consider Scott's comment in Chapter 5 with regard to the weekly company 'forecast meeting').

For these reasons, musicians do not necessarily experience music companies, they experience relationships with individuals employed by them with whom they may bond closely, and on whom they come to rely whether bonded or not. Similarly and equally, these individuals do not necessarily form relationships with an act as if this is a distinct and self-conscious entity. Rather, they form separate sets of relationships, firstly with the artist manager as the representative of the act. Secondly, with some but not all of the musicians involved, if the act is a band, because almost inevitably, there will tend to be dominant members within a band. This is why so many of the 'formal' accounts of the Music Industry identified in Chapter 1 are so wide of the mark. There are balance sheets and company reports for the business press to discuss and there will be executives who act as the mouthpiece for them and with whom the Music Industry can be identified. In turn, it is these figures that the government lionises when it suits them to care, and whom the education system can be overly impressed by, but the reality is that industry is carried out in and through incessant and myriad highly personalised and therefore highly charged relationships that are prone to break down.

Music industry relationships are prone to break down for a multiplicity of reasons, where five general ones would be:

1. Given that nobody knows what will be a 'hit', all parties, are always driven to behave as if they are on the verge of great success, because, until proved otherwise, this might be true. This hyper-intensity then has the peculiar logic that it is only sustainable if it is sustained, and while it is, it is difficult to be rational and clear about strategic choices.
2. Relationships break down because musicians are mostly young and will have invested what they see as their 'whole lives' in making music and in the 'dream' of success (the only difference between *X Factor* hopefuls and 'indie' ones is that the latter are cool enough not to say this). Amalgams of desire and ambition are poor sources

of measurement for musicians to evaluate their status as texts, businesses and commodities.

3. Relationships break down because, mostly, symbolic goods are market failures and, whether the relationships formed are stable or not, company representatives will be practising strategies of risk management even as they conduct what can be emotional entanglements with musicians. This is the root of the feeling of 'betrayal' that so many musicians report when 'deals' are lost.

4. As a point connected directly to the previous one, music and especially record company employees (although this can be equally true of artist managers) can develop their own emotional engagement with the translation of particular texts into symbolic goods. In this way, one of the 'prices' of 'value-adding' for all parties is that different individuals may make an emotional investment in the text or the process of transformation into the symbolic good, only to find their contributions overridden and even disparaged. Managing industrial production here becomes the act of managing an emotionally charged environment. Volatility of working relations and fragility of goods-in-progress is a particularly lethal combination where the aim of market success is concerned.

5. How emotional intensity and the fragility of outcomes express themselves inside working alliances can take familiar 'biographical' forms: musicians clash with companies; personnel are sacked or move on; bands fight amongst themselves; managers are fired or desert. In all of this, given its dispersion and encounter-based character, rarely is a single individual truly 'in charge' of the overall process and able to contain its tensions and minimise its turbulence. When one is, or appears to be, they become the 'legendary' figures' of the Music Industry with Madonna, Peter Grant and Jerry Wexler as examples from each main 'camp'.

Star-Making Machinery

As comments on Greenfield and Osborne in Chapter 6 indicated, there is a tension between the alliance made between musicians and music companies 'on paper' and that which exists in reality. When musicians sign contracts with companies, it means acknowledging that the expertise they seek is embodied by the individuals with whom they come to work. In this way, what musicians enter is a working group of individuals drawn from different specialist backgrounds towards the market entry of a symbolic good. This could be called a 'supra-alliance'. In order to work together, to be organised in their pursuit of a symbolic good ready for market entry, this alliance will take on the characteristics of an organisation, but a temporary and informal one. This will be an unconstituted organisation, in the sense that not only is it informal, but it will not be recognised as an organisation by its participants. In this way, music industry becomes *ad hoc*, impressionistic and pragmatic, where none of these conditions are conducive to making fragile goods. Even so, members of the supra-alliance will still need to find a common ground and a common language for the work they do together; in turn this will involve them generating a common culture, with all that term's implications for shared values and ritualised forms of behaviour and speech. These temporary, low-allegiance but absolutely necessary cultures will either cohere or they will not; they will stand up to strain or they will not; they will survive their own self-generated stresses, or they will not. Mostly they do not: to understand why we need to see them in action.

As a way of beginning to penetrate the organisational character of supra-alliances as music industry, consider this composite of observations about the band's manager, Joe Kerr, recorded by Stokes in his discussions with Warner executives in the first weeks of Commander Cody's signing to them:

> With some guys it can get pretty hairy, but with a guy who's as solidly established as Kerr is, it shouldn't really be any problem.... For instance Joe is looking for TV exposure, but he doesn't have any LA contacts. That's the kind of way we can help too [as well as in booking a live show]. It's not that we're taking anybody's authority away or anything like that. It's just that there's a real need.
>
> (1977, p. 185)

We can return to this, but Stokes quotes another executive who asserts:

> When we've got a quarter of a million dollars invested in a bunch of high-school kids, do you think we want to watch their management piss it away?
>
> (1977, p. 185)

What underscores and drives both quotes is a sense of complete and absolutely certainty on the part of the record company personnel. Not only do they have the 'contacts', they have the expertise and the knowledge that the manager and the musicians are evidently considered to lack. Additionally, the explicit reference to the investment made in what the second executive clearly regards as unworldly business partners is particularly telling – here, the company executive is concerned with his company's investment, to the exclusion of all other considerations. The first executive, though, is equally hard-nosed, where the reason that 'it can get pretty hairy' is because, by implication, he and his company is indeed in the business of 'taking…authority away' and, by inference, they fear it being resisted. Kerr is only allowed his limited autonomy because he has been evaluated, in advance, as a 'guy who [is]…solidly established'. Here, a record company enters an alliance that is substantially an alliance in name only – they understand their needs and they set the parameters of what they will and will not accept in regard to them from the outset. This is an example of the formation and implementation of company strategy discussed in Chapter 5. It derives from a *realpolitik* that is rarely voiced or made explicit. In any case, the day-to-day management of alliance relations is left to single individuals. In this day-to-day activity, acts will be keen for constant updates but will rarely act as a business entity in its own right which leaves the manager to glean what the company or companies truly think of them and their prospects.

To exemplify this point, and to open up others for exploration, during the writing of this book, one set of my respondents finished an album for a major record company. I discussed with them the process of signing and recording in the months leading up to the release. Even at that stage there was disquiet in their ranks ('it's like *Alice Through the Looking Glass*'). Even so, an expensive video was made for a first release, a second release was slated and the release date for the album was fixed. Subsequently, review copies went to press. Yet, when the due date arrived, the company declined to release the album and my second interview was with a band which was experiencing the shock and disorientation of no longer being signed. Their rationalisations make for salutary reading and, astonishingly, they begin with the 'mud against the wall' analogy:

> It's so clichéd…it's a shame to even discuss it…they take an artist; they throw them at the wall with their half a million pounds each; they see which one sticks; and they try and make all the other ones like the one that stuck.

In representing her experience in this way, this particular individual, lead singer and main songwriter fronting the band, still needs to recount her particular experience in terms of an incoherent set of working relations. As she put it,

> The thing that is very strange for an artist is that there's no way in and no way out of a major label, at all. There's no guidance, no-one holds your hand and explains what's going on. When you get signed to a major label, it's so fast. You're chucked into this brand new world.

Very tellingly, given the non-release of the album, the act did not work with a Product Manager (which suggests that the release schedule was only ever provisional), instead they worked with A&R on choosing a producer and then with the Marketing Department on designing 'campaign' materials. There was considerable conflict over the creation of these materials, to the extent that a keenly anticipated 'creative autonomy' in terms of, exactly, self-presentation seemed simply to be not on offer. This was the source of another band member's reference to 'Alice'. He was particularly angry and baffled at the company's resistance to the band's ideas in this central, symbolic and textual, regard. Worse, inside this increasingly tense and rapidly deteriorating situation the artist manager appeared to take the record company's side. As the lead singer put it,

> As (we) signed, it (*the previously healthy relationship with the manager*) fell apart. He didn't know what to say. He should have been more of a Rottweiler really, and he wasn't, he was a 'yes man'. [...] He would say 'yes' to them a lot and then he would try and back *me* down.

To briefly digress here, in another interview with an act that endured an almost identical experience (much money spent on an album that also reached the press review stage and was then not released), their lead singer made the exactly opposite point about a manager perceived as being equally derelict,

> He was so aggressive all the time, 'I'm not having this for my band', and so on.... We were unhappy about a lot of things, we were quite a Bolshie band – about the singles, the sleeves. I was very concerned that I didn't want to be marketed as a woman...we were a group, a band, we each had our role to play...and (the manager) absolutely supported us in all of that. He was important but I wonder whether we were right.

To return to the previous act, relations between them and the manager deteriorated to the point that, at the point of the second interview they had become locked in a legal dispute with each other. In another interesting parallel with the second act, their lawyer proved a source of advice and solace but, at the time of writing, the dispute was becoming deeper and more painful – substantially because the artist management contract included a 'sunset clause' (a clause which allows the manager to go on earning a commission after the agreement has been terminated). In this instance the clause provided for the manager earning a 15 per cent commission on works completed during his engagement for an eight-year period. In both instances, what is notable, and also consistent and generalisable, is the invidious position of the manager. As was discussed in Chapter 4, inside the production relations of symbolic goods, the artist manager is either 'shop steward' (which is what makes the use of 'Bolshie' – an abbreviation of 'Bolshevik' – so revealing) or 'foreman', but in both instances the record company was in control of its investment. If the record company does not continue to invest then there is little incentive for a live performance agent to organise tours, and little incentive for a music publisher to actively 'work' the act's songs because they will not enjoy the special status of being a 'hit' act.

We gain a strong sense of how resolute companies can be from Stokes, but this is a resolution with wide tolerances. To reiterate the points made in Chapter 5, one of the key risk-management strategies employed by record companies, especially major ones, was, and remains (though now with some modification as a later example will explore), to over-sign acts in an attempt to reduce the impact of the inflexible reality of symbolic production that 'nobody knows' which texts will make market-successful symbolic goods. What this means is that, truly, very little 'mud' is thrown compared with how much is gathered. Furthermore, sometimes over-signing can be strategic in a different way; as a senior music industry lawyer put it to me,

> I did have a strong feeling that (a major company) were from time to time signing acts just in order to shut out their rival companies. It made me wary of accepting deals from (that company) where they seemed to be willing to out-bid everyone else without really thinking about it.

The 'without really thinking about it' is significant because it suggests that this particular company might have no specific desire for an act that they still sign. In the absence of such desire, there will be no drive to work with them and no pre-determined bespoke game plan through which to convert them into market-successes. Something of this order was certainly sensed by the lead singer of the act under discussion; she felt strongly that the company had signed a similar and, to this extent at least, rival act which appeared, briefly, to promise big sales and so drained resources from the promotion of her act's album. Whether or not this is an entirely accurate supposition is not the point. What is, is that her company had signed a similar artist at exactly the same time, which meant, in turn, that its resources were divided between these two acts and, obviously, among yet others – you can recall Marsh's observation from Chapter 5, 'and you do that for nine acts at a time'. It is no wonder that this particular act felt so bewildered. Bewilderment is a persistent condition when discussing the aftermath of failed deals with formerly 'signed' musicians. It is a bewilderment at the inconsistencies and what appears to be the illogic at work in transforming texts into symbolic goods. This is a bewilderment that is shaped, very often, by a deeper sense of hurt; as the lead singer observed about what she experienced as an abrupt transition between dealing with A&R and dealing with the marketing department: 'I got on with my A&R guy (but) they disappear … it's like, "What, you were my best friend for the last month!" '

It is important to return to 'bewilderment' for what it can be argued to tell us about the specific nature of the music-industrial process, generally. Before doing this, or as a way to begin it, it is worth considering how a representative from a major record company understands the process the musician found so frustrating.

Welcome to the machine

This particular senior record company executive is not one from the company involved with the musicians quoted so far, but this individual is certainly someone able to speak with authority on the practices of the major companies. His background (in common with other figures that I interviewed and will draw into this discussion) lay first in making music and then in joining an independent record company. This is a familiar journey for many record company and music industry personnel and therein lies not just a 'problem', but the nub of what allows the Music Industry to go on, in the expression used in Chapter 5, 'tumbling into the future', always just ahead of being consumed by its contradictions. That its contradictions fail to consume it is also a factor of the location of those contradictions themselves, as will be argued subsequently, but here we need to register, firstly, the ex-musician's and the ex-'indie' record company employee's own discomfort with the 'corporate environment':

> To go into a big corporate concern with meetings with accountants and making formal speeches and formal presentations of your artists; I mean, you know, I used to have to stand up every Monday morning to the whole company and present the singles of the artists, it was like working in the Ideal Home Exhibition!

Yet, as he goes on to say, 'I kind of got into it, eventually' where the 'it' he got into remains very much the practice and process that the disgruntled act discussed previously:

> I got to realise that if you were gonna break your act through the company you had to kind of do it in that kind of way so I sort of changed my colours for the surroundings, really and got dug into it.

This getting 'dug into it' then brought with it a set of expectations about the most efficient way of working with new signings on the transformation of texts into symbolic goods; where these devolved onto the following:

> A good manager; you couldn't not sign a fantastic act because their manager was crap but sometimes you kind of feared for an act if the manager wasn't able to sell its artist inside the company like *you* have to sell the artist inside the company, and a lot of them couldn't. [...] they don't know how to, in a more sophisticated way, how to present their acts and how to present their acts to a body of workers who have to work the act over lots of other acts that they have to work, you know, and how to present their act to a bunch of managing directors of fifteen record labels all over Europe, you know, blokes who are working with (very big stars) you've got to be able to present your act to them, you know, in a very positive way. [...] if you want them to work for your act you've gotta make sure that they understand all the qualities that your act have and why they should work a little bit harder on it than they do on (a big star).

This observation is revelatory in inter-related ways. Firstly, it confirms the risk-management practice of 'over-signing' by major record companies; secondly, it demonstrates that some acts can fail to become prioritised inside a company, with the result that their market failure is a self-fulfilling prophecy; thirdly, this could also be taken to indicate the complete absence of creative autonomy as a meaningful experience for musicians. What concerns me, most, at this point is that the musicians' implied solution to this reality, this *realpolitik*, is to rely on the ability of an artist manager to prosecute their case throughout their time with the company. This then raises the question of how best to effect that 'sophisticated . . . present(ation)'. Most revelatory of all is his description of what a manager should not do, and why:

> They (the record company employees) should feel part of this act and they should feel excited if the act gets a break and if you go into them talking to them as if they're a bunch of arse-holes, right, then they'll just, the moment you leave, walk out the door, they'll forget you and the next manager will come in who's a nice guy and tries to bring them in and get them to be supportive of the act and brings the act into meet them (and so on) they'll work harder on his act [. . .] you've got to treat them in the right way and a lot of people couldn't do that very well or didn't suss it.

What is of central importance inside this set of multi-dimensional observations is the executive's emphasis on the need for the manager to effect what is essentially an emotional bond with the act ('should feel part of the act . . . should feel excited').

To return to the musicians already encountered, the poignancy in the remark, 'What, you were my best friend for the last month!' needs to be explored in the context(s) provided by the executive. When an act is 'signed', when they achieve their 'deal', it is impossible for this not to be registered as the sense of being recognised as 'special', as 'talented', as already 'somebody'. 'Making it' is a horribly imprecise metaphor: for example, 'making' can be understood as creating something tangible, when what is really created is an intangible alliance towards an intangible outcome. 'Making it', can also be understood in the sense of arriving somewhere, where making it, then suggests that the 'it' 'made', is somewhere special and important: the summit of a mountain, the end of the rainbow. The signing of a deal and beginning to work on records and preparing tours can only be an emotional experience, because these are exciting activities in and of themselves, especially when contrasted with being in a mundane job, or in no job at all. The problem then is not only is there no force in the musicians' lives to rein in this excitement, there is the expectation that significant, industrial figures must be made part of this excitement as the pivotal condition of the industrial process itself (if the record company is not excited by the act, then why should anyone else be?).

Yet this is an industrial process; it is the manager's job to get record company, and, by inference, other types of music company employees, 'to be supportive of the act (so that) they'll worker harder on his act'. When this all goes wrong, as it does in the vast majority of cases, the act is left to deal with the fact that the often very strong emotional bonding they have experienced (when they, themselves, are in heightened emotional states) is simply a stock, a standard, aspect of the industrial process. As the lead singer of the band quoted previously put it:

> They say things all the time to keep the artist happy. You can see it; it's horrid; it's really bad acting;

As another member of the second act with a similar experience expressed it to me: 'Oh yeah, they really love you – until you're dropped, and then it's "are you still in the building?"'

Alliance

The hurt and also disgust in these comments above is echoed continuously in encounters with musicians who have either not enjoyed or not sustained market success; but the strong temptation to dismiss such remarks as 'sour grapes' and as 'self-pity' needs to be resisted. In dismissing the testimony of formerly signed musicians, and in failing to listen to the complaints of the 'unsigned', what is missed is not just that the hurt experienced is a direct outcome of the conduct of music-industrial production; it is to remain completely and dangerously ignorant of the role played by the internalisation of emotional pain, and by 'rationalisation' generally, in the off-setting of the contradictions of that particular industrial process. Ultimately, music industry 'works', but it works because so many people suffer it to work. I will return to this point, below, here I want to register that music industry personnel deal with market failure in a completely contrasting way, but one I hope to show draws from the same well of, essentially faulty and circular, rationalisation.

In interviewing the principal protagonists in one particular experience of market success, I was struck not so much by how divergent the accounts produced were, but by the extent to which aspects of the collective experience that should have been factually unequivocal (such as why one record company was chosen above others) were not just remembered differently, but conceived differently by representatives of the key constituencies. There is insufficient space here to explore this particular case study in the kind of detail that would make its exploration fully productive, but its essential contours are that what had been constructed as an 'indie' band enjoyed a very big, mainstream hit single. The hit single lost the act its critical acclaim (and limited but growing fan base); while, at the same time, it did not generate comparable levels of sales for the album from which it was taken; where this meant, in turn, that the act did not 'cross over' into the mainstream and so generate a new and much larger national and international audience that would have sustained the career all parties anticipated. In both market and popular-cultural terms, the act could not go 'forwards' or 'backwards' and, even though several subsequent hit singles were registered and more albums were released, the act was dropped comparatively soon after this major success. In this example, a working alliance produced both success and failure.

It has already been argued that there is a strongly emotional dimension to cultural production. What emotions are stirred and how individuals deal with their emotions, particularly over time, is an important factor in their shaping of accounts of experiences. In addition, and this is the key point here, rationalisation can be argued to be constructed through a set of common 'filters'. To a certain extent these are accounts of personal 'Odysseys' and, rather like the *Odyssey* itself, they can be argued to be 'built from a ... flexible repertoire of formulaic elements' (Price and Thonemann, 2011, p. 104). Evidence for and of these 'formulaic elements' will be discussed below, what concerns me is that I asked the principals involved in a working alliance which produced a very well-known UK hit record how success came about and why it was not developed and sustained. How these accounts were shaped showed me, unsurprisingly perhaps, that different principals remember differently, not just because they each make a different contribution to the whole, but because each has a different stake in the whole. The question then is how, through what mechanisms, were these different stakes coordinated in ways that produced such contradictory outcomes over the short and medium term?

To summarise these accounts means to lose almost all of their richness, although to explore in detail risks compromising the anonymity promised to those concerned.

1. The dispersal of the industrial process of the transformation of texts into symbolic goods means that no one experiences every part of the process. This means that the different parties are prone to

conceptualise its overall strengths and weaknesses in contrasting and even radically different ways. In this instance (and given the geographical separation of the record company from the act's base of operations), what was notable was the how limited the musician saw the contribution of the record company A&R man. As far as the musician was concerned, it was the band's music that produced the success; where the record company executive was concerned it was his actions that produced the success by winning his company to the act through a strategy of co-ordinated independent releases which generated favourable press and radio attention.

2. The fact that each has their own area of practice means that the whole is conceived through the lens of their particular specialism. What was extraordinary about the accounts of the transformation of a rough 'demo' of what became the hit song into the released record was how the record company executive attributed this entirely to the appoint of a record producer, while the musician felt that the song was evidently a 'hit' waiting to happen. The artist manager remembered the song with mixed feelings, but attributed what he saw as the record's 'cheesiness' to the song itself rather than to the production. The choice of term smacks strongly of *post hoc* rationalisation. There was no reported objection to its choice as a single and no objection to it as unrepresentative of the band's repertoire seemed to have been raised at the time or features as a factor in these later accounts.

3. Symbolic goods are intended to communicate, but no producer can be certain that what is received is what they intended to be communicated. In this particular case, how the main songwriter saw himself (as a new 'Tom Waits'), how the band anticipated its future ('I wanted us to be as big as U2 and I thought we were capable of doing it at the time'), and how the record company saw them, initially at least, ('The Residents, Zappa . . . our Jonathan Richman') were at complete variance. Towards his vision of the act, the A&R man argued, 'we've got to get a plot, but it can't be a normal plot'. The manager's collusion with this 'plot' was then what rebounded on all parties. In this way it was the 'story' of the act, rather than its sound that sent mixed signals to the market. As previous remarks have argued, texts are not inviolate, they do not have fixed boundaries, so it is that 'value adding' actions can be inappropriate additions to existing texts even as they produce immediate value.

4. Success does not unify narratives or even, necessarily, make working alliances more coherent and transparent; rather, the reverse can be true. As remarks in the second point testify, years after the event,

each party sees their contribution as the decisive one and, conversely, the failure to capitalise on success (literally as well as metaphorically) as the responsibility of some other force: the musician – 'I think we signed to the wrong label'; the artist manager – 'the song sold, not the band' – the record company executive (who moved on during the success of the single) – 'I wasn't there to A&R them' (in the less-successful aftermath).

The industrial process sketched in this way is a blend of the utterly specific and the substantially general that makes the Music Industry so difficult to study. As Stokes did, it would be possible to fill an entire book with the 'story' of the musicians, manager and music companies involved in this particular hit and its painful postscript. As it is, what the episode can be taken to show is that alliances can 'work', but they can also fail to work. Here, we have a company willing to give a persistent employee his 'head' (there was, at first, strong resistance to signing the act in question). Large companies can do this because they are geared to absorb losses as market successes pay for them. To an extent, in this instance, how the employee creates the initial success is largely from his own enterprise; which, in turn, suggests that forms of creative autonomy do exist within the industrial process, but these are not necessarily 'artistic' spaces. Such can be the power of big companies, this 'enterprise' need not proceed with the co-operation of the other parties, although in this case, it involved the full co-operation of the manager. The mutuality which existed between the A&R representative and the artist manager was pursued entirely in the interests of clients they both believed in, but it still proved to be counter-productive. Clearly, this comment is made with the luxury of hindsight, a hindsight which also argues that the musicians were culpable in supporting a strategy that eventually thwarted them even as it launched them so powerfully.

From the interviews I conducted there seemed to be no real evaluation of the manager's actions as they were taking place; rather, the musicians exhibited the destructive frustration of people simply wanting to 'get on with it', without asking too many hard questions of the 'it' with which they wanted to be 'getting on'. What this says is that musicians can have 'tunnel-vision'; they push a manager for progress and, because this pursuit of progress involves frequent trips away from them, co-ordinating not just the efforts but the understanding of all three parties is easily allowed to drift or, more accurately, is never genuinely constituted. In this case, there is also no evidence that the manager stood back from his own entanglement with the A&R person in a way that might have helped the musicians evaluate the choices made and decisions taken. Whether they would have taken the time out to make such an evaluation is moot. From the company's perspective, their upper echelons also did not critique the 'plot' cooked up by their A&R man; they were happy to reap the rewards of his efforts; and frustrated that those efforts refused to maintain their original, high-yielding capacity.

So it is that this particular 'supra-alliance' was not genuinely under anyone's control – the musicians deferred too readily to the manager's 'authority' ('I had plenty of contacts in the industry'); the manager deferred too readily to the only person in 'the industry' who would take him seriously; the company stood back and hoped their employee 'go it right'. That the employee appeared to, and then appeared not to, was not addressed by the company. This failure to address is characteristic of an industry that continues to exhibit some of the worst habits of the entrepreneurialism at its heart. In this instance, the fact that individual in question found a better position so was not there to 'debrief' is a contributory factor to the lack of evaluation but, more pertinently, debriefing (and, with it 'knowledge management') is regarded as a distracting soul-searching. As the senior executive quoted previously put it,

> The ones that fail you quickly forget, you only remember the successful ones [. . .] if you're gonna go around trying remembering the failures, you're gonna get miserable.

It is important that we recognise this candid observation for what it is. Firstly, its a callous but supremely honest confirmation of the centrality of emotion to the working practices of music companies (evident in the need to avoid being 'miserable'). Secondly, its intricate entanglement with the formulation, and therefore the formation of a particular kind of working knowledge, one that prizes the tacit over the explicit. Specifying the chemistry of emotion and tacit knowledge then leads to a final understanding of 'music industry'.

Rationalisation, contradictions, contradiction

What made the example above a successful exercise in value-adding by a music company was that the representative of a record company inside a supra-alliance had a vision which he could share with the artist manager to which the latter, in turn, won his clients. What was shared was a commitment to a story; a story that helped to bring influential media conduits to channel that music to readers and listeners whom the alliance hoped would translate into a paying audience for later symbolic goods. Considered in this way, the co-ordination of the alliance was achieved by the A&R man; the issue of the management of the process of converting the text into symbolic goods is more problematic.

The market-entry strategy failed because the alliance was co-ordinated around an idea more than it was actively managed towards a set of realisable goals. Once the market took up the act, no force in the alliance could correct the course which had been set. In many respects this is not dereliction by the manager (as the two previously cited acts argued); rather, once events had been set in motion, the manager concentrated on the immediate, logistical needs of the act rather than the strategic needs of the symbolic good of which the act was part; as the musician put it 'he (was) a good organiser'. Furthermore, it shows that definition of the text counts most towards its cohesion as a symbolic good and, in this case, the initial definition seemed to be enough. What it is difficult to appreciate without experiencing it first-hand, or else it being tracked ethnographically in a comprehensive way, is the scale and intensity of events surrounding a hit record. In the absence of the close direction of a central figure, or a central strategic hub involving several key figures, events can quickly amplify an initial margin of error and take definitions of symbolic goods into areas which dictate the likely reception of further goods from the same act. In my discussions with them, the manager determined that the record company had been at fault in the handling of the success of the single – promoting it at the expense of the album from which it came and failing to counter-balance the reversal in the market position of the act the single's success induced. Clearly, the A&R man's leaving for another post was a contributory factor here, because no new supra-alliance replacement appears to have been found, but the willingness of the record company to believe that the act would simply continue to make its impact is a complacency that can only be traced to the 'chemistry' that can be provoked between emotion and tacit knowledge.

The absolution of market entry companies from the market failure of the majority of symbolic goods can be heard being rehearsed regularly at the music industry conferences that are now a staple of music industry life in the UK. Time and again, whether from platforms or in conversations surrounding such events, the music industry orthodoxy is that, just so long as an act has 'great songs' then all of the rest (market success, company profit, acclaim for the act) simply follows, almost without a need for effort and certainly not an industrial effort that subordinates music and musicians to profit-driven goals. In this version of the industrial process, music itself (in an ineffable but irresistible way) rather than the actions of companies decides whether demand will be satisfied by the supply embodied as a particular symbolic good. This conception allows music industry personnel to be redrawn as handmaidens of 'great songs'; their actions become sanctified as the ability to identify a great song and to bring it to 'the public'. In turn, all of the inconvenience of the fact that their efforts overwhelmingly produce market failures (market failures of what, at some point, they judged to be 'great songs' and potentially 'hit acts') is finessed away. Market failure is not their responsibility, it is the responsibility of the musicians whose work was not sufficiently current, insufficiently idiomatic to connect with, confirm or animate a structure of feeling that would have led to their own celebration and to the company's profit

This view was certainly clear in the A&R man's analysis of the subsequent failure of the act; where his assessment is the polar opposite of the musicians':

> (They) took the easy route of being slapped on the back by the cool guys (in the press) for turning (their) back on the mass market; on accessible recordings and on hits, and so (their) next album was devoid of hits, of anything remotely like a hit, devoid of all the exuberance and charm, of pop charm, that the first album had.

Versus:

> We recorded I think some of the darkest songs *ever* written [...] We recorded I think, and most fans would say, the...masterpiece.

In this confrontation, one party thinks that the songs stopped being 'great', the other that they became greater: yet both are misguided in their assessments. Why music users elect to purchase one symbolic good over another is that they believe, or can be persuaded to believe, that some aspect or aspects of a symbolic good are useful to them. While music is at the core of symbolic goods produced through music industry, by the Music Industry, its idiomatic currency is carried by the text. It is carried by each aspect of it as a signifying whole. While a 'hit' act can sometimes go on pleasing a loyal audience and animating structures of feeling within that audience, not every record by Elvis Presley or The Beatles or Madonna or Oasis needed to be 'great' or even 'good'.

An act which retains its currency goes on selling records, tickets and merchandise.

Where the acts featured in this discussion were concerned, they either failed to make it to the popular cultural 'launch pad' or failed to go into 'orbit'. Once 'in orbit' there is a kind of popular cultural 'gravity' that eventually drags all symbolic goods back to Earth. This is because 'people' change, 'times' change and meanings made from signifying goods change with them. In turn, because all parties to music industry approach their joint work in a discourse that is centred on music even as they all work on the wider dimensions of the text, their 'common ground' is always likely to be formed from materials inadequate to the strain and tension that will inevitably be generated between them. It will be inadequate because what is required is a language rooted in the material needs of production and market entry. What is on offer is the common culture forced into being by the needs of the supra-alliance. This common culture will be constructed discursively through signifying practices all parties believe they have in common – a sensitivity to, and an expertise in, 'great songs'. The alliance speaks in unverifiable and romantically expressed ideals; consequently, its constituents do not so much talk music when they should be talking business, they talk music loosely as if they were talking business.

That music industry as a form of production developed as a discourse of ideals is rooted both in the rise of music industry in the 19th century and in the nature of the symbolic good itself. What all parties discuss is a symbolic whole (the sound, the look, the story of the act) and, as such, they can only discuss such symbols through other ones. Moreover, they all discuss this symbolic whole in terms of an anticipated future state, and so a loose discourse becomes looser still; it becomes more speculative and more emotive. In addition, as Chapter 2 argued, what the institutionalism of music not only allowed and encouraged, but depended on, was the granting of the right to a designated group of people to speak with authority about music, where this 'authority' could only be effective if it was subscribed to by music users (and all musicians begin as music users). Against this background, the Music Industry can be a treacherous place for musicians because the authority of pop is tacit and informal.

To elaborate this last point, as Chapter 2 argued, the institutionalisation of popular music followed the pattern set by that of 'classical' music with the exception that, in the classical institution it was scholars who judged while in the Music Industry it was the rapidly coalescing practices of the entrepreneurs. What linked the institutions was that both sets of power-holders deferred to 'the music' as if music itself decided who should be acclaimed or who should be top of the bill. In this way, the 'expertise' associated with organising the market entry of symbolic goods was underwritten by a specialist 'knowledge' that only those in the institution were held to possess (what made 'great music'); in turn, this 'expertise' and 'knowledge' underscored the authority and therefore the power of the 'experts'. In a world of over-supply, the personnel of music companies are never wrong, because some investor, somewhere, is always right: as long as there are 'hit acts', the Music Industry works. The problem with this logic is, of course, that mostly, the Music Industry doesn't work; it produces vastly more failures than success. Music companies prosecute and survive this fact through a combination of the actions and attitudes discussed previously. It is difficult to see them as a general and industrial process, but industry is ever present in the seething biographies of every act, signed and unsigned, in all their intriguing distinctiveness and often depressingly general similarity.

Conclusion

Musicians, artist managers and music company employees can be argued to construct their accounts of the industrial process through various filters that derive from conceptions of music and what makes it successful that have accumulated in the period since its commercialisation. Musicians go on wanting to 'make it', but without ever being able to identify what 'it' they are trying to 'make' and how this will come about. The other constituencies share this imprecision, but are drawn to rationalise from a different but connected set of materials which derive from the notion that there is a 'knowledge' which, though substantially tacit, is accessible in and through the experience, rather than any explicit accounts or theorisation, of the senior figures of the Music Industry. This is why, when they are asked questions, music company figures tend to answer with anecdotes, where these are more productively understood as parables, specific stories intended to exemplify general, even universal, truths.

The preponderance of tacit over explicit knowledge in the Music Industry is essential if the claims to expertise and knowledge are to go on ensuring the power and authority of music companies over musicians. In a sector founded on tacit knowledge, 'old hands' keep their jobs because of a 'gut instinct' they have shown in the past and are judged to have retained; new entrants are spared induction and professional development regimes because what is valued about them is that they, too, have shown an alertness to cultural trends and change. Managerial innovation is rare and attention to managerial practices is limited, because the industry goes on insisting that the abilities it values cannot be taught; so it is that managing, even in the face of profound change, tends to remain what it always has been – routine that, once learned, is continuously repeated. As Adorno recognised so long ago (and as 'the cultural industries approach' finds it difficult to throw off); the Music Industry exerts a standardising cultural force, because its key driver is the maintenance of the 'standard' of the 'expertise' of companies towards the formulae that continue to show a return on investment.

Capturing all of this in action continues to present an enormous challenge to researchers. Identifying the composition of supra-alliances of musicians, artist managers and music company personnel forms the core of this challenge, but not only are their interactions dispersed, so much of what counts towards the responses made to decisions is an internal and internalised sense-making practice, rather than a set of decisions recorded as minutes and accessible to scrutiny. Given the emotional dimension of so much music industry activity, its working relations are more usefully understood as working relationships. As such, they are relationships that can be even more precarious than the ones we enter into in our personal lives. Further, this level of precariousness is not confined to the world of 'the majors' and the heartlands of the Music Industry; as Chapter 1 put it, music companies are myriad and the majority of the companies that make up the Music Industry are very small indeed, even so, the observations made in this chapter can be scaled down to the smallest 'project'. In all sets of working, music-industrial relationships, each supra-alliance is a working unit; they are all temporary configurations; they are all isolated from each other; and many of them are never destined for completion – mainly because investors are 'taking a punt' and prove reluctant to complete 'projects' (literally projections into an unknowable future) without, usually impossible to achieve, 'guarantees' that their investment is not going to be lost.

In all of this, what remains in place (so far, at least) is the Music Industry as the collection of frameworks and practices referred to previously and, with it, the teeming shoals of musicians seeking audiences and acclaim. Investors in making symbolic goods in music are necessarily driven to make profit from their sale. The investment of capital requires reciprocation from musicians with the investment of emotion. Even so, the needs of profit are satisfied by practices that may conflict fundamentally with the emotional needs of musicians to be recognised and acclaimed. On this basis, how 'the greatest (managerial) challenge of all' is met is, deliberately or not, largely at the expense of musicians' emotional well-being. So it is that, the contradictions of this form of production never truly surface to the point that the industry needs to reorient, or at least modify, its production practices. This is because its primary contradictions (waste and the failure to manage it) are 'reconciled' by being internalised by its key participants. Until the triumph of managerialism, workers confronted the contradictions of the production process by challenging it through industrial action. Musicians are workers too, but their need to behave like businesses, and act as commodities (while thinking of themselves as 'artists') and always against the idiomatic 'clock', means that such actions are unlikely to be taken in this branch of cultural production. The result is that bewilderment, frustration, anger and despair are the predominant emotions when discussing the majority experience of music industry, with the majority of those who have experienced it: the question then is, is this changing under the impact of recent technological, social and political upheaval? This is the subject of the next, and final, chapter.

8
Digitisation and Music Industry

The argument made in the previous chapter was a culmination of those made before it and it consisted of five core elements:

1. Musicians organised as 'acts', seek audiences. Audiences bring recognition and the possibility of acclaim for ability, sensibility and inventiveness, but they also offer the monetary income to sustain the role of a musician.
2. In organising themselves to be 'used' – to be attended to and enjoyed – musicians offer themselves as a text in their totality. The value users find in a music act derives from its textual totality and so involves the music it makes, how its members present themselves together with the ways in which their actions are explained or contextualised.
3. In order to find audiences acts must enter markets. In entering markets, acts seek to form alliances with companies whose expertise lies in music-market entry.
4. While acts and companies have vested interests in market success, these interests are not identical: musicians may want acclaim above other considerations; companies must seek profit and growth regardless of other considerations. Ultimately, there is a defining tension between the two which always problematises the working alliances they form.
5. In preparing them for market-entry, music companies 'add value' to acts. This added value is what converts texts into symbolic goods. To add value to a text involves value adders having access to that text. This 'access' cannot fail to be registered as impacts on the original conception of the text. 'Impacts' need not necessarily be negative and an act might offer the strongest definition of its own work. Even

177

so, neither eventuality is certain; so it is that the value-adding process is usually a fraught one and always tense because musicians, artist managers and music company representatives might conflict with each other, separately and together, over the finished form of the symbolic good.

In making this argument, an undercurrent has been that innovations in technology, while fascinating in their own right, have never fundamentally reconfigured the core inter-dependencies activated through 'music industry' (and misrepresented as the 'Music Industry'). Even so, it is debatable whether any previous period of technological change has been as far-reaching and as transformative as the ongoing impact of digitisation. The question then is whether this particular round of technological change continues to leave the inter-dependencies between musicians, music users, music companies, music and markets relatively undisturbed.

It would not be hyperbole to argue that advanced capitalism is experiencing an industrial revolution and, as Chapter 2 argued, the industrialisation of music is very much an outcome of the first Industrial Revolution. This is not to say that there have not been profound periods of technological innovation since the late 18th and early 19th centuries. Equally, the impact of electronics and petrochemicals in the early part of the 20th century continues to reverberate and, to an extent, much of the reality of the 'digital revolution' could be seen as an extension of this revolution, rather than a new phase in its own right. For example, I type this claim on an electrically powered plastic device; except, of course, this particular 'electrically powered, plastic device' is only made possible by the combination of electronics with binary logic. Machines driven by binary code allow information to be saved, stored and retrieved and always in the form of a perfect copy ready for instant access and transmission. Moreover, it is what constitutes digital 'information' that has been so decisive in registering an array of impacts on culture – the ability not only to digitise analogue originals of all kinds of texts, but to manipulate those digitised originals is what deepens and transforms the impact of digital technologies on expression and communication. In turn, these transformative impacts on culture cannot fail to affect cultural industries and especially music.

Technology and the Music Industry

As Chapter 2 argued, what made the Music Industry a viable one was the legally enforceable right of the originators of texts to be recognised as the only person or persons allowed to make copies of the original work. Commerce in music was facilitated by the creation of companies whose business model was predicated on the buying and exploitation of copyrights – music publishers and record companies bought the rights of songs and recordings from their originators and sold copies of them; venues offering music either as the main source of pleasure or as an enhanced dimension of their offer (radio, films, bars, hairdressers and so on) needed to pay licences and royalties for their use of songs and recordings owned by those companies.

This system was never watertight – once printed or recorded, illegal copies of originals can be made utilising identical reproduction methods. Until the introduction of the Compact Cassette in the mid-1960s, such illegal copying and distribution could be survived by the music publishing and recording industries for the very basic reason that copyists ('bootleggers' as they were called after gangsters who made 'copies' of alcoholic drinks during the Prohibition Era in the USA) required exactly the same physical infrastructure that they themselves required; and physical infrastructure can be traced. Cassette copying was different. It was different because cassettes were legitimately and legally produced by a powerful electronics manufacturer (the Philips company of Holland), which was also one of the major record companies of the day. This was a contradiction in the fundamental sense that a business based on copyright ownership was providing the means for potential copyright infringement. Even so, cassette production was industrially survivable for two main reasons. Firstly, because recording devices cassettes promised to be highly lucrative (by making tape recording cheap and accessible to the 'mass' market) and so worth the risk of supporting. Secondly, as pre-recorded devices for music reproduction they promised to be more profitable than vinyl albums (they could be reproduced *en masse* far more quickly using simple equipment and they cost less in storage and delivery). The problem was, of course, that their capacity to record music cheaply stimulated illegitimate as well as legitimate use of cassettes. More pertinently, they raised the issue of what constituted 'legitimate' use where copyrighted music was concerned.

The music cassette was a pivotal, transitional device for the fundamental reasons that, culturally rather than legally, it gave music users a defining sense of control over, and with it ownership of, music. Additionally, it obviated the need to pay for music and so helped to devalue that music (if it can be recorded effortlessly and cheaply why does it cost so much in the first place?). The introduction of the 'Walkman' by Sony further reinforced and extended the pleasures of cassette copying by adding portability and immersion in a mobile, personal soundtrack to sequencing playlists and sharing them with friends. The record industry eventually fought back (in the form of the campaign 'Home Taping is Killing Music') against a practice that it itself had enabled. Cassette recording could also be argued to be the point at which music users began to question the role and practices of the major record companies; those companies did not seem to be any poorer and neither were prominent musicians noticeably leading less glamorous lives.

As it transpired, this incipient tension between music users and record companies was concealed rather than eradicated by the technological coincidence of the introduction of the Compact Disc during the heyday of the Walkman. The Walkman was first mass-marketed in 1979, the same year that Philips introduced the Compact Disc (CD); Sony had been working on a parallel technology and came to co-operate with Philips on the development of a consumer version. As a result cassettes and CDs co-existed throughout the 1980s and into the 1990s. Quite quickly, the major record companies enjoyed a boom in revenue as large numbers of customers replaced their vinyl collections with CD versions of the same albums which resulted in excessive profit: firstly because when re-releasing CD 'catalogue' albums at full price, production costs were minimal and secondly because this new format was overpriced. Despite these windfall profits, the 'CD boom' would go on to prove something of a pyrrhic victory for the major record companies, because not only could it be argued that their profiteering further eroded customer loyalty, but the intrinsic attractiveness of the CD as a digital medium – binary encoded sound – stimulated and reinforced the appetite for control over recorded sound that the cassette had made possible. Added to that, digitised sound had already 'escaped' the monopoly of the record companies; the combination of continuous innovation and economies of scale meant that, at an accelerating rate through the 1980s, digital instruments (sequencers, drum machines, synthesisers and samplers) came within reach of even 'new entrant' musicians.

With the introduction of Musical Instrument Digital Interface (MIDI) technology and cheap (initially cassette-based) forms of multi-track recording (the first TASCAM Portastudio was released in 1979), musicians were able to take the notion of 'home taping' into realms unanticipated by the 'Home Taping is Killing Music' admonition. In little over a decade, recording lost its (cost-ensured) mystique as an activity that only musicians invested in by major record companies could enjoy. Certainly, in the 1980s 'high-end' recording studios remained viable businesses as issues of acoustics, fidelity and engineering and production expertise continued to limit the reach of 'bedroom' producers.

Equally though, new genres (notably hip-hop and dance music) evolved around this ease of access to digital instruments and their growing commercial success forced record producers, studio owners and, eventually, record companies to rethink their practices. If we 'fast-forward' to and through the coming of the 'worldwide-web', MP3, CD 'ripping', faster and faster modems, file-sharing, social networking, 'user-generated content', broadband, Wi-Fi and smartphones, then it is little wonder that a report into the steep decline of the recording industry published in 2011 by the globally active management consultancy, Bain and Company, could provoke the widely reproduced headline, 'The Death of the Music Industry'.[1] What is notable about this judgement, though, is that John Perry Barlow, co-founder of the Electronic Frontier Foundation, had already declared the 'death of the music industry' in 2000[2] – ahead of most of these developments and well in advance of the recording industry's woes. This is not to argue that Bain and company were late or Barlow was prescient, but to problematise the very idea of 'The Death of the Music Industry'.

The end of music industry?

Clearly, the Music Industry is not dead, partly because it is an entity that does not exist and so cannot die, but more importantly because people and businesses go on paying for symbolic goods in music on a vast scale. In attempting to identify what has changed, and so what this means for music industry, it is worth considering why claims about the death of the Music Industry seem plausible; and also why such claims are often made with relish.

It is still a colloquial practice to make the fortunes of the recording industry stand for those of an undefined Music Industry. On this basis, it is plausible to claim that the Music Industry is dead because the practice of 'file sharing' appears to have made the major record companies the first corporate 'victims' of the internet. This apparent victimhood is evidenced by two main factors: firstly a precipitous decline in sales revenues through the 2000s (in the USA, down from $14 billion in 1999 to $6 billion in 2009)[3]; secondly an equally steep decline in the number of major record companies in the same period. BMG first created a joint venture with Sony in 2004, only to be bought out by Sony in 2008; EMI and Warner Music both face uncertain futures as acquisitions of non-music financial and industrial conglomerates (Citigroup and Access Industries, respectively). The temptation to relate these phenomena and to trace both to file sharing is compelling, but this conclusion needs to be resisted for two reasons. Firstly, because, a decline in revenue notwithstanding, the weaknesses of BMG and EMI as companies were as much a product of corporate decision making in the years surrounding file-sharing as they were an inability to withstand a shrinking market for album sales. Secondly, the weaknesses of major record companies, generally, are traceable to longer-term trends than the sudden on-set of file sharing; however much this may have negatively affected record sales.

To consider this last point, one of the great ironies for the major record companies is that the years of the foundation of their greatest prosperity – the rise of the album – were also the years when the questioning of the role of the record company began to surface. The designation of the rock musician as an 'artist' repositioned the tension between 'art' and 'commerce' within pop music for the first time (arguably, Jazz had been re-designated from 'popular' to a form of 'art' music by this time). The role of rock in 'counter-culture' then intensified the question of why rock music seemed so implicated with big business. The major record companies were alert to this tension and used a range of strategies – for example, advertising in the 'underground' press; creating new, less obviously corporate labels – to offset it. Also, hippies wanted albums and therefore needed to swallow the uncomfortable fact that they were expensive to make. In this, it helped to consider technology as an autonomous force – there could be no excessive 'progressive' rock without excessive expenditure and (for those who cared) the reluctant recognition was that no other entity but major labels could foot the bill.

The coming of punk rock tends to be presented as popular culture's rejection of the idea that only big record companies could make records. Whether this is an accurate representation of punk as a phenomenon is beyond my remit here but certainly the period of its emergence allowed anti-corporatism in music to resurface and to become politically charged through the practice of 'Do it Yourself' (DIY). Despite the fact that the leading punk acts all signed to major record companies, DIY and with it the notion and practice of anti-corporatism, suffused popular music culture and, arguably, remains active there. Record companies, certainly the major ones, never enjoyed brand loyalty; the loyalty of customers was always, however temporarily this might have been in the vast majority of cases, to specific acts and to what they represented as specific pleasures of textual use.

Considered in these terms, the relish with which 'The Death of the Music Industry' is pronounced is driven, in part, by the tenacious anti-corporate strand in popular culture, but it is a relish that is enjoyed indiscriminately, for its popular character rather than for reasons of genuine, material, pro-popular change. Instead, in music-industrial terms, what has truly changed is that the major record companies have lost their monopoly positions in recording and in distribution, as well as the guarantee of their business model based on the certainties of the intellectual property (IP) framework. To an extent all of these deficits are traceable to differing impacts of digitisation on that business model but, again, the internet is not some vengeful, technological *deus ex machina* – it is a technologically informed cultural practice that exists within and against wider social and cultural contexts, even as it reimagines them. On this basis it is cultural change – beginning with attitudes towards the (CD) album but continuing more profoundly to question music use itself – that underscores the instabilities of record companies. Taken as a whole, if we continue to confuse the Music Industry with the practices of the recording industry then defining change appears to have taken place. On the other hand if we remember that music industry is how the original efforts of musicians become realised as symbolic goods then even the dramatically changing fortunes of record companies does not mean necessarily that music industry has been affected in similarly substantial ways.

Continuity and discontinuity

It can be difficult to be precise about when seeds sown in earlier times germinate and their subsequent blooms cross-pollinate as an 'industrial revolution'. Certainly at the beginning of the second decade of the 21st century the music industries look very different than they did in the mid-1990s. 1996 was perhaps the year that now represents the high point of the 'old' system – a time in which, from a UK perspective, Take That, Oasis and the Spice Girls could sell millions of records, undertake world tours and enjoy hits in the USA, but also one that saw the launch of 'Bowienet'. Bowienet was not the first artist website, but it is in both conception and execution that David Bowie was particularly prescient; as he expressed it on the site's launch:

> I wanted to create an environment where not just my fans, but all music fans could be part of a single community where vast archives of music and information could be accessed, views stated and ideas exchanged.

It is the use of 'not just my fans, but all music fans' that is so striking; the anticipation of what the internet would come so quickly to represent for music users – 'vast archives of music and information' – except that Bowienet envisaged this access at a price, and quite a steep one (given that these were 1996 prices):

> For only dlrs 19.95 per month you'll be able to use BowieNet as your Internet service provider (with the first month's fee waived for a limited period). For those who would like to remain with their current internet provider you can access **http://www.davidbowie.com** for only dlrs 5.95 per month

In terms of 'execution', what marked out Bowienet was the digital download release of *Telling Lies* from the album *Earthling*. The three-track download was free to subscribers, it was released three months ahead of its 'official' release by BMG and, of course, it acted as a marketing device for the website, the album, and for Bowie himself, by this time in commercial eclipse. Undoubtedly, the first MP3 download (and a 'free' one at that) made available by a huge star with the co-operation of his record company is a significant moment, a metaphorical 'line in the sand'. But it is not as if all aspects of every constituent of the music-industrial process were instantly transformed as a result; far from it, many of those aspects continue to remain comparatively untransformed, for example:

1. Demand for music remains extremely strong and, consequently, music seems no less ubiquitous than it did before the internet and the permeation of the digital into communication and leisure activities. There are now more uses for music than previously (in ringtones; as support for user-generated content on YouTube; as a distraction while contacting call centres, among them). Live music has undergone a renaissance (if an uneven one), particularly in the form of the willingness of audiences to pay premium prices for some types of live music events. Additionally, the proliferation of television channels, the pervasiveness of gaming, the continued economic health of the film industry and the implication of all of these with marketing and advertising both online and offline has intensified the business-to-business demand for music.
2. As music continues to be in high demand, so musicians keep on offering themselves to potential audiences. Furthermore, the first decade of the 21st century saw the rise of 'reality' music shows that existed by drawing on and reinforcing the institutionalised orthodoxies referred to in the previous chapter. So it is that a handful of

singers – Leona Lewis and Susan Boyle among them – have achieved success by a caricature, but still a compelling caricature, of 'making it'. In this way musicians are encouraged to construct themselves in familiar, pre-digital ways.

3. The laws of Intellectual Property continue to apply, where they can. Online and in terms of file sharing and user-generated web content, IP is recognised more in the breach than in observance but this is not true of business-to-business transactions. Music publishing continues to thrive and new models are contesting older ones. In addition, Apple's iTunes has succeeded in embedding the habit of paying for downloads amongst an impressive percentage of internet users.

4. The major record companies continue as significant concentrations of capital and, as such, are still the force to which emergent acts turn even when they may have achieved market awareness by other routes.

5. Taste making has not disappeared and the media still tend to operate in 'conventional' ways, which means that market entry still involves, but is no longer restricted to, convincing programme producers and magazine editors to alert their audiences, as target markets, to new releases.

6. Musicians still cannot necessarily self-organise, and so remain reliant on alliances with market-entry specialists, although whether in the same ways and with the same consequences remains to be seen.

These continuities are both substantial and important, and their persistence should act as a corrective to proclaiming 'The Death of the Music Industry'. The problem with this corrective, though, is that discontinuities have occurred and developed since circa 1996 and that the idea that the Music Industry is now indeed fundamentally changed remains a persistent and persuasive position. To identify and discuss all of the 'discontinuities' would involve a full-length study in its own right (see, for example, Wikström (2009) for such a study). Consequently, in order to discuss how and to what extent the core interconnections which define music industry have been subject to what is clearly accelerated and defining change, we need to recognise that 'the internet', as 'technology', is not a mysterious and autonomous force like gravity, magnetism or electricity. Digital connectivity has certainly instantiated and enabled change in cultural practices, but what is important to consider is that these changes have occurred within the context of far wider experiences of socio-economic and political change – notably the impact on workforces of Neoliberalism as a political project.

Music industry is 'different' not just because major record companies entered crisis; or because musicians can distribute music as files without recourse to record companies; or because music users can share files and 'generate content' and so find new pleasures in music; it is 'different' because music use is subject to strongly countervailing forces, forces that internet use is not proof against. To discuss the interplay of these forces we need to take each one of the facets of recent 'discontinuity' in turn: the impact of digitisation on musicians, music companies, and music users; followed by the impact of wider political change on the interactions between all three.

Digitisation and musicians

If we focus on the mass of musicians attempting to create and sustain frameworks for active involvement in music, then digitisation has made two primary impacts – on accessible recording technology and on self-management. To begin with recording, the increasing ease of access and use of Digital Audio Work-Stations (DAWs) has been a prevalent feature of music making and recording since the introduction of Pro Tools in 1991. Steinberg's introduction of 'Virtual Studio Technology' into its already successful Cubase digital recording software in 1996 accelerated this take-up. Both Cubase and Avid Pro tools had become 'industry standard' digital recording software before this date but the CD-ROM version of Cubase 3.2 gave musicians 'studio access' without needing to pay studio costs; 'home recording', often to a high-standard, has been the result. Since then, home recording technology has increased in sophistication as well as in accessibility in the dual sense of ease of use and cost. Further, DAWs introduced following Cubase and Pro Tools and, subsequently, Logic Pro could be argued to be more genre-inflected, with Apple's *GarageBand* and Image-Line's *Fruity Loops* favouring, although not exclusively, rock and dance, respectively.

Clearly, there is more to emulating a recording studio than a MacBook Pro and compatible software – ordinary houses and non-dedicated commercial premises rarely come with adequate space for full band recording, particularly in terms of isolation of instruments; they are not designed acoustic spaces and most 'unsigned' musicians cannot afford the standard of microphones and associated 'outboard' equipment that might match the sound of a record made in a costly studio. Nonetheless, DAWs allow pre-production to high standards and so contribute to musicians' control over creative choices and, in intensely competitive arenas, could be argued to contribute also to an increased self-esteem and self-worth; for example, by taking away much of the frustration of not being able to record and develop material and by reducing dependency on external investment to achieve those goals. Furthermore, not all music genres are as dependent as rock music on the recording of live instruments (and not all rock is dependent on high fidelity recording). Additionally, the ability to make and release recordings quickly erases the economic dependency of musicians on record companies as recording companies.

In the UK, grime music, in line with its antecedents in DIY-informed UK dance music, could be argued to be entirely a DAW phenomenon; which, in turn, has had repercussions for the degree of self-management enjoyed by its players. This has given the genre a level of self-sufficiency, but to move beyond the confines of its informal economy involves contracting with 'mainstream' music companies. The dynamics of a scene that is marginal in a variety of often illegitimate senses (a reliance on pirate radio, for example) may not be not the best preparation for such engagement. In a discussion with two of their members, the grime act Roll Deep reflected negatively on their first comparatively brief experience of a major label deal with EMI.

> When we joined the label the MD just wasn't interested, he didn't get us. Then, as soon as the first single got to number 11 he was all over us, he kept saying 'the next one's top three, the next one's top three' but when it only got to 24 he lost interest and they dropped us.

What is instructive here is that Roll Deep as a collective of producers and performers enjoyed status inside the informal economy of grime, but lacked preparation for the formalities of a working alliance with a major record company.

What could be argued to prepare acts for such an engagement – and to bypass some of its defining aspects – is the array of internet services and applications which support musicians' self-organisation. At the time of writing, several hundred such services and applications can be identified. These range from sites offering unsigned acts advice or exposure; sites that offer unsigned acts the opportunity to create profiles of themselves; applications that encourage fanbases to crystallise from 'traffic' to and from profile websites; applications that allow acts to sell music files and merchandise to newly acquired fans; applications for co-ordinating 'content' (video, news and blog posts, as well as music) so that it multiplies opportunities for exposure; sites that allow acts to find gigs and to engage existing and potential fans in the progress of tours or individual gigs; and services that allow acts to track progress, or otherwise, in every aspect of each of these practices.

The usefulness of these resources, individually as well as collectively, is not clear-cut – some are irrelevant; others will quickly become eclipsed; still others are time-consuming and are negatively rewarding: keeping up a blog may not add more users, while neglecting it erodes a sympathetic audience. What is more pertinent is that the energy required to maintain an online profile needs to be balanced with the energy necessary for an offline presence. In this, it is not so much that acts can't keep up online activities when engaged in offline ones – the rise of smartphones eliminated that problem – it is that there is more to management than organisation of effort, vital though this is. As comments in Chapters 3 and 4 indicate, musicians exist in torsion, dragged in different directions by differing aspects of the role of musician; meanwhile artist managers are also torn by competing demands and by competing conceptions of their own role. Together, acts and their managers need to develop coherent strategies for career progress and appropriate and accurate metrics for measuring both; they need to deal with endemic tensions and random contingencies; they need to be able to prioritise and co-ordinate actions and be able to articulate the 'why' and the 'how' of both. If they enjoy the appropriate resources, which, globally, many still do not, all acts can now create music and an online presence quite literally from their bedrooms. If they are inventive they can bring themselves to the attention of investors able to offer them growth and if they are astute they can engage in this growth on something approaching their own terms. To this extent, and as later examples will seek to demonstrate, digitisation has changed music industry, but not transformed it beyond recognition – complete self-sufficiency remains limited in a market economy.

Digitisation and music companies

If we consider the music industries separately from the tribulations of the recording industry, the emerging common sense was that the live performance industry would be the great beneficiary of this change because live performances cannot be replicated. Live performances could also attract additional revenues by streaming coverage of gigs on the internet for payment; where streaming, in turn, would attract sponsorship and advertising revenues. The flaw in this optimistic scenario was that, for 50 years it was record companies that made 'stars', and as declining tour and festival revenues began to demonstrate,[4] without new stars to go and see, music users would be reluctant to pay the escalating costs for tickets. For example, at the time of writing, Live Nation, the behemoth of the live performance industry, continues to struggle.[5] Similarly, music publishing has been able to take advantage of the proliferation of television channels and their advertising. Furthermore, it benefits from the continued strength and appeal of gaming and cinema: publishers supply businesses in both sectors with licensed music 'content'. Here digitisation has been a positive boon, but this happy picture is also not without its blemishes. Both gaming and audio-visual companies refuse to be dictated to – the large games firms, such as Electronic Arts, have enough bargaining power to enforce 'buy-outs' for the use of 'catalogue' tracks rather than consent to pay royalties on sales (Tessler, 2008). Similarly, TV producers are as likely to scour the internet or start-up digital music publishers for the copyrights of unsigned acts as they are to negotiate the costly use of songs and tracks by established acts and writers.

Interestingly, given the reported generally negative impact of music users' online practices on them, record companies are to an extent, discovering advantages in the popularity of social networking. With so many internet users willing to be highly visible in sharing their tastes, record companies are at last learning the value of knowing their customers. Of music industry commentators, it is Scott Cohen who most consistently discusses the flaws of the 'old' record industry model versus the opportunities afforded by a new one, provided that those companies are alert and flexible enough to seize those opportunities and create such a new model. His emphasis is very much on how, before they were forced to take notice of them, record companies had no real interest in their customers – they released an album by an act and, if this was a follow up to a previous one, they expected the people who had been there two years before to still be there and to be eager to buy, even though they had been neglected in the interim. This is the 'push' economy that is in stark contrast with the emergence of the 'pull' economy celebrated by internet activist David Bollier:

A 'pull economy' – the kind that appears to be materializing in online environments – is based on open, flexible production platforms that use networking technologies to orchestrate a broad range of resources. Instead of producing standardized products for mass markets, companies use pull techniques to assemble products in customized ways to serve local or specialized needs, usually in a rapid or on-the-fly process.

> (Bollier, D. On the Commons.org 2 September 2006)

In implicitly subscribing to this view, Cohen's points out that ground-breaking initiatives such as Radiohead's *In Rainbows* and Nine Inch Nails' *Ghosts I – IV* are notable not so much as new business models but because,

> Really what made it special and why those succeeded was because those were two artists that understood that they needed to maintain a relationship with their audience, the business model was irrelevant, any model they did was gonna work.
>
> (At Music Ally, 18' 31")[6]

For Cohen it is a 'relationship', the building of 'community' that counts in selling records, where the heart of such relationships is all about inclusion and inclusiveness; as he argues,

> Every community, and when I say 'community' I mean social net-working like MySpace or Facebook, . . . has two very distinct aspects, the first is for the ability of the audience to get a 'behind the scenes' look, to get information that nobody else has. The second is the abil-ity to impact or influence the outcome of some event. You need those two things in order to have 'community'.
>
> (At Music Ally c. 21' 40" ')

In making this argument he uses the 'reality' TV shows as his paradigm; in them the 'behind the scenes' look is the contrived, sympathy-creating narrativisation of the contestant's lives; the 'influence' over 'the out-come of some event' is the voting process. Similarly, acts and record companies now look for ways of winning and maintaining the atten-tion of fans – from a relentless use of Twitter to provide instant reactions to events great and small, to providing 'stems' so that music users can create their own remixes of tracks they may have bought. Seemingly with 'content' still so central to multimedia pleasures (and inclusion and inclusiveness now replacing exclusion and exclusivity) the fortunes of music companies appear to rest on a trade-off between 'lawlessness' and 'democracy' – customers can be brought back on-side, back within IP frameworks, just so long as record companies are willing to work harder at keeping them happy within those frameworks by making users feel part of the 'creative' process. This can also mean that, as Radiohead and Nine Inch Nails demonstrated, the transition between old and new, push and pull, is realised by making different offers: the uses of symbolic goods are, in part, tied to the ability to access modifications through payment. As Cohen puts it,

> You want to focus on the user…particularly your best users. The Music Industry has essentially had a single model strategy for the last fifty-plus years, if you are a fan of a band you can buy an album, if you are a casual fan you can buy an album, if you want to give someone a gift you can buy an album, it's the identical product with the identical price points with just different content on it. What I've found is that you create stuff for your super-users, they spend a lot more money…If I think of an analogy it would be the travel industry, they don't make one hotel room, all the same price, all the same shape; they recognise that some people want to stay in a five star hotel and…other people want to stay in a youth hostel.
>
> (At Digital Derry.org, c. 1' 10")[7]

Because fans are now making themselves accessible as never before, acts and record companies can monetise fandom in increasingly efficient ways. The increasing ability of record companies to operate online is, so far at least, a case of too little, too late and this in turn affects the practices and fortunes of other 'traditional' types of music companies in the other music industries. The problems of the recording industry run deeper than a turn away from buying CD albums; the success of the recording industry business model was that it was a quintessential 'push model' and the conditions for its 'push' – the willingness, indeed the need, for media companies more widely to collude with it (Hirsch, 1969) – have been both eroded and dramatically reformulated. In considering music users' use of music, it is not so much that the usefulness of music is now unrecognisably different from its pre-1996 condition; it is that industrialised music has always been the core of a more complex symbolic good. Digitisation has enabled the disaggregation of such goods with the result that the pleasure taken in music is now, more explicitly and with more user-effect than ever, not just the pleasure of the text, but pleasure in engagement with the text.

Digitisation and music users

As Chapter 6 argued, from the perspective of music users, the digital music watershed was the generalisation of the Napster peer-to-peer file sharing programme in 1999. In turn, Napster only 'worked', and became the nemesis of the recording industry, because the sudden technological confluence of internet-centred developments (the ease of use of MP3; CD-ROM drives as a standard hardware device in home-PCs; increased modem speeds) allowed an existing cultural propensity to use music to fashion personalised soundtracks and soundscapes, first evident in cassette usage two decades previously, to be reproduced on a vastly wider canvas. The recognition of this new means to satisfy an 'old' desire was capitalised on by Apple's marketing campaign 'Rip, Mix, Burn' in 2001. What does not follow though, despite all the evidence of a huge decline in sales of recorded music is that, as the International Federation of the Phonographic Industries (IFPI) continues to insist, piracy is the main cause of the decline in sales.[8]

The defining issue is that music users can access music that they find satisfying without buying it and this can only problematise historically embedded profit-seeking production routines. The fact that music users can directly access each other and, to a previously unimagined extent, popular music acts means that they have developed expectations about those relations that demand to be fulfilled. It is here that the problems of record companies bear on music industry, because some aspects of change in the nature of music use have come to bear on choices made in the production of symbolic goods – whether specifically or more generally. Several distinct trends can now be identified in various stages of their emergence and consolidation, where the big winners from the perspective of major companies and their most successful acts are the alliances that have found ways to maximise their fortunes in uncertain times.

To begin with the issue of file sharing, it is a diversion to explore IFPI's campaign here, but just the designation 'piracy' conveys the degree of hostility of an industry based on Intellectual Property towards those in breach of its laws. The problem is that the hostile pursuit of file sharers (with the Recording Industry Association of America – RIAA – as the most robust of IFPI's national members) helped to make stronger and more overt what had lurked beneath the surface since the 1970s; namely the belief of music buyers that, once purchased, they owned the music they had bought and were free to do with it what they wanted. In insisting that file sharers were 'criminals' and 'pirates', the major record companies effectively declared war on their customer base which, by any measure, is a reckless course of action, especially since the Apple campaign appeared to legitimise the practices of ripping pre-recorded CDs and moving playlists of them to internet-accessible hard drives so early in the process. Arguably, to thwart music users when they want, expect and believe they have power over recordings is the true rift in relations between record companies and their customers – one which musicians are advised to tread warily around since Metallica did all signed acts so much harm with their own aggressive posturing against the new digital habits of their die hard fans.

The more likely reasons for the fall in sales of recorded music derive from different aspects of the CD album. For example, the internet revealed how overpriced it was (especially on a country-by-country comparison); online sellers could sell albums more cheaply because they did not require the same retail mark-up; personal computer users came to learn how cheap blank CDs were which acted as 'proof' that CDs were overpriced; record companies supported the market saturation of magazine cover-mounted CDs which tended to devalue them as objects; and, eventually, the major retail chains undercut record retailers by making CDs loss-leaders, although this latter development occurred substantially after file sharing became so prevalent. It is against this background that file sharing was the *coup de grâce* of the CD album; not because it represented theft but because, as the term 'file' indicates, what is used is not necessarily the whole album but a track or tracks from one. Digital sales cannot match CD revenues because music users are buying single tracks where once they bought entire albums; at the same time, record companies are persisting with a largely unmodified version of 'traditional' practices, because they have yet to rethink their business model as one of service provision rather than copyright owning.

What made record companies vulnerable at a time of great challenge was associated with how they spent the windfall profits of the CD boom – essentially on marketing budgets that had escalated to a point that almost any album released needed to achieve very high sales indeed to recoup this exorbitant outlay. On this basis, it was not so much illegal file sharing that intensified this vulnerability, but the disaggregation of the album that rapidly eroded the allegiance to the idea of the album and therefore to the practice of buying them – and this at exactly the time when record companies had made themselves 'prisoners' as well as the beneficiaries of huge sales. Moreover, digitisation has amplified and extended the sensation of disaggregation to the level of the text itself, and it is this qualitative leap that means that the old position cannot be recovered.

The rise of DAWs and with them the parallel rise in the production of easily accessible word, still and moving image software has given music users the power to become not just types of musicians, but circulators of texts. This is the significance of the earlier observation that digital files are open to 'manipulation'. For example, where YouTube is concerned 'user-generated content' is now a source of immense pleasure. The cultural industries can only envy from the sidelines the consolidation of this practice; they can also be enraged. For example, Constantin Film continues to attempt to restrict satirical re-edits of its film *Der Untergang* (Downfall). These humorous parodies of a tortured speech by Hitler in his last days are an example of an internet meme. Memes are one of the key phenomena of social networking and user-generated content. They proliferate because to modify already modified materials, and so virally generate them, only requires easily learned skills in video-editing. This low barrier to entry to what is, precisely, cultural production means that the same texts can be adapted continuously in response to social, political and cultural events; a phenomenon that companies would be glad to monopolise, but the days of cultural-industrial monopoly appear to be over, completely. As a result, adaptation seems the only viable strategy for companies in the cultural industries, generally; but with memes and virality only two of its immersive dimensions, the question truly is, 'adaptation to what?'.

The internet is increasingly relocating to tablet computers and smartphones. This intensifies its usability and this, in turn, has intensified the internet as a site of commerce. For example, the sale of 'apps' is now big business as are opportunities for social gaming and the ability for people to assert their tastes and values through social networking services. Strategies of adaptation need to be as fast moving as are these fast evolving practices. The term 'Industries' suggests by the connotative weight of the term that they are not fast moving; but what this study is concerned with is 'industry' in the sense of control over the application of effort. To explore whether and how this is changed and is changing involves considering the wider social contexts within which culture exists and to which culture is a response.

Discontinuity as a way of life

So far, with regard to the impact of digitisation on the recording industry several landmarks and watersheds have been identified such as the introduction of the cassette; the introduction of the Walkman; the introduction of the CD; the introduction of MIDI; the launch of Pro Tools; the launch of Cubase VST; the introduction of Bowienet; the creation and proliferation of Napster; the rise of social networking. All of these are fascinating, both in their own right and in the bearing they have on each other and on music practice, music use and music business. The problem is that, if we write accounts of the Music Industry or music industry in terms only of music-specific developments we fail to see the bigger picture in which these technologies have their different degrees of efficacy and cultural purchase.

If we return to the mass marketing of the Walkman in 1979, this was, in the UK, also the year of the election of a Conservative administration with Margaret Thatcher as Prime Minister. Thatcher was a radical conservative in the sense that her policies were informed by the economic theories of Milton Friedman and Friedrich Von Hayek. Friedman was an advisor to Ronald Reagan who became US President in 1981. Between them, Thatcher and Reagan, after Friedman and Von Hayek, oversaw the onset of government policies informed by 'Monetarism'. Monetarism was an attractive economic theory for enthusiasts of capitalism because the formerly dominant theory, Keynesianism, seemed unable to address what had become intractable problems in the UK and US economies during the 1970s, notably rising unemployment and inflation. The additional dimensions of Monetarism had a significant impact on social and cultural life: the 'cure' for these economic ills was not restricted to economic policies, but became part of a wider political project for which Thatcher and Reagan became figureheads. This project is identified as 'Neoliberalism' and its practice and ideology hinges on repealing national laws that its adherents believe limit or frustrate the operation of global 'free markets'.

Discussing whether Neoliberalism is a 'good' or 'bad' system or ideology is beyond the remit of this study, but what its onset can be argued to signal was the ending of commitments made to some of the worst affected populations of countries involved in the Second World War. These commitments in the UK especially to welfare provision and to full employment have been identified as limitations on free markets and have, where feasible and in different ways, been replaced by policies that emphasise individual self-responsibility for the conditions of life: housing, and provision for health, education, employment, pensions and insurance. At the same time policies of 'deregulation' have allowed capital to 'migrate' with the result that much employment has been transferred to countries in which wages are lower, employment laws less rigorous and where 'tax breaks' exist for investors. These processes have combined to create new work and new workforces in the 'Western' economies, especially in those sectors that had once relied on 'mass' workforces in primary and secondary industries.

Characterised as a 'Precarity' by Hardt and Negri (2001) what were formerly mass workforces have been forced to adapt to lives shorn of collective resources and replaced by individual uncertainty. The effect of this has, in Sennett's words,

> left many people's lives in a fragmented state; the places they work more resembling train stations than villages, as family life is disoriented by the demands of work.
>
> (Sennett, 1998, p. 26)

This 'fragmented state' of people's lives can only produce a demand for cultural materials that help to make sense of, and, more importantly, help in surviving this way of life. Fragmentation and disintegration are fundamentally unsettling conditions, and it can be argued that there is an innate impulsion to reverse these conditions and to reclaim a sense of affiliation. It follows that if older cultural forms are not adequate to the task, then this work will be done by creating new ones. The first problem that arises is that older cultural forms are inscribed by commercial imperatives and practices: in our case, making and selling albums. It is against this background that the internet exerts an appeal: digital 'connectivity' allows individuals the opportunity to pursue places, identities, roles and all of their associated meanings in virtual communities. The second complicating factor is that virtual communities will be experienced differently from work- and location-based ones because they have, and so reflect, different material conditions of existence. Moreover, as Scott Cohen has been shown to argue, they too can be exploited for commercial purposes. Therefore, when we discuss online communities we must see them as collectives of disparate individuals who will be differentiated in their offline lives by the 'countervailing forces' referred to previously. These countervailing forces are the ones that recompose the workforce and the lives of the majority populations of the heartlands of 'the West', and through this process, force individuals to seek solutions to crises that are crises not just in terms of employment, but in terms of personal ontology.

Life and lifestyle

One of the great ironies about rock music was that it explicitly celebrated music's ability to express a set of values. The 'counter cultural' values condensed in the exhortation 'turn on, tune in, drop out' revolved around a rejection of the values of 'straight society' and echoed earlier but far less generalised precedents in various phases of 'Bohemianism'. What gave the counter-culture its social power was the high social visibility of its advocates and the apparent threat to social order in their advocacy of free love, communal living, a rejection of 'consumerism', and the taking of psychedelic drugs to provoke mystical experiences. As the most visible members of the counter-culture were the new 'rock stars', rock music became, briefly and incoherently, the soundtrack of the 'alternative lifestyle'. That this initial episode was both under- and over-cooked both by participants and by sections of the media is not the issue; rather the issue is that during the brief life of the counter-culture several 'genies' escaped from several 'bottles' and they have never returned.

The first of these 'genies' was the commercial realisation that, if rock was a soundtrack for an 'alternative lifestyle', then different music genres could be the soundtracks of different lifestyles. In the early 1970s, product endorsement; commercial tour sponsorship; and the appearance of rock and pop stars in adverts were some way in the future, although the Rolling Stones had advertised Rice Krispies years before. The coming of rock decisively fractured the notion of pop as a single, mass, teenage market and marketing and advertising agencies were alert to this sea-change. Additionally, the strong allegiance that young people involved in the counter-culture movement showed not just to rock bands, but an incoherent set of alternative values, indicated that record companies would need to factor value-sets into the records they made and therefore into the acts they signed. Symbolic goods are commodities, and no commodity will be produced without its producers being able to answer fundamental questions about the market for such commodities – 'who will buy?'; 'why?'; 'what is the competition?'; 'how can we defeat the competition?'. These are the questions that tend to be subsumed by the emphasis on the need for 'great songs' discussed in the previous chapter; and also the source of the reliance on tacit knowledge in the Music Industry also discussed there. As it is, anyone who answers these questions plausibly, and with some occasional good results, becomes a leading figure in 'the Industry'. This is why entrepreneurialism continues to inflect cultural production, and why the potent combination of the rise of digitisation during the time of Neoliberalism represents one of the most extreme challenges to entrepreneurialism in the production of symbolic goods in music so far experienced. To understand how this challenge is being met and in order to gauge its consequences for music industry we need to revisit the watershed year of 1996.

The mid-90s in the USA were also years in which a range of albums sold in huge quantities, including ones by Alanis Morrisette, Hootie and the Blowfish, and Celine Dion, but 1996 is also notable because this was the year in which Tupac Shakur was murdered. He died while his album *All Eyez on Me* was also selling in enormous quantities (nine times platinum). The, apparently retaliatory, murder of his rival The Notorious B.I.G in March 1997 could be seen as a point of transition in the popular cultural consolidation of hip-hop, together with R&B, as an industrial form in the sense that the energies of its leading figures and their respective record labels were diverted from murderous rivalries into the expansion of business empires. Following the lead of Russell Simmons some years before, Sean Combs (P. Diddy/Diddy) and Shawn Carter (Jay-Z) both progressed as record company owners and, more significantly, as entrepreneurs more generally. While the careers of all three men are not identical, the diversification and capitalisation, of music 'profile' into non-music goods and services – clothing, restaurants, drinks and toiletries among them – has been made possible by the profound industrial-cultural change encapsulated in, but not fully explainable by, the phenomenon of 'branding'.

As Naomi Klein demonstrated in *No Logo*, the rise of branding was a beneficiary of Neoliberalist deregulation in the sense that the phenomenon of 'Globalisation', as a term given to the effects of relaxing capital flows and restrictions on terms and conditions of employment, encouraged the previously discussed 'migration' of jobs. This strategy was not driven simply by the pursuit of cost-reduction; nor even by a desire to reassert control over labour; it was more that companies had begun to realise that what they sold was, in Klein's words, 'not a product but a way of life, an attitude, a set of values, a look, an idea' (2001, p. 23). Many major companies in 'the West' relocated physical production to cheaper regions in order to concentrate on enhancing what Lash and Lury refer to as the 'sign value' (2007, p. 7) of their goods or services; the paradox resulting from this process was that companies sold 'lifestyle' products to the very people whose jobs were lost to relocation. It is reasonable to argue that the response to feelings of 'disintegration' is to seek forms of reintegration, therefore in buying such consumer goods, the precarious workforce seeks the restoration of community as members of a logo's community, with all of the 'values' and sense of 'attitude' its brand has been marketed to convey. The steps back from here to music are both well marked, and treacherous.

What is at stake in music's relationship to 'lifestyle' is represented in two opposed tendencies – one towards democracy and collectivity (the internet as a means for freedom of expression; music as a source of asserting alternative values); the other towards compliance and conformity with capitalism (the internet and music as vehicles for marketing commodities and, so, for maintaining the commodity system). Consider this pronouncement from the UK's primary 'specialist music marketing agency' (Frukt, 2010, p. 5)

> Smirnoff's URthenight pulls of (an) interactive trick, positioning a Facebook group as the very creative hub of its series of music/club nights and inviting consumers to dictate how the events take shape. So many efforts at online engagement feel like 'tagged on' afterthoughts, but this is a consummate lesson in making your digital platform feel like the heartbeat of your activity. Moreover, correct in its realization that people aren't always just super-interactive for the sake of it, consumers are clearly and appropriately incentivized for their participation.
>
> (2010, p. 16)

The tension between 'alternative' and 'conformist' is captured here in the use of this example of a digital campaign as a 'best practice case study' by a marketing company. What counts for them is that Smirnoff's own marketers pulled off a 'trick'. The trick is to create participation – where Cohen's formula of the combination of community with an ability 'to impact or influence the outcome of some event' (Cohen, 2008) is the incentive for participation and, vitally, brand-identification. But clearly this influence is trivial; consumers are not allowed access to the architecture of their consumption, only to its momentary decoration. In this the strength, but also the weakness of the 'new position' of consumers is revealed: they (or a majority of them) access the internet and because they do they may not be attending to pre-digital forms of advertising, hence their attention must be won by companies. To this extent, to use a very old-fashioned phrase, consumers are 'sovereign' and must therefore be treated with respect, but it is the obverse here that produces results for companies. If consumers are 'on the internet' and mostly 'on Facebook' companies know where they are, know who they are and can figure out ways to involve them in marketing strategies towards brand identification and the loyal purchasing patterns this can produce.

New contradictory states define music use; because they are no longer concentrated at the end of media-channels, the attention of music users is now at a premium and companies that profit from trade in symbolic goods in music must work to attract this attention if they are to stand any chance of it being monetised. Attracting and maintaining attention means conceding that activities and types of access to acts and texts that were formerly deemed unacceptable are now either positively encouraged or no longer actively discouraged. Music users, whether legitimately or illegitimately, now access the whole of the text that is the heart of the symbolic good – they manipulate recorded sound as tracks for their YouTube and blog posts; they produce 'mash-ups'. Moreover, they expect, and are allowed, 'access' to their favourite acts, from 'tweets' before, during and after concerts to an expectation of constant maintenance of blogs, including an allowance for interaction; opportunities to remix tracks; decide on album track listings; decide on single releases; enjoy backstage visits; and receive personalised releases of albums and allied merchandise at premium prices. All of this means that acts must embrace the commercial practices their supporters define themselves through; they can no longer take 'sabbaticals'; they can no longer disappear, sometimes for years, into expensive studios and be out of contact for all that time save for the occasional, carefully manicured press 'exclusive'. Under current conditions, to be out of sight is to be out of mind; while to be 'in sight' can involve being in the sight created for music by a branded good. Driven by these currents and considerations, the adaptation to new realities, referred to previously, is taking on a discernible form as 'music industry'.

From B-boy to Bieber

One of the key dimensions to the emergence of hip-hop culture was its sheer marginality. As authors such as Rose (1994), Forman (2002) and George (2005) discuss, the major record companies, together with the wider Music Industry, were resistant to the new cultural form. Consequently, as with music hall in the 19th century, music entrepreneurs led the way in hip-hop's irresistible penetration of popular culture. Where hip-hop, in the USA, and dance music, in the UK, were concerned, demand was met in informal economies (block parties and illegal raves, respectively). Quite rapidly, through entrepreneurial initiatives, these informal economies spawned more-or-less familiar forms of music industry and became formalised, standardised and institutionalised in the way that Music Hall did over a century previously. In the routinisation of the new genres, the existing music-industrial structures were modified by the ways new entrants did their business but, in turn, those new entrants experienced reciprocal modification.

Certainly, this is true of Def Jam Recordings. Founded by Rick Rubin and Russell Simmons in 1984, Def Jam was eventually sold to Universal Music Group in 1998, but long before this, notably through his *Phat Farm* clothing company, Simmons had demonstrated that the 'unmet demand' in hip-hop extended beyond music. The symbolic goods in music produced by Def Jam and other, at first marginal labels such as Death Row Records, Bad Boy and Roc-a-Fella, stimulated the accumulation and realisation of vast new stores of symbolic capital. The cultural impact of hip-hop helped to drive a wider resurgence of black popular music in the USA with Antonio (L.A.) Reid as the key entrepreneur of R&B. Between them, hip-hop and R&B acts enjoyed enormous and increasing prosperity throughout the 1990s, and so it comes as no surprise that it is this sector of the recording industry that has adapted most quickly to the changes wrought both by Neoliberalism and by digitisation – they remained the most entrepreneurial sector and in many ways had most to lose.

At the time of writing, Beyoncé Knowles represents the strongest, but by far certainly not the sole, example of a popular music act as a brand. She is at the centre of a spider web of branded goods, product endorsements, collaborations and film roles. Again, it is Madonna who represents the template, but the contribution of Russell Simmons was to develop brand logic into commodities that could extend the original brand in a sympathetic way. Popular music success now consists of three main components:

1. Selling what you can; capitalising as widely and as quickly as possible, but never too crudely. This latter point was the lesson of the Spice Girls break-up.
2. Never stop working; never be out of the spotlight. Beyoncé's four studio albums have been released with 'orthodox' time delays between them (2003/6/8/11) but these have been supplemented by four further live albums in the 'gaps' together with a remix album; two extended plays; and 25 singles in her own name and 17 further collaborations. The ever busy Beyoncé, if not in the throes of releasing and touring an album or releasing her own singles, is appearing on singles by 'credible' others – among them Jay-Z, Justin Timberlake, Usher, Alicia Keys and Lady Gaga.

The third dimension is the latest addition to the panoply and is pioneered by Scott Braun, manager of Justin Bieber, the biggest star, so far, to be associated with (rather than an outright product of) social networking. In being jointly interviewed with Troy Carter, Lady Gaga's manager, Braun first outlined how he sees the role of the artist manager,

> Your strategy is to help continue to grow your brand and then look at the opportunities for how your brand can grow other businesses that can sustain as their own brand.
>
> (Braun, YouTube c. 2'.30")[9]

He then went on to argue that social networking platforms, while hugely influential and highly lucrative, are not static. As the rise and fall of MySpace demonstrates so starkly, no web platform is unassailable; there is constant innovation in software and hardware – to the extent that, with the rise of applications on tablet computers, PCs and smartphones, leading internet analyst Chris Anderson declared worldwide web 'dead' in 2010.[10] Braun identified that what he is on the lookout for is what will replace Facebook, Twitter, YouTube and the other internet giants, for the reason that:

> The power our artists have created for themselves on Facebook, on Twitter, on Youtube are very, very valuable for launching these new platforms. (We are responsible for) more than (sixty percent) of the traffic on Vevo…these are all platforms on which people are making lots of money and we're responsible for it and we're not participating.
>
> (Braun, YouTube c. 3'.49")[11]

Braun's point is a vital one to understand; what he is suggesting is that, because successful acts drive traffic on internet platforms, they should participate in the earnings enjoyed by those platforms and, moreover, not in the form of royalties, but in the form of equity. Considered in this way, the third component of prospering in changing contexts is to own the means of change. Ultimately, as Braun has realised, with conventional record sales and revenues declining, the 'real' money is in owning part or all of the platforms that users access to seek out not just individual symbolic goods, but the symbolic capital they represent and activate.

Conclusion

Digitisation in and of itself has had a profound effect on music making and music use; consequently it has impacted on music companies, notably and especially those that make up the recording industry. Even so, the effects of digitisation must be seen in the wider context of social change with which it has coincided. Digitisation has registered its greatest impact on the recording industry and because the recording industry has been central to the music industries for five decades, unsurprisingly the severe instability of major record companies has had, and is continuing to have, reverberations throughout the Music Industry as a whole. Music and musicians continue to provide the texts that are transformed into symbolic goods by largely entrepreneurial practices, although these are always subject to forces of consolidation and standardisation. Inside this, the internet is something of a battle ground between contending social processes. This contention can be seen in the internet's equivalent propensity to support DIY efforts in music making and in music industry, while simultaneously offering significant opportunities to commercialise social networking and other internet-driven pleasures.

In these powerful and contradictory contexts, music industry needs to negotiate conflicting forces. In this negotiation, two 'continuities' persist above all others: there is a constant surplus of musicians and 'nobody knows' which symbolic goods will be market successes. If we live in 'fragmented' times then these are represented by market fragmentation in symbolic goods. There is a very definite and seemingly robust 'pop' mainstream in which the industry of Beyoncé, Pink, Kanye West, Jay-Z and Rihanna and their contemporaries thrives. In essence, their music is a soundtrack to a desperate aspiration towards a 'safe', fulfilling and exciting celebrity lifestyle as a solution to the loss of certainties in life itself. Many other niches now co-exist with mainstream pop, all of which involve musicians striving to be heard, to be noticed, and to be taken seriously. Among these, many involve the 'old' ways of record companies. The internet means that no one need wait to hear or hear about music and musicians. This access to what had always been an anonymous mass of aspirant musicians' over-supply is having the effect of recasting the 'nobody knows' element that so much of the business strategy of cultural production has always rested on, but not in a way that necessarily favours acts or favours musicians.

Reference to 'nobody knows' has been made persistently throughout this book because it defines so much about cultural production. The Music Industry has always been subject to the impacts of technology; long before the CD, the internet and 'apps' there was electronic recording, broadcast, 'talking pictures', television, tape recording, vinyl, transistors and multi-track recording. Yet, in the wake of all of these impacts, there remained music companies creating contractual relationships with musicians aimed at satisfying demand for music, always in ways that involved those musicians ceding a proportion of the revenue they accrued, and a proportion of their control over the texts they created to those companies, on the basis that companies could argue their monopoly of skill, expertise and knowledge. This 'expertise' was always based on the 'track record', of the company or of individuals in the company, who somehow 'knew' when 'nobody knows'. But in a digital world where I can write music, record simultaneously as I write, and circulate to 'the world' the instant I am finished, just so long as I have created a presence through channels and amongst communities receptive to my actions, much of that acclaim and recognition that musicians seek can be mine within moments and, allowing for time zone differences, within hours. This 'changes the game'; but what it doesn't change is that I am unable to monetise this cultural production; what doesn't change is that I am unable to make headway offline.

Today music companies, now joined by companies who are used to dealing in the symbolic dimensions of goods of other kinds, still have a role to play in securing the market entry of acts and in sustaining their market success should this be brought about; but now those companies expect to earn from all, from 360°, of the musician's efforts. Digitisation has brought 'democracy', but it has brought with it its obverse, autocracy. Music industry is still a field of, and a battle for, power – the power to decide who controls effort and who decides what efforts are appropriate to market success. Until musicians are in complete control of their effort, they will still need to contract with specialists in market entry; and even if musicians control market entry as well as controlling music, they will still be involved in industry because their efforts are focused on market success rather than expression in and for itself. Music industry is inescapable; that is why, even as so much changes, it is essential that it continue to be understood in all its fascinating detail and in all its continuing complexity.

Notes

1   Music and Industry

1. As reported by the director, John Landis, 29 April 2008, available at today.msnbc.msn.com.
2. 'Nobody knows' is an essential concept in this study. As work by Caves is a book-length study in which the concept is prominent I will attribute its use to him.

2   Industry and Music

1. Compare and contrast the work of authors such as Florida with the baleful statements of IFPI.
2. This is contested by Peter Bailey who cites his own PhD work as the source for this insight.
3. Bailey (1978); Kift (1996).
4. See Fabbri (1981) at www.tagg.org/others/ffabbri81a.htm.
5. Schumpeter (1949).

3   Musicians in Four Dimensions

1. In Making Popular Music (2000). Toynbee's argument is a rich one and deserves more substantial engagement than can be offered here.

4   Artist Managers

1. Perrone, Pierre 20 May 1999 at http://www.independent.co.uk/arts-entertainment/obituary-rob-gretton-1094674.html.
2. Perrone, Pierre 20 May 1999 at http://www.independent.co.uk/arts-entertainment/obituary-rob-gretton-1094674.html.

5   Music Companies and Music Industry

1. See references to Straw and others.
2. Music Week Directory, UBM Information Ltd London.

8   Digitisation and Music Industry

1. At Business Insider, www.businessinsider.com.
2. At www.spack.org/words/napster.html.

3. At money.cnn.com who were quoting a report by Forester Research money.cnn.com/2010/02/02/news/companies/Napster_music_industry/ (accessed 3 October 2011).

4. See, for example, Cochrane, G. (2011) 'Music Festivals Struggling Due To "Overcrowded" Market. IBBC News (online) at www.bbc.co.uk/newsbeat/ 14446562 (accessed 3 October 2011).

5. See, for example, 'It's a rough road for Live Nation' at www.upi.com/ Business_News/2010/06/21/Its-a-rough-road-for-Live-Nation/UPI-400612771 38441/.

6. http://musically.com/blog/2008/11/19/video-qa-with-the-orchard-founder-scott-cohen/.

7. http://digitalderry.org/big-thinking/scott-cohen-from-the-orchard-talks-about-making-music-pay/ (accessed 3 October 2011).

8. http://www.ifpi.org/content/section_resources/dmr2011.html.

9. http://www.youtube.com/watch?v= r-mGQZPk2-U.

10. The Web is Dead, Long Live the Internet, Anderson, C & Wolff, M. http:// www.wired.com/magazine/2010/08/ff_webrip/all/1.

11. http://www.youtube.com/watch?v= r-mGQZPk2-U.

Bibliography

Adorno, T. & Horkheimer, M. (1977/1944) 'The Culture Industry: Enlightenment as Mass Deception', in Curran, J., Gurevitch, M., and Wollacott, J. (eds), *Mass Communication and Society* (London: Edward Arnold), pp. 349–83.

Adorno, T. (1990) 'On Popular Music', in Frith, S. and Goodwin, A. (eds), *On Record: Rock, Pop and the Written Word* (London: Routledge), pp. 301–14.

Anderson, C. & Wolff, M. (2010) 'The Web is Dead, Long Live the Internet' 17 August 2010 http://www.wired.com/magazine/2010/08/ff_webrip/all/1 (accessed 3 October 2010).

Attali J. (1985) *Noise: The Political Economy of Music* (Manchester: Manchester University Press).

Bagehot, R. & Kanaar, N. (1998) *Music Business Agreements* (London: Sweet & Maxwell).

Bailey, P. (1978) *Leisure and Class in Victorian England: Rational Recreation and the Contest for Control* (London: Methuen).

——(1994) 'Conspiracies of Meaning: Music Hall and the Knowingness of Popular Culture', *Past and Present* 144: 138–70.

Banks, M. (2007) *The Politics of Cultural Work* (Basingstoke: Palgrave Macmillan).

Barfe, L. (2004) *Where Have All the Good Times Gone? The Rise and Fall of the Record Industry* (London: Atlantic Books).

Barlow, J. (2000) 'Napster.com and the Death of the Music Industry', 12 May 2000, at www.spack.org/words/napster.html (accessed 3 October, 2011).

Barna, E. (2011) *Online and Offline Rock Music Networks: A Case Study on Liverpool, 2007–2009*, unpublished PhD thesis, University of Liverpool, UK.

Barnard, S. (1989) *On the Radio: Music Radio in Britain* (Milton Keynes: Open University Press).

Bayton, M. (1998) *Frock Rock* (Oxford: Oxford University Press).

Becker, H. (1963) *Outsiders: Studies in the Sociology of Deviance* (New York: The Free Press).

Becker, H. S. (1982) *Art Worlds* (Berkeley, CA: University of California Press).

Bennett, A., Shank, B. & Toynbee, J. (eds) (2006) *The Popular Music Studies Reader* (London: Routledge).

Bilton, C. (2006) *Management and Creativity: From Creative Industries to Creative Management* (Oxford: Wiley-Blackwell).

Blanning, T. (2008) *The Triumph of Music: Composers, Musicians and their Audiences, 1700 to the Present* (London: Penguin).

Bourdieu, P. (1984) *Distinction* (Cambridge, MA: Harvard University Press).

——(1993) *The Field of Cultural Production* (Cambridge, Polity Press).

Burkart, P. (2005) 'Loose Integration in the Popular Music Industry', *Popular Music & Society* 28(4): 489–500.

Burnett, R. (1996) *The Global Jukebox: The International Music Industry* (London: Routledge).

Business Insider, www.business.com/these-charts-explain-the-real-death-of-the-music-industry-2011-12 11 February 2011 (accessed 3 October 2011).

Caves, R.E. (2000) *Creative Industries* (Cambridge, MA: Harvard University Press).

Cavanagh, D. (2000) *The Creation Records Story: My Magpie Eyes are Hungry for the Prize* (London: Virgin Books).

Chambers, I. (1985) *Urban Rhythms: Pop Music and Popular Culture* (New York: St. Martin's Press).

Chanan, M. (1995) *Repeated Takes: A Short History of the Recording Industry and its Effects on Music* (London: Verso Books).

Chapple, S. & Garofalo, R. (1978) *Rock 'N' Roll Is Here To Pay: The History and Politics of the Music Industry* (Chicago, IL: Nelson-Hall Company).

Cloonan, M. (2007) *Popular Music and the State in the UK* (Aldershot: Ashgate Publishing).

Cochrane, G. (2011) 'Music Festivals Struggling Due To "Overcrowded" Market'. IBBC News (online) at www.bbc.co.uk/newsbeat/14446562 (accessed 3 October 2011).

Cohen, S. (1991) *Rock Culture in Liverpool: Popular Music in the Making* (Oxford: Oxford University Press).

——(1993) 'Ethnography and Popular Music Studies', *Popular Music* 12(2): 123–38.

——(2008) 'Video Q&A with The Orchard founder Scott Cohen'. Music Ally at http://musically.com/2008/11/19/video-qa-with-the-orchard-founder-scott-cohen (accessed 3 October 2011).

Currid, E. (2007) *The Warhol Economy: How Fashion, Art & Music Drive New York City* (Princeton and Oxford: The Princeton University Press).

Davis, H. & Scase, R. (2000) *Managing Creativity: The Dynamics of Work and Organization* (Buckingham: Open University Press).

Denisoff, R.S. (1986) *Tarnished Gold: The Record Industry Revisited* (New Brunswick, NJ: Transaction Books).

DiMaggio, P. & Hirsch, P. (July/August 1976) 'Production Organizations in the Arts', *American Behavioral Scientist*, 19(6): 735–52.

Du Gay, P. & Negus, K. (1994) 'The Changing Sites of Sound: Music Retailing and the Composition of Consumers', *Media, Culture and Society* 16: 395–413.

Du Gay, P. & Pryke, M. (eds) (2002) *Cultural Economy: an Introduction* (London: Sage).

Dyer, R. (1998) *Stars* (London: BFI).

Fabbri, F. (1981) A Theory of Musical Genres: Two Applications. At www.tagg.org.

Finnegan, R. (1989) *The Hidden Musicians: Making Music in an English Town* (Cambridge: Cambridge University Press).

Fiske, J. (1992) 'The Cultural Economy of Fandom', in Lewis, L.A. (ed.), *The Adoring Audience* (London: Routledge), pp. 30–49.

Florida, R. (2010) *The Great Reset* (London: HarperCollins Business).

Forman, M. (2002) *The 'hood Comes First: Race, Space and Place in Rap and Hip Hop* (Middletown, CO: Wesleyan University Press).

Frith, S. (1983) *Sound Effects: Youth, Leisure, and the Politics of Rock 'n' Roll* (London: Constable).

——(ed.) (1987) *The Industrialization of Popular Music* (London: Sage Publications Ltd).

——(1996) *Performing Rites: on the Value of Popular Music* (Oxford: Oxford University Press).

——(2000) 'Music Industry Research: Where Now? Where Next? Notes From Britain', *Popular Music* 19(3): 387–93.

——(ed.) (2001) *The Cambridge Companion to Pop and Rock* (Cambridge: Cambridge University Press).

Frith, S. & Marshall, L. (eds) (2004) *Music and Copyright* (Edinburgh: Edinburgh University Press).

Frith, S., et al. (eds) (1993) *Rock and Popular Music: Politics, Policies, Institutions (Culture: Policy and Politics)* (London: Routledge).

Frukt Music Intelligence (2010) *Brands & Music Manifesto* (no details). www.fruktmusic.com.

Gabriel, Y. (2008) *Organizing Words: A Critical Thesaurus for Social and Organization Studies* (Oxford: Oxford University Press).

Garfield, S. (1986) *Expensive Habits: The Dark Side of the Music Industry* (London: Faber and Faber).

Garnham, N. (1990) *Capitalism and Communication* (London: Sage Publications Ltd).

Garratt, S. (1998) *Adventures in Wonderland – A Decade of Club Culture* (London: Headline Book Publishing).

George, N. (2005) *Hip Hop America* (London: Penguin).

Gillett, C. (1970/1983) *The Sound of the City: The Rise of Rock and Roll* (New York: Pantheon Books).

Greenfield, S. & Osborn, G. (2007) 'Understanding Commercial Music Contracts', *Journal of Contract Law* 23: 248–68.

Gretton, R. (2008) *1 Top Class Manager* (Manchester: Anti-Archivists).

Gronow, P. (1998) *An International History of the Recording Industry* (London: Cassell Academic).

Hardt, M. & Negri, A. (2001) *Empire* (Boston, MA & London: Harvard University Press).

Harron, M. (1988) 'McRock: Pop as Commodity', in Frith, S. (ed.), *Facing the Music: Essays on Pop, Rock and Culture* (London: Mandarin), pp. 173–220.

Hennion, A. (1992) 'The Production of Success: An Antimusicology of the Pop Song', in Frith, S. and Goodwin, A. (eds), *On Record: Rock Pop and the Written Word* (New York: Pantheon), pp. 185–206.

Hesmondhalgh, D. (1996) 'Post-Fordism, Flexibility and the Music Industries', *Media, Culture and Society* 18(3): 468–88.

——(2002) *The Cultural Industries* (London: Sage Publications Ltd).

——(2007) *The Cultural Industries*, 2nd ed. (London: Sage Publications Ltd).

Hesmondhalgh, D. & Baker, S. (2011) *Creative Labour: Media Work in Three Cultural Industries* (London: Routledge).

Hesmondhalgh, D. & Negus, K. (eds) (2002) *Popular Music Studies* (London: Hodder Arnold).

Hirsch, P. (1992) 'Processing Fads and Fashions: An Organisation Set Analysis of Cultural Industry Systems', in Frith, S. and Goodwin, A. (eds), *On Record: Rock Pop and the Written Word* (New York: Pantheon), pp. 127–39.

Hirsch, P.M. (1969) *The Structure of the Popular Music Industry: The Filtering Process by Which Records Are Preselected for Public Consumption* (Ann Arbor, MI: University of Michigan Press).

Horner, B & Swiss, T. (eds) (1999) *Key Terms in Popular Music and Culture* (London: Wiley-Blackwell).

IFPI Digital Music Report (2011) www.ifpi.org/content/section resources/dmr2011.html (accessed 3 October 2011).

Island Records: Music College interviews, DVD, unnumbered, Island Records, Island 50, 1959–2009: Marketing.

Jones, E. (1998) *This is Pop: The Life and Times of a Failed Rock Star* (Edinburgh: Canongate Books).

Jones, G. (1985) 'The Gramophone Company: An Anglo-American Multinational, 1898–1931', *The Business History Review* 59 (1), Spring: 76–100.

Jones, M. (1997) *Organising Pop: Why So Few Pop Acts Make Pop Music*, Ph.D Thesis, University of Liverpool.

——(1999) 'Changing Slides – Labour's Music Industry Policy Under the Microscope', *Critical Quarterly* 41(1): 22–31.

Jones, S. (1992) *Rock Formation: Music, Technology, and Mass Communication* (London: Sage Publications Ltd).

Justin Bieber & Lady Gaga's managers speak on the internet http://www.youtube.com/watch?v=r-mGQZPk2-U (accessed 3 October 2011).

Keat, R. & Abercrombie, N. (eds) (1991) *Enterprise Culture* (London: Routledge).

Kift, D. (1996) *The Victorian Music Hall: Culture, Class and Conflict* (Cambridge/New York: Cambridge University Press).

Kirschner, T. (1998) 'Studying Rock: Towards a Materialist Ethnography', in Swiss, T., Sloop, J. and Herman, A. (eds), *Mapping The Beat: Popular Music and Contemporary Theory* (Oxford: Wiley-Blackwell), pp. 247–68.

Klein, N. (2001) *No Logo: No Space No Choice No Jobs* (London: Flamingo).

Kusek, D. & Leonard, G. (2005) *The Future of Music: Manifesto for the Digital Music Revolution* (Boston, MA: Omnibus Press).

Laing, D. (1985) *One Chord Wonders: Power and Meaning in Punk Rock* (Milton Keynes: Open University Press).

Lash, S. & Urry, J. (1994) *Economies of Signs and Space* (London: Sage Publications Ltd).

Lash, S. & Lury, C. (2007) *Global Culture Industry* (Cambridge: Polity Press).

Lee, S. (1995) 'Re-Examining the Concept of the "Independent" Record Company: The Case of Wax Trax! Records', *Popular Music* 14(1): 13–31.

Leonard, M. (2007) *Gender and the Music Industry* (Aldershot: Ashgate Publishing).

Leyshon, A. (2001) 'Time-Space (and Digital) Compression: Software Formats, Musical Networks and the Reorganisation of the Music Industry', *Environment and Planning* 33(1): 49–78.

Leyshon, A., Webb, P., French, S., Thrift, N., & Crewe, L. (2005) 'On the Reproduction of the Musical Economy After the Internet', *Media, Culture & Society* 27(2): 177–209.

Loudon, E. (2010) *Performing the Popular: The Context, Composition and Creation of Liverpool Music Hall*. Unpublished PhD thesis, University of Liverpool, UK.

Mankowitz, W. (1960) *Expresso Bongo* (London: Ace Books).

Middles, M. (1996) *From Joy Division to New Order: The Factory Story* (London: Virgin Books).

Middleton, R. (1990) *Studying Popular Music* (Milton Keynes: Open University Press).

Miège, B. (1979) 'The Cultural Commodity', *Media, Culture & Society* 1(3): 297–311.

——(1987) 'The Logics at Work in the New Cultural Industries', *Media, Culture & Society* 9(2): 273–89.

——(1989) *The Capitalisation of Cultural Production* (New York: International General).

Music Managers Forum (2003) *The Music Management Bible* (London: SMT).

Music Week Directory 2010 (London: UBM).

Negus, K. (1992) *Producing Pop: Culture and Conflict in the Popular Music Industry* (London: Hodder Arnold).

——(1993) 'Plugging and Programming: Pop Radio and Record Promotion in Britain and the United States', *Popular Music* 12: 57–68.

——(1995) 'Where the Mystical Meets the Market: Creativity and Commerce in the Production of Popular Music', *The Sociological Review* 43(2): 317–39.

——(1996) *Popular Music in Theory* (London: Polity Press).

——(1999) *Music Genres and Corporate Cultures* (London: Routledge).

——(2001) 'The Corporate Strategies of the Major Record Labels and the International Imperative', in Gebesmair, A. and Smudits, A. (eds), *Global Repertoires: Popular Music Within and Beyond the Transnational Music Industry* (Aldershot: Ashgate Publishing), pp. 21–32.

Negus, K. & Hesmondhalgh, D. (2002) *Popular Music Studies* (London: Hodder Arnold).

Negus, K & Roman-Velazquez, P. (2000) 'Globalisation and Cultural Identities', in Curran, J. and Gurevich, M. (eds), *Mass Media and Society*, 3rd ed., Arnold, 2000, pp. 329–45.

News.bbc.co.uk/cbbcnews/hi/chat/your_comments/ . . . /2248416.stm 10Sep 2002 (accessed 3 October 2011).

Peterson, R. & Berger, D. (1971) 'Entrepreneurship in Organisations: Evidence from the Popular Music Industry', *Administrative Science Quarterly* 1(16): 97–107.

——(1975) 'Cycles in Symbol Production: The Case of Popular Music', *American Sociological Review* 40(April 1975): 158–73.

Price, S. & Thonemann, P. (2011) *The Birth of Classical Europe: A History from Troy to Augustine* (London: Penguin).

Robson, J. (2006) *Finding the Female Fan: A Feminist Ethnography of Popular Music in Sheffield.* Unpublished PhD thesis, Sheffield Hallam University, UK.

Rogan, J. (1989) *Starmakers and Svengalis* (London: Futura Publications).

Rose, T. (1994) *Black Noise: Rap Music and Black Culture* (Middletown, CO: Wesleyan University Press).

Ross, A. (2004) *No Collar: The Humane Workplace and its Hidden Costs* (Philadelphia, PA: Temple University Press).

Savage, J. (1991) *England's Dreaming: Sex Pistols and Punk Rock* (London: Faber and Faber).

Schumpeter, J. (1949) *Economic Theory and Entrepreneurial History – Change and the Entrepreneur* (Cambridge: Harvard University Press).

Sennett, R. (1998) *The Corrosion of Character* (New York: W.W. Norton & Co.).

——(2006) *The Culture of the New Capitalism* (New Haven & London: Yale University Press).

Shepherd, J. (1991) *Music as Social Text* (Cambridge, MA: Polity Press).

Shuker, R. (2002) *Popular Music: the Key Concepts* (London: Routledge).
——(2007) *Key Concepts In Popular Music Culture* (London: Routledge).
Smith, C. (1998) *Creative Britain* (London: Faber & Faber).
Stokes, G. (1977) *Star-Making Machinery: Inside the Business of Rock and Roll* (New York: Random House).
Strachan, R. (2007) 'Micro-independent Record Labels in the UK: Discourse, DIY Cultural Production and the Music Industry', *European Journal of Cultural Studies* 10(2): 245–65.
Stratton, J. (1982) 'Between Two Worlds: Art and Commercialism in the Record Industry', *The Sociological Review* 30: 267–85.
——(1983) 'Capitalism and Romantic Ideology in the Record Business', *Popular Music* 3: 143–56.
Straw, W. (1997) 'Communities and Scenes in Popular Music', in Gelder, K. & Thornton, S. (eds), *The Subcultures Reader* (London: Routledge), pp. 469–78.
Tagg, P. (2002) www.tagg.org Notes on Semiotics of Music.
Tessler, H. (2008) 'The New MTV? Electronic Arts and "Playing" Music', in Collins, K. (ed.), *From Pac-Man to Pop Music* (Aldershot: Ashgate Publishing), pp 13–26.
Thornton, S. (1995) *Club Cultures: Music, Media and Subcultural Capital* (Cambridge: Polity Press).
Toynbee, J. (2000) *Making Popular Music: Musicians, Creativity and Institutions* (London: Arnold).
UPI 'It's a rough road for Live Nation' at www.upi.com/Business_News/2010/06/21/Its-a-rough-road-for-Live-Nation/UPI-40061277138441/ (accessed 3 October 2011).
Wikström, P. (2009) *The Music Industry: Music in the Cloud* (Cambridge: Polity Press).
Williams, R. (1963) *Culture and Society 1780–1950* (Harmondsworth: Penguin).
——(1983) *Keywords: a Vocabulary of Culture and Society* (London: Flamingo).
Zwaan, K. (2009) 'Sop You Want to Be a Rock and Roll Star? The Determinants of Career Success of Pop Musicians in the Netherlands', *Poetics* 37(3): 250–66.

Index

Note: Page numbers with 'n' in the index refer to notes in the text.